The Scottish Political System Since Devolution

From New Politics to the New Scottish Government

Paul Cairney

imprint-academic.com

Published in the UK by
Imprint Academic, PO Box 200, Exeter EX5 5YX, UK

Published in the USA by
Imprint Academic, Philosophy Documentation Center
PO Box 7147, Charlottesville, VA 22906-7147, USA

ISBN 9781845402020

A CIP catalogue record for this book is available from the
British Library and US Library of Congress

For my lovely partner Linda,

our beautiful children, Evie, Alfie and Frankie,

and our smelly but handsome dog

(who can be seen here:

http://smallvillagebigdog.wordpress.com/)

Table of Contents

List of Tables

List of Abbreviations

AMS	Additional Member System
ASBO	Anti-social Behaviour Order
CAP	Common Agricultural Policy (EU)
CCR	Collective cabinet responsibility
CCT	Compulsory Competitive Tendering
CFP	Common Fisheries Policy (EU)
COSLA	Convention of Scottish Local Authorities
CPD	Continuous Professional Development
CSG	Consultative Steering Group
DCA	Deparment for Constitutional Affairs
ECHR	European Convention on Human Rights
ECtHR	European Court of Human Rights
EIS	Educational Institute for Scotland
EU	European Union
EYF	End Year Flexibility (Scottish Executive savings from assigned budget)
FM	First Minister
FOI	Freedom of information
HMIe	Her Majesty's Inspectorate of Education
IGR	Intergovernmental relations
JMC	Joint Ministerial Committee
LCM	Legislative Consent (Sewel) Motion
LSVT	Large scale voluntary transfer (council housing stocks)
LTS	Learning and Teaching Scotland
MLG	Multi-level governance

MMP	Mixed Member Proportional (electoral system)
MOU	Memorandum of Understanding
MP	Member of Parliament (Westminster, UK)
MPA	Ministerial Parliamentary Aide (later Parliamentary Liaison Officer)
MSP	Member of the Scottish Parliament
NCT	Negotiating Committee for Teachers
NDPB	Non Departmental Public Body (quango)
NEBU	Non-Executive Bills Unit
NHS	National Health Service
NICE	National Institute for health and Clinical Excellence
PFI	Private Finance Initiative
PPP	Public Private Partnerships
PR	Proportional representation
PSA	Public Service Agreement
Quango (QNG)	Quasi–autonomous Non-Governmental Organisation
SCC	Scottish Constitutional Convention
SCF	Scottish Civic Forum
SCVO	Scottish Council for Voluntary Organisations
SEPA	Scottish Environmental Protection Agency
SFT	Scottish Futures Trust
SMC	Scottish Medicines Consortium
SNCT	Scottish Negotiating Committee for Teachers
SNP	Scottish National Party
SOA	Single Outcome Agreement
SPADs	Special advisers
SPCB	Scottish Parliament Corporate Body
SPICe	Scottish Parliament Information Centre
SQA	Scottish Qualifications Authority
SSP	Scottish Socialist Party
STUC	Scottish Trades Union Congress
STV	Single transferable vote (not Scottish Television)

Preface

I wanted to start the book with something punchy about the importance of Scottish devolution. I settled on 'Devolution in 1999 was a major event in Scottish politics' but, as a careful academic, instantly felt the need to qualify this statement to death—which would defeat the purpose. Instead, I decided to qualify it here. There are two standard qualifications. The first is that devolution is a 'process, not an event'. This statement is generally attributed to former Welsh Secretary Ron Davies who used it to assure Welsh people that their initial devolution settlement would be improved as devolution became popular and its institutions and politicians more mature. However, it is also used by commentators in Scotland to counter the sense of a devolution 'settlement' which will go no further. Devolution *is* going further even if independence doesn't happen.

Second, we play down the importance of that event in two main ways. We identify points of continuity in Scottish politics, suggesting that administrative devolution existed long before political devolution and that key institutions—relating to education, local government, the legal system and the church—are decades or centuries old. Indeed, Kellas' (1989) famous argument is that a 'Scottish Political System' existed before 1999. We also question the novelty of 'new politics', a rather vague term generally used to describe our hopes and dreams regarding devolution (Mitchell, 2000). But, still, devolution in 1999 was a major event in Scottish politics. We can say the same for the next sentence on the shift from a unitary to a quasi-federal state, and then my suggestion that we have a new political system. These are problematic statements but I don't want you to fall asleep before I get past my introductory paragraph. Just go with it if you know the unitary/union state/quasi-federal literature or the political system debate already, ignore it, or read up on it (I recommend McGarvey and Cairney, 2008) and come back to this book later.

This study of Scottish devolution draws heavily from the devolution monitoring programme led by Robert Hazell in the UCL's Constitution

Unit. The Scottish Devolution Monitoring effort has been led by Graham Leicester, James Mitchell, Peter Jones, Akash Paun, Charlie Jeffery, Nicola McEwen, and Paul Cairney (also note the Constitution Unit's 'Devolution and Health' reports, which ran from 1999–2001). There have been many contributors to the individual parts of the Scottish reports on which I draw: David Bell, Eberhard Bort, Julie Brown, Paul Cairney, Alex Christie, John Curtice, John Harris, Charlie Jeffery, Michael Keating, Peter Lynch, Lynne MacMillan, Nicola McEwen, Neil McGarvey, James Mitchell, Akash Paun, Kirsty Regan, Nicholas Rengger, Jane Saren, Philip Schlesinger, David Scott, Mark Shephard, Alan Trench, Barry Winetrobe, and Alex Wright. I would like to take this opportunity to thank them for their hard work. I have this nagging feeling that some contributors will think that I am just pinching their work and calling it my own, when in fact I am trying to get the most out of these reports. In particular, I would like to thank Neil McGarvey and Barry Winetrobe, who read most of the chapters and gave me some very useful comments. Further, Michael Clancy from the Law Society of Scotland reminded me of the importance of the ECHR to public policy in Scotland and John Curtice provided some figures to complete chapter 7. Final thanks to Anthony Freeman, Imprint Academic, for being so patient.

I originally thought of this book as an 'impact' output, as part of the Research Councils UK focus on the effective dissemination of knowledge from academics to practitioners (and vice versa). Then, like many people, I realised that impact means something else (note: I don't claim to know what it is—just that I know it is something else). The project was funded initially (1999–2005) by the Leverhulme Trust and the Economic and Social Research Council (http://www.ucl.ac.uk/constitution-unit/research/research-archive/archive-projects/devolution-monitoring99-05). From 2006–9 it was funded by the Economic and Social Research Council, Ministry of Justice, Scottish Executive/Government, Scotland Office and Wales Office (http://www.ucl.ac.uk/constitution-unit/research/research-archive/archive-projects/devolution-monitoring06-09). As far as I know, this is the first book to draw conclusions from a comprehensive reading of the reports, but it should not be the last.

The reports present a problem for referencing. The aim of referencing is that the reader can use the reference to check or follow up the text in the original source. In my opinion the best way to do this is to depart slightly from the Harvard system, to note in the text the month as well as the year of publication (e.g. Shephard, August 2002: 8) so that the reader can go instantly to source (using the weblinks above, or going through the Constitution Unit if those links change) rather than fish around the bibliography (they are not listed there!). Some early reports have no authors attached to sections, so I list the month, year and page. I have all of the reports on file, and so can keep this document on one side and click to open the reports on the other. It's a good system (once you get used to looking for page numbers at the bottom, not in the Adobe box at the top) and I recommend it to you (although, of course, you will be holding a hard copy unless you are sneaking a look at a few pages on Google books). I suspect that, although this is a stand-alone book, you will get more out of it if you follow up the reports. This system also helps me avoid looking like I really enjoy referencing myself (imagine Cairney, 2008a; 2008b; 2008c; 2008d). I do enjoy it sometimes (see Cairney, 2011), but don't want it to look that way. Barry Winetrobe told me that the reference style often breaks up the flow of the text. I have tried to amend it to make it better, by putting the report references to the end of a paragraph when possible, or at the end of a sentence if not, but some sections might still be a pain. Any references to the *State of the Nations* chapters (and to related reports series, such as the early quarterly and annual reports on health) just use Harvard.

Final notes: I generally use 'Scottish Executive' to refer to the Labour-Liberal Democrat coalition government from 1997–2007 and 'Scottish Government' to refer to the SNP government from 2007 onwards. I generally use the term 'Secretary' to refer to the most-senior minister in a Scottish government department (and 'Scottish Secretary' for Secretary of State for Scotland — a UK Government post). This is a longstanding UK convention (short for 'Secretary of State') that became more established from 2007 when the Scottish Government started using the term 'Cabinet Secretary' (but note that this term refers to a senior civil servant in the UK). One of the monitors has one of those amusingly-rude typos that you find in the Private Eye. I'll give a small prize to the first person to spot it.

Paul Cairney
University of Aberdeen
paul.cairney@abdn.ac.uk

Chapter 1

Introduction

Devolution in 1999 was a major event in Scottish politics. Devolution as a whole is described by Hazell (2000: 3; 5) as an 'extraordinary achievement'; a set of decisions to 'transform a highly centralised unitary state into a devolved and quasi-federal system of government in the space of only three years', without leading to the 'break-up of Britain'. Leicester (2000: 14) reports the idea that the Scottish Parliament's first election is 'an opportunity for a new start and the turning point in Scotland's fortunes'. Much of this 'new start' came hand in hand with the idea of 'new politics', or the pursuit of a collection of institutional, process and cultural differences (Mitchell, 2000) to produce something 'more inclusive, consensual and less adversarial than Westminster' (Hazell, 2000: 10). The Scottish system was designed, in Lijphart's (1999) terms, to be a 'consensus' rather than a 'majoritarian' democracy, with a proportional electoral system designed to produce a new party system and foster a sense of cooperation between government, Parliament, 'civil society' and the wider public.

While much of the subsequent literature has challenged or qualified the image of new politics, and the difference that new institutions have made, we still have a new political system following devolution. Kellas' famous argument (made from 1973 to 1989) is that Scotland had, before devolution, most aspects of a political system, including: a population with high levels of Scottish national identity, producing a desire to introduce or maintain policymaking institutions at that national level; and, a means for people in Scotland to articulate and aggregate their interests (1989: 211). It maintained the Scottish institutions that reflected and reinforced national identity (a separate legal, education, church and local government system) and developed the Scottish institutions to articulate (Scottish media, interest groups, MPs) and respond to (the Scottish Office) Scottish demands, as well as the administrative autonomy necessary to carry out Scotland-specific policies. Consequently, the system would be complete with the introduction of a Scottish Parliament with legislative powers (1989: 162).

While there were many critics of Kellas' arguments (see McGarvey and Cairney, 2008: 245–6), relatively few would question the idea that Scotland has a political system now — even though our understanding of the idea of a political system is changing. In other words, Scottish devolution now provides a means for 'political socialization and recruitment' (through the Scottish Parliament and Scottish Government civil service), 'interest articulation' (Scottish elections) and 'interest aggregation' (Scottish political parties and interest groups) and a means to address Scottish demands and make policy on that basis (2008: 10). However, this takes place within a wider system of 'multi-level governance' (Bache and Flinders, 2004; Cairney, 2012b) in which power is dispersed across levels of government, and Scottish institutions have become interdependent with local, UK and EU institutions. It has become a new political system which operates within a wider national and supra-national system.

It is also a system that has already changed enough to produce realistic demands for further devolution — a process that began to take serious shape from 2007 and accelerated from 2011.

The Scottish Election of 2011 produced a landslide victory for the Scottish National Party (SNP). It secured 69, or 53%, of 129 seats under a voting system designed to make such majorities highly unlikely. Proportional representation is generally designed to produce a party system in which: the largest party forms a coalition government with at least one other party, as Labour did with the Liberal Democrats in 1999 and 2003; or, a minority government, as the SNP did in 2007. However, the Scottish Parliament's Mixed Member Proportional system does not make it *impossible* to gain a majority of seats without a majority of the vote because it is not entirely proportional.

The election result signifies a notable reversal-of-fortunes, with the SNP now dominating the constituency vote at the expense of Labour when, in the past, the SNP received most of its seats from the regional lists and Labour dominated the constituency vote at the expense of almost all other parties. As a result, we have moved very quickly from a Labour-dominated political system, focused on the importance of devolution and 'new politics', to an SNP-dominated system characterised by a curious mix of very competent devolved government, which receives minimal attention, and the prospect of further constitutional change, which receives maximal attention. There is also a new UK Government context, with Labour (1997–2010) replaced by a Conservative-led coalition with the Liberal Democrats.

Consequently, our attention has moved quickly from a consideration of Scotland's new political system and its style of politics towards the potential for a new devolved or independent era in which we reconsider Scotland's relationship with the UK, EU and wider world.

The Devolution Monitoring Project

The aim of this book is to consider this new era through the lens of contemporary history, comparing the current and future operation of a Scottish Government and Parliament to the institutions that developed following the first elections to the Scottish Parliament in 1999. It does so by drawing heavily on the devolution monitoring project, led by the UCL's Constitution Unit (and Professor Robert Hazell in particular). The project produced regular reports of the 'implementation of devolution' in Scotland, Wales and Northern Ireland from 1999. From 2000, it produced reports on developments in the English regions and the 'Centre'. The reports were produced for approximately 10 years, ending in 2009. They were supplemented by regular *State of the Nations* volumes that used the reports to produce a year-in-the-life of devolution.

The nature of the monitoring project changed markedly over time. Frequent changes to the size, structure and focus of the reports reflected, to some extent, the organic growth of the project as more commentators became involved and more became known about the scale and significance of devolution. By the mid-2000s, when the devolution settlement was more settled, the reports sought to provide a systematic set of questions for each devolved territory:

- **Changes in the Constitution** — How is the devolution settlement evolving? What further powers have been transferred? What further powers are sought by the devolved assemblies? What is the response of the UK government and Parliament?

- **Changes in Public Policy** — What difference does devolution make? What innovations are there in public policy? Experiments; successes; failures? How much policy divergence is there? How much policy transfer?

- **Changes in the nature of Politics** — How different are the 'new politics' of the devolved institutions? How consensual or majoritarian are the devolved assemblies? How effective are they in terms of scrutiny? How innovative are they? Do any of these innovations get transferred?

- **Changes in public attitudes** — What is the attitude of the public to: the autonomy of the devolved institutions, and the question of independence; the division of powers between the devolved governments and UK government; and the performance of the devolved governments and UK government?

- **Changes in intergovernmental relations** — What are the relations between the UK government and devolved government: bilateral or multilateral; formal or informal; cooperative or competitive?

- **Finance** — How are the devolved governments funded? How would they like to be funded? What tensions arise, and how are they resolved?

- The Scottish reports also produced sections on **the media** and **political parties**, exploring the extent to which they influenced attention to, and the development of, new politics, public attitudes, public policy and intergovernmental relations.

The aim of this book is to produce a detailed account of that ten year project in Scotland, exploring its links to the Scottish devolution literature, and using the results to situate this new era of SNP Government within a useful context. The monitors provide at least three kinds of academic value. First, they give a strong sense of the value of contemporary history, providing a perspective on events from 1999 that we may no longer hold. At the very least, it is interesting to note that much was written on the assumption of Labour dominance for many years to come. Second, they provide much-needed detail on policy processes. For example, the monitors generally confirm the picture of informality in intergovernmental relations, but they also provide key details on periods of tension between Scottish and UK Governments (chapter 5).

Third, they help us understand the context in which the 2011 SNP Government will operate. For example, chapter 3 shows that there is a clear imbalance of resources between the Government and Parliament. This imbalance was most clear from 1999–2007, when the Labour-Liberal Democrat coalition had a majority in plenary and committees, and used it to push through an extensive legislative programme with minimal opposition. However, it did not disappear from 2007 under SNP minority government. The Scottish Government made more concessions, and opposition parties made more amendments to legislation, but the vast majority of legislation was still passed by the Government following fairly limited scrutiny by Parliament. This is the context for the analysis of a SNP majority government: it will enjoy a parliamentary majority, but we should not exaggerate the difference that makes. Further, as chapter 8 discusses, it will be able to re-introduce policies rejected from 2007-11, such as a minimum price for alcohol and perhaps a replacement for council tax, but relatively few SNP policies were opposed effectively by opposition parties before 2011. In more general terms, we can say that the SNP Government from 2011 will harbour no illusions or expectations regarding 'new politics'. As discussed in this chapter (below), the monitors show us that the new Scottish political system is often not markedly different from its UK counterpart. Further, in the absence of coalition or minority government in Scotland, the differences may be even less apparent.

The aim of this chapter is to outline that sense of contemporary history provided by the early reports, including the shifting role of media coverage. It then outlines the initial coverage of 'new politics' in the reports as a way to structure the first part of the book. It goes on to identify areas of interest not covered fully in the reports before setting out the structure for the remainder of the book.

Contemporary History

It is striking that, after only twelve years, much of the early devolution commentary reads like a description of history. The first main example is Mitchell et al's (2001: 49-40) discussion of the association between the first First Minister Donald Dewar and devolution as an 'event rather than a process', or 'a fitting culmination of his career ... rather than a new and radical phase of political activity'. This image was reinforced at the time by Alex Salmond's decision to step down as SNP leader in July 2000, following 'private declarations early in his leadership that he had no intention to serve more than a decade' (2001: 50; and a poll suggesting that his departure would make little difference—August 2000: 18; see also May 2000: 17; 19). While the idea of devolution as a box to be '"ticked off" as delivered' was challenged more by Dewar's successor Henry McLeish, he did not serve long enough to make a lasting impact (2001: 49-50) (the First Ministers were Donald Dewar May 1999-October 2000, Henry McLeish October 2000-November 2001, Jack McConnell November 2001-May 2007 and Alex Salmond from May 2007). This image of devolution already seems historical. It was challenged in 2007 following the Alex Salmond-led SNP's first election victory, which prompted moves towards extending devolution further (chapter 10). It was then blown away by the SNP's victory in 2011 which made it almost certain that Scotland would have an independence referendum, even if there is a weak link between a vote for the SNP and a vote for independence (chapter 7).

The second example regards an initial sense of satisfaction or optimism in the early coverage. For example, while we may now take devolved institutions for granted, it is only 10 years ago that Mitchell et al (2001: 50) note: 'the Executive has been scrutinised in a manner and to an extent unknown before in Scottish history'. The same chapter also draws on the early evidence to highlight a new Executive-Parliament relationship based on the ability of MSPs and committees to influence government legislation or introduce their own (and, in some cases, choose their own Deputy Presiding Officer—Shephard, February 2002: 12). The early experience suggests that Scottish ministers 'cannot dominate the running of the parliament in the same way that their UK counterparts can in the House of Commons' (2001: 57; Shephard, February 2001: 15; Shephard, May 2001: 13). However, by 2002, this was not the view of 15 MSPs interviewed by the Scottish Council Foundation; many bemoaned the extent of Executive dominance (of both the introduction and amendment of legislation) backed up by the party whip (Shephard, August 2002: 8). Shephard's (June, 2003: 10) suggestion that the reduction of the Scottish Executive coalition majority from 15 to 5 may increase the potential for 'parliamentary leverage' also did not prove to be prophetic. By 2007, the reports had become more sceptical about the idea of parliamentary power even under a minority government which made some important concessions at the beginning of its term: 'The small size, MSP turnover and legislative loads of committees may still undermine their abilities to scrutinise, amend and initiate legislation. The gulf in resources between Executive and Parliament remains' (Cairney, September 2007: 21).

The third example is interesting in the light of concerns from 2007 about the stability of minority government. Many early reports expressed concern about the stability of *coalition* government (in much the same way that we see concerns in the UK from 2010), particularly when the Liberal Democrats were portrayed as tricky coalition partners when pursuing their policy aims (Mitchell, February 2001: 5). In fact, the coalition held for 8 years and only seemed 'loose' in the lead up to the 2007 Scottish Parliament elections (Cairney, January 2006: 13).

Other examples of key issues to revisit include: coverage of the Scottish Parliament building which, according to Mitchell (2004: 35; see also Shephard, May 2004: 8; November 2004: 8), came to 'symbolise the extravagance of devolution'; concern in 2004 about the prospect for ballot paper confusion in the 2007 elections (Wright, May 2004: 29; Scott, January 2008: 76-7); and, Mitchell's (2004: 37) discussion of the speed with which the Scottish media came to equate Scottish politics with the Parliament and Executive rather than the wider political system associated with 'new politics'.

MSPs, Expenses and the Media

One of the first subjects discussed by the first report (November 1999: 10) and Leicester (2000) in the first *State of the Nations* is MSP expenses — an issue that demonstrated an often remarkable degree of print media hostility to the Scottish Parliament despite its initial optimism about devolution (or perhaps because of its unrealistic hopes). Although there is now an impetus for Westminster to learn from Holyrood's expenses and second-homes system (Cairney, May 2009: 28–30), the monitors remind us that Scotland's system developed as much through partisan debates, self-interest and a response to intense media criticism as any higher sense of propriety that preceded public attention. In particular, the Scottish Parliament has been dogged by the issue of different allowances for constituency and regional MSPs — a debate made more contentious by the makeup of the Parliament in which most constituency MSPs were Scottish Labour and most regional MSPs were from the opposition parties (i.e. before the SNP-Labour reversal in 2011).[1] A cross-party group chaired by (SNP) Mike Russell produced recommendations for a £36000 staffing allowance and £10000 local office costs allowance. Labour sought unsuccessfully to amend this plan to give regional MSPs 60% of both costs, while the Liberal Democrats amended it successfully (using the coalition majority) to maintain the salary costs but ensure that if one party had more than one list MSP in the same region then the costs are reduced (£10000 for the first MSP plus £3000 for each additional MSP, to be divided equally among them).[2]

The inability of MSPs to agree on this (one of the first votes in the Scottish Parliament) and other issues, such as seating and the length of parliamentary recesses, was pounced on by a media which 'had a field day watching the undignified squabble' (Leicester, 2000: 20). 'Serious damage was done' to the image of the Scottish Parliament because the public's first impression was influenced by 'a pasting in the press' between the first election on 6th May and the state opening on 1st July (followed quickly by the 'Lobbygate' scandal, in which lobbying firms

---

[1] Note a similar example of party politics in Wales, regarding Labour plans (in the White Paper on further devolution in 2006) to stop list candidates running constituency campaigns.

[2] See Scottish Parliament Official Report 8.6.99 cols. 280-330 http://www.Scottish. parliament.uk/business/officialReports/meetingsParliament/or-99/or010704. htm

promised privileged access to Scottish ministers — see chapter 8). Much of this coverage was denounced by Presiding Officer David Steel as 'bitch journalism' which, as well as being a remarkably inappropriate statement to make, sums up the early political-media relationship and gives a sense of the tone for subsequent media coverage (interrupted briefly by 'hypocritical' press reports following the death of Donald Dewar in 2000 — Mitchell at al, 2001: 51).

Although more agreement among MSPs could be found in 2002, when the Scottish Parliament revisited MSP pay, the issue remained controversial because the parliamentary vote effectively gave MSPs a 13.5% pay rise by moving from a system based on senior civil servant salaries to 87.5% of MP salaries. It also introduced allowances for major party leaders (£21000 for parties with 30-plus members and £11000 for 15–29) and entrusted the Scottish Parliament Corporate Body (SPCB) to act on behalf of MSPs in the future (Shephard, May 2002: 11; see also Earle, 2007: 5; Scottish Parliament Official Report 21.3.02 cols. 10577–87). Attention to MSP costs also became an annual media event following the publication of expenses by the Scottish Parliament Corporate Body (e.g. BBC News, 2003). However, it did not reach a crisis point until 2005, following various freedom of information requests by journalists for more detailed breakdowns of expenses, prompting Keith Raffan to resign as an MSP and David McLetchie to resign as leader of the Scottish Conservatives (Cairney, January 2006: 22; Bort, January 2006: 40; Lynch, January 2009: 112–13; Curtice, January 2006: 78–9) and a feeling among politicians, including Presiding Officer George Reid, that the constant attention undermined the Scottish Parliament's reputation as a transparent body (particularly since the Scottish Executive had also come under criticism for its spending — Winetrobe, November 2004: 7; Winetrobe, April 2005: 4). This prompted the SPCB to publish in December 2005 a much more detailed account of expenses and initiate in June 2006 an online search facility on the Scottish Parliament's website.

Yet, the levels of unwanted attention did not end there. Instead, there was a shift in media attention to the possibility of MSPs making a profit from sales of their second homes in Edinburgh (the mortgage interest was funded via MSP expenses) which prompted First Minister Jack McConnell to encourage George Reid to reform the system (Cairney, May 2006: 20). While the original intention of George Reid was for the SPCB to produce a legacy paper for consideration by the new Parliament in 2007 (Scottish Parliament, 2006), his successor Alex Fergusson commissioned an independent review to take a 'first principles' approach to the allowances of MSPs and the extent to which centrally provided services (particularly relating to office equipment) could replace allowances (Scottish Parliament, 2007; Earle, 2009). The Langlands Review recommended abolishing the payment of an allowance to meet mortgage interest payments (by phasing it out by 2011) and setting a cap on claims for overnight stays for MSPs in eligible areas. While this was accepted by the Scottish Parliament in June 2008, the debate also took us back to the very first party conflicts regarding office and staff allowances for list and constituency MSPs (see also Wright, June 2003: 44 on the perceived inequalities between list and constituency MSPs; see also Lundberg, 2006). Although Langlands recommended that the latter receive £62000 and the former £45000, the Scottish Parliament voted to amend the motion and grant all MSPs £54620 (although the principle of shared office costs for regional MSPs was maintained). Thus, again, the media was able to report that the parties were divided despite voting themselves a significant rise in allowances (Langlands prefers the term 'reimbursement of expenses' — Cairney, September 2008: 17).

Therefore, while Westminster may have much to learn from Holyrood, the experience of the first decade suggests that we should not look back with rose-tinted spectacles (the same can be said about the registration of non-financial interests — Shephard, November 2002: 8). The media coverage in Scotland may not have reached the heights of the equivalent scandals in Westminster, but they were still significant (Bort, January 2006: 41; Bort, September 2006: 26–7).

Changes in the nature of Politics:
New Politics and Unrealistic Expectations

(1) The 'Capability-Expectations Gap'

The idea of new politics, as a departure from 'old Westminster', was part of a 'rallying call for the architects of devolution' and, as such, a lens through which most evaluations of Scottish political success have been conducted ever since (McGarvey and Cairney, 2008: 14). It was promoted (by 'elites' — Mitchell, 2004: 16) for two main reasons. First, it became linked to the unsuccessful referendum on Scottish devolution in 1979 followed by a long spell of Conservative government which increased attention to the 'democratic deficit' — when the Scottish electorate voted for one party, Labour, and received another, Conservative. The new campaign for devolution took shape following the set-up of the Scottish Constitutional Convention (SCC) — a collection of political parties (primarily Labour, Liberal Democrat and Green), the Scottish Trade Union Congress, Scottish Council for

Voluntary Organizations, religious leaders, local authorities and civic organizations — in 1989 (McGarvey and Cairney, 2008: 34). The SCC sought to reinvigorate elite, media and popular support for devolution by addressing the concerns associated with previous devolution proposals and articulating a new vision of Scottish politics based on narratives of its past. This rhetoric became inextricably linked to dissatisfaction with the democratic deficit and a feeling that devolution could have saved Scotland from the worst excesses of Thatcherism (McCrone and Lewis, 1999: 17). Indeed, the SCC vision was developed at the same time that many of its participants were acting as the unelected opposition to Conservative government rule. Thus, the remote, top-down and unitary UK state was contrasted with a vision of consensus for Scotland based on a narrative of Scotland's political tradition and longstanding propensity for the diffusion of power, combined with popular and civic participation in politics (Cairney, Halpin and Jordan, 2009). The SCC (1990; 1995) articulated hopes for:

> participatory democracy in which the Scottish population would seek to influence decisions made in Scotland directly rather than through a ballot box which seemed so remote; pluralist democracy, in which interest and social groups would seek to counter policies 'unsuitable' for Scotland at all levels of implementation; and deliberative democracy, in which a separate level of debate about the direction of UK policies implemented in Scotland could take place (McGarvey and Cairney, 2008: 244).

Second, it followed a perceived crisis of popular disenchantment with politics, producing the potential for a Scottish Parliament to be seen as yet-another layer of bureaucracy or source of yet-another pool of self-serving politicians with no meaningful link to, or care for, their populations. In both cases, the devolution agenda embodied hopes for a new style of politics far removed from 'Old Westminster' as the main source of discredited policymaking. While some attention was paid by the architects of devolution to the 'consensus democracies' (and Nordic politics in general), most was devoted to making sure that old politics was left behind.

In this context, a key theme of the early quarterly and annual reports is the extent to which the capabilities of the new Scottish Parliament were 'talked up', well beyond the ability of devolution to solve the democratic deficit and improve accountability (Mitchell, 2004: 16). This produced an 'expectations gap' regarding devolution and its ability to fulfil the hopes associated with new politics or to be 'the panacea for Scotland's ills ... Parliament simply did not have the powers to meet the expectations that Scots had of it ...[producing] the largely negative media and public assessment of its initial performance' (Mitchell et al, 2001: 48). While this gap narrowed over time, it was caused more by reduced expectations than any positive effect of the Parliament itself (2001: 48), when politics gradually became 'more rooted in what is possible than in what is desirable' (Macmillan, November 2000: 3).

(2) The Scottish Parliament

New politics was based on a range of perceived defects of the UK system, including an electoral system that exaggerates government majorities, excludes small parties, concentrates power within government rather than Parliament and its committees, and encourages adversarialism between government and opposition (McGarvey and Cairney, 2008: 12–13). Thus, it referred partly to the selection of a proportional electoral system and all that this produces, including the strong likelihood of coalition, the need for parties to bargain and cooperate and, hopefully, a consequent reduction in partisanship and rise in consensual forms of politics. To foster a sense of 'power sharing' between government, parliament and the public, the parliament was set up as a hub for popular participation (including a new public petitions process) and vested with an unusual range of powers. In particular, while the Consultative Steering Group (a cross-party group charged with producing the principles, procedures and standing orders of the Scottish Parliament) recognised the 'need for the Executive to govern', or produce most legislation and make most expenditure decisions, it also envisaged a stronger parliamentary role (Scottish Office, 1998; McGarvey and Cairney, 2008: 90). It recommended: the fusion of Westminster's standing and select committee functions, to enable members scrutinising legislation to develop subject based expertise; the ability of select committees to call witnesses and oblige ministers and civil servants to attend; and, the ability to hold agenda-setting inquiries and to initiate legislation if dissatisfied with the government response. Crucially, the committees were also charged with performing two new roles to 'front-load' the legislative process and make up for the fact that, in the absence of the House of Lords, there would be no revising chamber. First, they would have a formal pre-legislative role, charged with making sure that the government consults adequately with its population before presenting legislation to parliament (McGarvey and Cairney, 2008: 91; 104). Second, they would consider both the principles of legislation and specific amendments to bills before they were discussed in plenary.

Yet, although the Scottish Parliament's powers are strong when compared to most West European legislatures, they are weak when compared to the Scottish Government (McGarvey and Cairney, 2008: 127; Cairney, 2006). From 1999–2007 we can explain much of the imbalance of power in terms of the decision by Labour and the Liberal Democrats to form a governing majority able, through a strong party whip, to command a majority in plenary and all committees. As chapter 3 discusses in detail, this unequal relationship is reflected in the monitors. They report immediate concerns about the lack of parliamentary resources to scrutinise departments and legislation, the negative effect of the Scottish Executive's legislative schedule on parliamentary scrutiny, the tendency for the Scottish Executive coalition to use its majority to change parliamentary rules to protect its position, and the enjoyment by Parliament of sporadic wins in the context of a fairly powerless position. Chapter 3 also argues that this imbalance of power did not disappear in 2007 when the SNP formed a minority government. Rather, it demonstrated that governments could further most public policy without recourse to the Scottish Parliament and that there is a huge gulf in resources between the Government and Parliament.

It is also worth noting how little the Scottish Parliament features in chapter 8's discussion of public policy. While members' bills looked like they might represent an important source of policy, it is worth looking back at the first list (May 2000: 25–7) to note the limits to their ambitions. Most member's bill proposals soon became little more than agenda setting tools. Some notable exceptions include the eventual Protection of Wild Mammals bill (Winetrobe, February 2002: 50; it was sold as the fox hunting ban but, when implemented, did not stop fox hunting) and Tommy Sheridan MSP's abolition of poindings and warrant sales, which removed distinctly Scottish practices (the sale of someone's possessions to pay off debts—a practice that arose famously when local authorities sought to collect 'poll tax' debts). Sheridan's bill is also memorable because it was one of the very few examples of a member's bill passing despite initial Scottish Executive opposition. The May (2000: 25) monitor reports that the 'Scottish Executive had to accept defeat in the face of a report from three Scottish Parliament Committees ... and a rebellion amongst its own backbenchers'. What it did not appreciate at the time was how rare these practices would become (McGarvey and Cairney, 2008: 103; also note that Sheridan and other MSPs were not happy with the replacement to poindings and warrant sales—Winetrobe, August 2001: 48–50; February, 2002: 51). The novelty of the Education Committee's bill introducing a Children's

Commissioner was also not apparent at the time (Winetrobe, May 2002: 63).

(3) New Avenues for Democracy

There is some hope in the first report that new forms of deliberative and participative democracy will represent more than 'empty rhetoric' following the announcement of Parliament funding for engagement. Engagement can involve: the promotion of meetings outside of Edinburgh; the use of 'citizens juries and panels to provide representative feedback; deliberative polling and consensus conferences; and inputs to wider forums such as a Youth Parliament and an Older People's Parliament' and Executive funding for the Scottish Civic Forum (November, 1999: 7). However, very few reports find anything to report. Indeed, the most frequently addressed issue regards the lack of funding for the SCF, forcing it to close (November 2001, 14; Winetrobe, August 2004: 6; Winetrobe, April 2005: 5; Cairney, January 2006: 18). Schlesinger's (August 2003: 14) section is the only entry discussing new avenues for democracy in a positive way.

Similarly, the reports are often as likely to report on the *numbers* of petitions (Shephard, May 2002: 10; Cairney, September 2006: 16; January 2007: 25) and their *existence* rather than their *effect* (Winetrobe, August 2002: 46; Winetrobe, November 2003: 52; Winetrobe, February 2004: 4; Scott, January 2006: 99; Cairney, January 2007: 29–30). Subsequent debates and further scrutiny are reported in relatively few cases (Winetrobe, November 2004: 9; Shephard, April 2005: 6; Cairney, January 2009: 48; Cairney, May 2009: 40). Nor has much come from the SNP manifesto proposal to 'allow for the best supported public petition in any year to be brought forward as a detailed legislative proposal' (Cairney, September 2007: 24) or from the Public Petitions Committee's decision to review procedures (Cairney, September 2008: 21). Overall, Mitchell (2004: 39; 2005: 37) argues that, 'Measured in terms of political power—the essential test of politics—these appear more symbolic than effective ... an elaborate democratic veneer sitting atop long-established processes'. These new and ineffective processes perhaps contrast with the more established reliance on pressure participants such as interest groups which, although more important, were discussed less often in the monitors (see below).

(4) The Scottish Executive and Civil Service

Many early portrayals of civil servants regarded them as a force of inertia; as a foil to the dynamic new Parliament and a strong tie to the

UK government (Ford and Casebow, 2002: 46; McGarvey and Cairney, 2008: 144). Much of this criticism was based on two types of unrealistic expectations. First, too much was expected of a government department set up originally to implement UK policy rather than research, consult on and produce new Scottish policy (Keating, 2005: 104; compare with Permanent Secretary John Elvidge's assessment, five years on—Winetrobe, November 2004: 6). Second, too much was expected of a civil service set up to be accountable to ministers rather than directly to the Scottish Parliament (Pyper, 1999; Parry and Jones, 2000: 53). The latter explains why Henry McLeish's attempts to give Labour MSPs direct access to civil servants appeared to fail: 'McLeish's notion appeared to be based on a local government rather than a British parliamentary model', or at least a system that threatened the notion of an 'apolitical civil service' (Mitchell et al, 2001: 54; November 2000: 4–5). The unanticipated divide between Executive and Parliament also extended to ministerial special advisers, originally housed in Parliament, who then moved to St Andrew's House (home of the Scottish Government) because 'they don't want to be hassled by backbench MSPs' (November, 1999: 4). Issues related to civil service/parliamentary relationships arose infrequently, perhaps because the initial expectations of the main players soon adapted to a fairly traditional decision-making process. However, they did not disappear—and it is worth noting John Elvidge's awareness of the still 'adversarial relationship between Executive officials and MSPs' in 2003 (Winetrobe, November 2003: 4).

What Can the Reports Not Do?

This focus on new politics shows us what the monitors can do when there is a common theme that can be tracked in different sections. In other cases, the reports may be ill-equipped to track issues that are difficult to pick up in quarterly reports. For example, progress on issues such as poverty, health inequalities and equality may be more long term affairs better suited to broader sweeps (although see Cairney, May 2006: 20 on the Finance committee inquiry on deprivation).

The monitors occasionally reported on the representation of women as an event (and occasionally note the general lack of representation of black and ethnic minorities). They also cover some flashpoints in relation to gender, such as: the charge that women were treated less favourably than men by the first Presiding Officer David Steel; that plenary is/was akin to a boy's club with a 'climate of sexism' (Shephard, May 2002: 12–13; February 2004: 6); the not-yet-realised idea that the occupation of MSP could involve job-sharing (Winetrobe,

August 2001: 39); Scottish Executive initiatives to encourage the participation of women in public life (Winetrobe, May 2002: 8); and a reduction in women in the Scottish Cabinet following the 2003 election (Winetrobe, June 2003: 5; see also Cairney, April 2007: 90 on the 'gender equality scheme' for public bodies). However, the project did not appear to track systematically the substantive representation of women or the role of women in public life or public policy — perhaps because so few women were involved in producing the monitor from May 2001.

Another thing the monitors cannot do well is predict the future. The best example may be the 2011 election result, which now colours a lot of the early monitoring coverage in the Labour-dominated years. Or, it may be the economic context in the early years of devolution. What has become clear now is that the first decade of devolution was accompanied by significant rises in public expenditure. The recent economic crisis, and subsequent agenda on UK and Scottish public sector retrenchment, presents a new lens through which to view early developments regarding public policy. It is occasionally suggested (e.g. in Bell's coverage of Barnett, chapter 9) that one of the biggest limits to policy innovation in Scotland is the budget settlement. Yet, we may look back on the first ten years of devolution as the best chance for Scottish governments to pursue relatively generous social policies.

Last but not least, the influence of interest groups and other 'pressure participants' (Jordan et al, 2004)[3] is perhaps the most notable absence in the reports, since policy networks or subsystems are generally the key focus in theories of public policy and policy analysis (Cairney, 2012b). The gap occurred partly because this type of investigation is generally supplemented by elite interviews. However, in this case, all is not lost because the reports do provide some useful context in their coverage of the Scottish Government (chapter 4), public policy (chapter 8) and the increasingly important matter of central-local relations (see below and chapter 6). To make the most of this material, chapter 4 introduces the literature on 'territorial policy communities' (Keating et al, 2009). The general idea is that devolution has provided new venues for interest group influence, prompting many groups to redirect their efforts to Scottish policy networks to influence policy. As chapter 6 discusses, these networks may now be changing further following the SNP Government's agenda on local government, which

---

[3] 'Pressure participants' is a term used by Jordan et al (2004) partly to show us that terms such as 'pressure groups' or 'interest groups' can be misleading because: (a) it conjures up a particular image of a pressure group which may not be accurate (we all think of unions or membership groups like Greenpeace); and (b) the organisations most likely to lobby governments most are businesses, universities and other types of government.

sees more discretion given to local authorities to deliver policy, and perhaps prompts groups to redirect their efforts once again to maintain their policy influence.

The Structure of the Book

Chapter 2 discusses the role of political parties as one of the main stumbling blocks to new politics in the Scottish Parliament, but also wider issues such as the level of party devolution, the brief role of small parties (largely from 2003–7) and shifts in party fortunes in UK and Scottish Parliament elections. Chapter 3 discusses the move from coalition government (1999–2007) to minority government (2007–11) as an important reference point for majority SNP Government from 2011. It discusses the limited extent to which the formation of a minority SNP government reignited the debate on new politics. Chapter 4 discusses the development of a new executive in Scotland, situating discussions of its new powers within the context of multi-level governance. It identifies the shift in focus from policy implementation under the Scottish Office (before 1999) to policy formulation and the need for greater policy capacity under the new Scottish Executive and Scottish Government. It argues that this need for policy capacity may be more useful than new politics in explaining the importance of 'territorial policy communities'. Chapter 5 discusses trends in the relationship between the Scottish and UK Governments and explores the extent to which the SNP has made a difference. Although it generally confirms a picture of informality and generally constructive relations, it also highlights particular areas of tension regarding the role of the Secretary of State for Scotland and Scottish Government attempts to play a greater role in EU and international affairs.

Chapter 6 discusses the Scottish Executive's relationships with local authorities, quasi-governmental and non-governmental bodies and explores the extent to which the new SNP government altered those relationships. It argues that the main SNP effect has been the development of a new relationship with local government, in which the latter enjoys more discretion and responsibility for service delivery. Focusing on the case study of education policy, it explores the move's effect on territorial policy communities. Chapter 7 tracks key changes in levels of national identity, public attitudes towards devolution and independence, attitudes to new Scottish institutions and the link between public opinion and particular policy initiatives. Chapter 8 charts, in depth, developments in Scottish public policy since 1999. Chapter 9 discusses how the Scottish Government is funded and the tensions that have arisen over the continued use of the Barnett formula, the limited range of economic levers in Scotland, the extent to which there is a Scottish Treasury, and the effect of an SNP government on finance debates. Chapter 10 discusses the extent to which devolution has satisfied calls for constitutional change, the constitutional issues that arose in the early years (such as the West Lothian question) and new calls for independence or a new devolved settlement (with sections on the National Conversation and Calman Commission). Chapter 11 assesses the overall effect of devolution so far, with a particular focus on the idea of policy success. In other words, can we say if devolution has succeeded or failed in any meaningful way and, if so, what measures should we use? Should we gauge devolution success in terms of the aims associated with new politics?

Chapter 2

Political Parties and Elections in Scotland

If anything sums up the obstacles to 'new politics' and a new political culture in Scotland following devolution, it is the role of political parties. Parties perform a range of positive functions, including providing an avenue for popular participation and using debate to educate the public in current political issues (McGarvey and Cairney, 2008: 46). They also pursue most strongly the electoral imperative; to win elections or enough seats to form a government. This practice may be positive, since fierce debate helps us think through hard choices, but it may also get in the way of new politics in a number of ways: parties may criticise before cooperating with each other; their pursuit of strong central control, to maintain an image of ideological coherence, may undermine the ability of individuals to cooperate across party lines; and, leaders may be under most pressure to 'perform' in Parliament and score party political points, rather than cooperate with each other to pursue common policy aims. The water in Scotland is also muddied by the wider UK picture, in which parties seek elections in multiple arenas and there are multiple sources of competition and historical distrust. For example, the fierce competition between Labour and the SNP in Scotland is supplemented by UK competition between Labour and the Conservative Party. Further, the latter is still markedly unpopular in Scotland – perhaps disproportionately so, given that it is not an electoral force – and it struggles to achieve any degree of formal cooperation with other parties in the Scottish Parliament (but not local government). The UK picture is also interesting because it shows us the degree of 'multi-level voting' that takes place with, most notably, Labour still dominating the UK General Election in Scotland but now coming second place to SNP in the Scottish Parliament (Jeffery and Herbert, 2011).

To demonstrate these points, the chapter is set up as follows. First, it outlines the multi-level nature of voting in Scotland: examining the extent to which voting in the Scottish Parliament is 'second order'; charting the extent of Labour dominance in UK General Elections in Scotland; identifying Labour's relative lack of success in Scottish Parliament elections; contrasting its performance with the SNP, which has begun to dominate Scottish Parliament elections while still struggling in general elections; and noting the performance of the other parties, including a brief rise in success for small parties in 2003. Second, it identifies minimal evidence to support the idea of a cultural shift in Scottish politics—a point made further in chapter 3's discussion of coalition and minority government. Instead, the electoral imperative is primary and, for example, fiercely fought by-elections show us that party competition is constant, operating throughout the development of new Scottish political practices from 1999.

Third, it identifies the selection of candidates and the selection of party leaders as key themes throughout the devolution monitor coverage. Both demonstrate the tensions between a pursuit of new politics and a pursuit of party coherence. The selection of candidates suggests that the successful adoption of new politics principles, most notably in relation to gender equity, requires a strong centralisation of the party, with the risk of undermining the ability of MSPs to cooperate as individuals or in committees. The selection of leaders, and expectations surrounding their performance, suggests that they find it difficult to reject the performance side of politics, in which they engage with each other in a form of theatre and their differences are exaggerated. Further, most Scottish leaders are subject to the constraints of a multi-level system in which there are pressures associated with different forms of competition; they are only responsible for certain policy decisions and may be subject to internal party constraints, particularly on issues such as constitutional change. Overall, new politics makes way for electoral competition and partisanship.

Shifts in Party Electoral Fortunes

A Second Order Election?

People vote differently in Scottish Parliament and UK General elections (Curtice, 2009: 61; Curtice, June 2003: 28; Paun, September 2007: 42). We may be tempted to describe it as a 'second order election', a rather vague term to describe two key features: turnout is lower; and, people use the opportunity to vote differently. The suggestion is that people think of this election as less important than a first order election (see also Cairney, May 2008: 83). Therefore, they do not bother to vote or they are more likely to use the opportunity to vote for another party, perhaps as a form of protest at the government in power and/or because they may have more than one vote. Consequently, the party occupying office in the UK Government attracts fewer votes in the second-order election, and opposition and smaller parties attract more votes. A further implication is that, while voters are free to choose how to behave, a second-order election may undermine the 'lines of electoral accountability' so important to the idea of a Scottish Parliament addressing the democratic deficit (Denver and Johns, 2010; exacerbated by the fact that few electoral campaigns stick to the issues associated with the policy responsibilities of the UK or Scottish governments).

However, as Denver and Johns (2010) argue, the binary first/second order distinction is misleading. They prefer the idea of a continuum, which shows that Scottish Parliament elections attract a higher turnout, and perhaps a greater sense of seriousness, than local and European elections. Further, the gap in turnout at UK and Scottish Parliament elections is falling, while the importance that voters attach to Scottish Parliament and General elections is similar (Denver and Johns, 2010; see also McGarvey, August 2001: 5-6 on the almost identical turnouts in 1999 and 2001). Voters also pay more attention to Scottish, not UK, issues when voting in Scottish Parliament elections (the percentage split is 52/34 in 1999, 54/27 in 2003 and 56/29 in 2007 – Curtice, 2009: 62). Indeed, this shift of focus from the UK to Scotland, combined with a strong sense of Scottish national identity and a demand of parties to 'stand up for Scotland', helps explain why the SNP does better in Scottish Parliament elections (2009: 62-3; a trend identified, by Jeffery and Hough, 2003: 211, in many political systems 'where territorial cleavages structure political debate differently across a state').

There is also some evidence that the Scottish Parliament often commands greater media attention or is considered more important by some parties. For example, the May (2000: 15) monitor reports Labour MP concerns that the performance of the Scottish Executive might harm their election chances, representing 'an interesting reversal of the theory of first and second order elections!'. Further, the Scottish Parliament (and some Scottish party leaders – McGarvey, August 2001: 40-1) became the media focal point for UK General Election campaigns in Scotland and parties such as the SNP and SSP saw the UK General election of 2001 as an 'opportunity to build up a profile and base for fighting the Scottish elections in two years time' (Mitchell, May 2001:

49). In 2007, the prospect of an SNP victory in the Scottish Parliament elections often overshadowed the prospect of a Scottish Prime Minister (Gordon Brown)(Lynch, January 2007: 65). In 2008, the popularity of Alex Salmond and the SNP Government appeared to be one factor in John Mason's win in the (UK) Glasgow East by-election (Lynch, September 2008: 87; Bort, September 2008: 28–31).

Denver and Johns (2010) also highlight the difficulty of attributing different voting patterns to the second-order nature of Scottish Parliament elections, since voters may also be swayed by the mixed-member proportional system that gives them two votes. Voters may use their second vote to support a smaller party—a practice that the Greens and Scottish Socialist Party exploited to great effect in 2003 (table 2.2)—without realising that this may undermine their support for their first choice party. Denver and Johns (2010) also demonstrate the link between voting behaviour in the Scottish Parliament and issues related to 'valence politics', which describes a tendency to vote in accordance with one's opinion of the party, the party leader, the government's record in office or one's prediction about another party's likely performance. Voters in 2007 appeared to support the SNP based on their negative evaluation of Scottish Labour's record in office (although note the SNP's hopes for a 'referendum on Blair'—Lynch, April 2007: 84) and their positive response to the SNP's image, its leader's image, its vision and its likely record in government (Johns et al, 2009: 207). Further, the SNP offered 'a more positive and Scottish-oriented agenda than Labour' (2009: 229; see also Johns et al, 2010). This suggests that voters were focused more on the Scottish Parliament than the 'first-order' UK.

While more detailed analysis is yet to come, the same can be said for the SNP's landslide victory in 2011. It was based largely on voter perceptions of the competence of the SNP in government, with some evidence of an *additional* second-order effect. In particular, the SNP benefitted most from the much-reduced Liberal Democrat vote (table 2.2) associated with its turbulent first year as part of the UK Coalition Government (see the Scottish Election Study website http://www. scottishelectionstudy.org.uk/). Voters make some reference to the UK context, but there is enough of a focus on Scottish politics and government to suggest that Scottish Parliament elections are not second order affairs. Instead, there is an often complex combination of Scottish and UK issues, such as when the SNP's stance on independence prompts some to vote SNP to pursue their beliefs on constitutional change, and others to choose a party most likely to 'stand up for Scotland's interests' (Johns et al, 2009: 212; see Curtice, January 2008:

56; November 2004: 19 on the SNP's higher scores on the 'looking after the interests of Scottish people' question). In other words, we should also not go too far in the opposite direction. For example, the success of the SNP in Scottish Parliament elections does not follow a notable rise in support for independence (see chapter 7).

Voting Behaviour in Scotland

We can begin to see the differences in voting by examining post-war voting patterns in UK General elections (table 2.1). The Scottish results show that the two main UK parties, Conservative and Labour, dominated votes and seats until the 1970s. From the 1970s, we can see two main developments. First, the SNP and Liberal Democrats became more serious electoral forces. The SNP commanded over 30% of the vote in October 1974 and the Liberal Democrats almost 25% in 1983 (as part of the brief Liberal Democrat/Social Democratic Party alliance). Second, it came largely at the expense of the Conservative party, particularly in October 1974, 1987 and, most importantly, since 1997 when it has failed to secure more than one seat. It did not undermine Labour in the same way. While Labour's share of the vote often dipped below 40% from 1974, it has always commanded a majority of seats during this period. Indeed, its share of seats has been above 69% since 1987. Combined with its showing in Scottish local authority elections throughout this period, Labour became known as 'Scotland's establishment party' (Irvine in McGarvey and Cairney, 2008: 52; although note that 'one of the biggest myths about Scottish local government is that it is dominated by the Labour party'—McGarvey, June 2003: 49). This image was particularly marked from 1979. The SNP vote suffered after 1979 when it became clear that devolution was off the agenda following a failed referendum (despite a small majority voting 'yes'—see McGarvey and Cairney, 2008: 31). In contrast, Labour remained Scotland's main party during 18 years of UK Conservative government from 1979–97.

Both outcomes contributed to the devolution agenda in the 1990s. The experience of Conservative government prompted many supporters of devolution to argue that a Scottish Parliament could have saved the Scottish population from a series of policies, associated with Thatcherism, that received relatively low support in Scotland. Further, the tendency for Scottish voters to choose Labour, but receive a Conservative government, contributed to the idea that devolution could address the 'democratic deficit' (2008: 32–6). These factors provide the key context to Scottish Parliament voting—the general expectation was that Labour would represent the largest party for many years to come. Combined with the new mixed member proportional system, in which no party is expected to gain a majority of seats, it became likely that Labour would form a coalition government with another party (see chapter 3 on the low likelihood of minority government).

As table 2.2 suggests, Labour became the Scottish Parliament's largest party in 1999 and 2003 and formed a coalition government with the Liberal Democrats from 1999–2007. It took until 2007 and 2011 for the SNP's victories to change Scottish politics fundamentally (the SNP win in 2007 happened 'despite the predictions of pundits' — Lynch, September, 2007: 64). Yet, we should not understate the importance of the result in 1999 by comparing it only with 2011. At the time, the 1999 result marked an important change in voting behaviour and outcomes. Most notably, Labour's share of the vote fell and the SNP's rose. The SNP was also much better able to translate its share of the vote into parliamentary seats. Labour became the largest party, but the SNP was also 'transformed from a handful of MPs at Westminster into a serious block of 35 at Holyrood: the official opposition' (Leicester, 2000: 15; Winetrobe, 2001: 180).

The more proportional voting system allowed the Conservatives to improve their position despite attracting fewer votes than in Westminster elections. It also allowed smaller parties and independents to win seats, although the 2003 high, in which the Greens and SSP took 13 seats (over 10%), now seems like a blip rather than a new settlement, particularly following the implosion of the SSP and the reduction of the Greens to 2 seats (for the SSP see Mitchell, November 2004: 41; Mitchell, April 2005: 39; Lynch, January 2006: 110–11; Bort, September 2006: 28–9; Lynch, September 2006: 61–5; January 2007: 72–3; April 2007: 85–6; September 2007: 74–5; January 2008: 102; May 2008: 82; for the Greens see Lynch, September 2007: 74; see also Bort, April 2007: 24 on the two horse race). The days when the SNP came under pressure from the SSP on the regional list (Mitchell et al, 2003: 136) already seem historical. The Liberal Democrats remained relatively unaffected because the concentration of their vote in particular (predominantly rural) areas allowed them to win constituency seats in both types of election (note that the SNP vote has traditionally been spread too thinly, particularly in UK elections — Curtice, 2009: 56). Then, in 2011, it suffered from its association with the UK coalition government, securing only 5 seats.

Table 2.1 UK General Elections, Results in Scotland, 1945–2010

	Labour			SNP			Conservative			Liberal Democrat		
	Vote	Seats	% Seats	Vote	No. Seats	% Seats	Vote	No. Seats	% Seats	Vote	No. Seats	% Seats
5.7.45	49.4%	40	59.7%	1.2%	0	0.0%	41.1%	27	40.3%	5.0%	0	0.0%
23.2.50	46.2%	37	52.9%	0.4%	0	0.0%	44.8%	31	44.3%	6.6%	2	2.9%
25.10.51	47.9%	35	49.3%	0.3%	0	0.0%	48.6%	35	49.3%	2.7%	1	1.4%
26.5.55	46.7%	34	47.9%	0.5%	0	0.0%	50.1%	36	50.7%	1.9%	1	1.4%
8.10.59	46.7%	38	54.3%	0.8%	0	0.0%	47.2%	31	44.3%	4.1%	1	1.4%
15.10.64	48.7%	43	60.6%	2.4%	0	0.0%	40.6%	24	33.8%	7.6%	4	5.6%
31.3.66	49.9%	46	64.8%	5.0%	0	0.0%	37.7%	20	28.2%	6.8%	5	7.0%
18.6.70	44.5%	44	62.0%	11.4%	1	1.4%	38.0%	23	32.4%	5.5%	3	4.2%
28.2.74	36.6%	40	56.3%	21.9%	7	9.9%	32.9%	21	29.6%	8.0%	3	4.2%
10.10.74	36.3%	41	57.7%	30.4%	11	15.5%	24.7%	16	22.5%	8.3%	3	4.2%
3.5.79	41.6%	44	62.0%	17.3%	2	2.8%	31.4%	22	31.0%	9.0%	3	4.2%
9.6.83	35.1%	41	56.9%	11.8%	2	2.8%	28.4%	21	29.2%	24.5%	8	11.1%
11.6.87	42.4%	50	69.4%	14.0%	3	4.2%	24.0%	10	13.9%	19.3%	9	12.5%
9.4.92	39.0%	50	69.4%	21.5%	3	4.2%	25.6%	11	15.3%	13.1%	8	11.1%
1.5.97	45.6%	56	77.8%	22.1%	6	8.3%	17.5%	0	0.0%	13.0%	10	13.9%
7.6.01	43.3%	56	77.8%	20.1%	5	6.9%	15.6%	1	1.4%	16.3%	10	13.9%
5.5.05	39.5%	41	69.5%	17.7%	6	10.2%	15.8%	1	1.7%	22.6%	11	18.6%
6.5.10	42.0%	41	69.5%	19.9%	6	10.2%	16.7%	1	1.7%	18.9%	11	18.6%

Note: the number of seats in Scotland fell from 72 to 59 following the post-devolution boundary review, exaggerating Labour's loss of support (Lynch, January 2006: 109).

Table 2.2 Scottish Parliament Election Results 1999–2011

	1st Vote	Seats	2nd Vote	Seats	Total Seats	% Seats
Labour						
1999	38.8%	53	33.6%	3	56	43.4%
2003	34.6%	46	29.6%	4	50	38.8%
2007	32.2%	37	29.2%	9	46	35.7%
2011	31.7%	15	26.3%	22	37	28.7%
Scottish National Party						
1999	28.7%	7	27.3%	28	35	27.1%
2003	23.8%	9	21.6%	18	27	20.9%
2007	32.9%	21	31.0%	26	47	36.4%
2011	45.4%	53	44.0%	16	69	53.5%
Conservative						
1999	15.6%	0	15.4%	18	18	14.0%
2003	16.6%	3	15.5%	15	18	14.0%
2007	16.6%	4	13.9%	13	17	13.2%
2011	13.9%	3	12.4%	12	15	11.6%
Liberal Democrat						
1999	14.2%	12	12.4%	5	17	13.2%
2003	15.4%	13	11.6%	4	17	13.2%
2007	16.2%	11	13.9%	5	16	12.4%
2011	7.9%	2	5.2%	3	5	3.9%
Green						
1999	0.0%	0	3.6%	1	1	0.8%
2003	0.0%	0	6.5%	7	7	5.4%
2007	0.2%	0	4.0%	2	2	1.6%
2011	0.0%	0	4.4%	2	2	1.6%
Scottish Socialist Party						
1999	1.0%	0	2.0%	1	1	0.8%
2003	6.2%	0	6.5%	6	6	4.7%
2007	0.0%	0	0.6%	0	0	0.0%
2011	0.0%	0	0.4%	0	0	0.0%
Other						
1999	1.7%	1	5.7%	0	1	3.1%
2003	3.4%	2	8.7%	2	4	0.8%
2007	3.1%	0	7.4%	1	1	0.8%
2011	1.1%	0	7.3%	1	1	0.8%

The difference in UK General and Scottish Parliament voting behaviour is best demonstrated in a comparison of the two main parties in Scotland. As table 2.3 shows, Labour always commands a higher share of the Westminster vote and seats than it does in the Scottish Parliament, while the reverse is true for the SNP. This emerging pattern prompted early monitors to talk up the chances of an SNP government in 2003 (August 2000: 17; see also Curtice, June 2003: 27), to be cautious about the implications of general election results for the Scottish Parliament (McGarvey, August 2001: 5), and to consider the argument accepted in most media that 'the SNP would struggle to be relevant post-devolution in a general election' (until they pursued the 'standing up for Scotland's interests' line more effectively—McGarvey, August 2001: 42). The difference was marked in 2007 when the SNP gained more Scottish Parliament seats than Labour for the first time, while only securing 10% of Westminster seats in Scotland (McGarvey and Cairney, 2008: 54). However, it is much clearer in 2011. While Labour gained more than two-thirds of Westminster seats in 2010, it secured less than one-third of Scottish Parliament seats in 2011. Conversely, the SNP secured 10% of the Westminster seats but a majority (54%) in the Scottish Parliament.

Table 2.3 Westminster and Scottish Parliament Elections,
Labour and SNP, 1997–2011

		Westminster			Scottish Parliament					
		Vote	No. Seats	% Seats	1st Vote	Seats	2nd Vote	Seats	Total Seats	% Seats
1997 and 1999	Labour	45.6%	56	77.8%	38.8%	53	33.6%	3	56	43.4%
	SNP	22.1%	6	8.3%	28.7%	7	27.3%	28	35	27.1%
2001 and 2003	Labour	43.3%	56	77.8%	34.6%	46	29.6%	4	50	38.8%
	SNP	20.1%	5	6.9%	23.8%	9	21.6%	18	27	20.9%
2005 and 2007	Labour	39.5%	41	69.5%	32.2%	37	29.2%	9	46	35.7%
	SNP	17.7%	6	10.2%	32.9%	21	31.0%	26	47	36.4%
2010 and 2011	Labour	42.0%	41	69.5%	31.7%	15	26.3%	22	37	28.7%
	SNP	19.9%	6	10.2%	45.4%	53	44.0%	16	69	53.5%

The Scottish Election of 2011 has to go down as the most exciting in its short history and probably for decades to come. The size of the SNP win was staggering. The most staggering part is that it gained a majority – given that the system seems to be designed to stop one party winning in this way. Indeed, the talk before devolution was that proportional representation was chosen by Labour to stop the SNP ever the getting the majority it needed to push hard on the independence agenda. Put more positively, the system is designed to make it unlikely that one party achieves a majority unless it gains a majority of the vote. PR is supposed to produce a different kind of party system in which the largest party forms a coalition government with at least one other party (as Labour did with the Liberal Democrats in 1999 and 2003) or a minority government (as the SNP did in 2007, performing the unlikely task of fulfilling a full 4-year term with 36% of the seats). However, MMP clearly does not make it *impossible* to gain a majority of seats without a majority of the vote because it is not entirely proportional. The explanation for the SNP's win comes from the role of first-past-the-post to elect 73 of its 129 MSPs. The SNP secured 73% (53) of those seats from 45.4% of the vote. While it received only 16, or 30%, of regional seats from 44% of the regional votes, this was not enough to offset its constituency majority.

The second surprise is how well the SNP did in the constituency vote. In the three previous elections it came well behind Labour: in 1999 Labour won 53 constituency seats to the SNP's 7; in 2003 the split was 46 and 9; and, even in 2007, the split was 37 to 27, with the SNP becoming the largest party on the back of its 26 regional seats (to Labour's 9). Now, 53 SNP compares to 15 Labour. The third is that the SNP did well in areas that used to be Labour strongholds. One of the most notable areas is Glasgow, where Labour won 10 of 10 constituencies in 1999 and 2003, then 9 in 2007. Nicola Sturgeon was the SNP's exception and, at the time, this seemed like a symbolic blow to Labour's dominance. In 2011, the SNP took the majority (5 of 9) of the constituency seats in Glasgow – a result that must seem like a crushing blow to Labour. In effect, we now have two eras in modern Scottish politics: the Labour dominated coalition from 1999–2007 followed by the SNP minority and majority governments from 2007–16 (note that the Scottish Parliament term will last 5 years to avoid coinciding with the next UK general election in 2015).

New Politics Versus the Role of Parties?

There are tensions between the idea of new politics, in which confrontational partisanship makes way for consensual party relations, and the traditional role of political parties in the UK. A key aim of parties is to compete with other parties in elections and demonstrate that their policies are superior to those of other parties (even though the manifestos of Labour, SNP and Liberal Democrats are often very similar — Mitchell, June 2003: 58). Further, since electioneering seems to take place continuously, rather than in the few weeks before an election, it is difficult for parties to juggle their competitive and cooperative roles. It perhaps requires a cultural shift, which may take decades to produce, as parties realise that they will need to cooperate with the same people over long periods (this seemed to take 20 years in Denmark — Green-Pedersen, 2001; Seyd, 2002). As chapter 3 discusses, this cultural shift does not appear to have taken place (yet).

There is some evidence of cooperation between two parties within the Scottish Executive (although see the discussion of Jim Wallace below), despite the appearance of divisive issues such as STV (single transferable vote) in local elections (Mitchell, February 2001: 52; Mitchell, May 2002: 60; Mitchell, May 2004: 55; chapter 6). However, government-versus-opposition partisanship tended to win over cooperation during Parliament-Executive relations. The monitor coverage of by-elections gives a sense of the constant competition between parties, taking place at the same time as new developments in parliamentary behaviour (for coverage of the first year of devolution, see February 2000: 18–22; May 2000: 21–2; August 2000: 15–16; see Mitchell et al, November 2000: 47–52 for an example of the coverage of local by-elections, analysed primarily as second-order indications of the popularity of the parties in Scotland; see Lynch, January 2007: 65 on the long lead up to the May 2007 election). Campaigning has also become big business, with the SNP spending almost £1.4m in 2007 and Labour over £1.2m (Lynch, January 2008: 101; new figures suggest that this gap is widening — Barnes, 2011).

The Selection of Candidates

We can see this tension played out in the selection of Scottish Parliament candidates. On the one hand, there is a new politics dimension to candidate selection, with the broad aim of 'devolution supporters' to 'broaden recruitment and create a more open political class, more representative of the country as a whole' (Keating and Cairney, 2006: 43). It included a specific commitment, expressed by the Scottish Constitutional Convention (1995), to pursue gender equity as well as a 'vaguer commitment to representativeness on other dimensions' (Keating and Cairney, 2006: 43). To a large extent, this involved addressing the overrepresentation of some social groups such as white middle-aged men, people with a private school education, elected officials from local government, and those with jobs which seem to relate primarily to gaining election (the 'politics-facilitating' professions).

On the other hand, this process requires that parties are controlled to a large extent from the centre—a situation that perhaps undermines the ability of MSPs to cooperate with colleagues in other parties. Labour and the SNP were particularly keen to ensure that 'better quality candidates would emerge than had been the case in the past', but critical candidates in those parties 'feared that the process would be used not only to weed out less impressive candidates but also to block anyone deemed insufficiently loyal to the leadership' (November 1999: 25). Indeed, 'it has been suggested that ideological tests were adopted to ensure that those selected and, more so, those elected were in tune with the thinking of the leadership of each party. This proved highly contentious within the Labour Party especially' (November 1999: 25). Labour's example is the most relevant, and it rejected two Labour MPs, Denis Canavan and Ian Davidson (Canavan went on to win his constituency seat as an independent). It was also the most committed to gender equity, and the only party to set up twinned, one man and one woman, constituencies.

We can find mixed evidence on these concerns. The November (1999: 25) monitor reports that 85% of Labour candidates agreed with the measures to further gender equity and 34% of SNP candidates felt that they should have had the same arrangement. Further, 30% of successful Labour candidates felt that 'leadership influence over the selection of constituency candidates was too great' compared to 12% in the SNP. The selection of regional candidates also had the potential to give party leaders considerable power. This power was exercised most by Labour, the party least likely to pick up regional seats (3 of 56 in 1999). In contrast, the SNP 'allowed its membership to choose the order of names for the list' (which made up 28 of its 35 seats, and half of all regional seats, in 1999) and 90% of candidates felt that the process was democratic (November 1999: 26; compare with the 'cauldron of tension' when regional candidates had to be re-selected before 2003, but note that this relates to *internal* competition—Mitchell, August 2002: 41-3).

The Liberal Democratic party perhaps sum up best the strong link between new politics and party control. It, as a member of the SCC, made a similar commitment to gender equity. However, its 'lack of central control allied with membership reluctance to put this into effect resulted in few successful women Liberal Democrat MSPs' (November 1999: 26). More generally, the evidence suggests that the most centrist party, Labour, is also the most socially representative. Indeed, Scottish Labour is generally the only reason for any difference in social composition between the Scottish Parliament and Westminster (McGarvey and Cairney, 2008: 231). It is the only party to achieve gender parity and Labour MSPs are less likely to be privately educated than their Westminster (and most Holyrood) counterparts (2008: 231).

The Selection of Leaders

Labour

Devolution quickly raised the issue of party leadership to the top of the agenda. For example, the May (2000: 17–20) report devotes considerable attention to leadership of the four main parties. Most attention relates to the Labour leadership, partly because Donald Dewar became First Minister at the age of 61 and soon became ill, and partly because of tensions between Dewar and Scottish Secretary John Reid, combined with the idea that UK Labour still had considerable control over the Scottish party and its future leadership (May 2000: 17; see also chapter 5). The speculation was *not* prompted by the prospect of a better leader (August 2000: 17). Dewar's death in October 2000, combined with the stipulation in the Scotland Act 1998 that a new First Minister must be elected in 28 days (designed largely to restrict the length of coalition government negotiations), prompted a process to replace him that overrode Labour party leadership rules. Henry McLeish won by a slim margin over Jack McConnell, a result that became significant a year later when McLeish resigned, to be replaced by McConnell. The former was generally characterised as gaffe prone, unpopular in the back benches and unable to provide strong leadership to a Labour party prone to in-fighting (Mitchell, February 2001: 3). The latter emerged from the first contest with a 'strong body of support' because he performed well, did not complain about the party election 'procedures which placed him at a disadvantage' and he did not make too much of UK Labour involvement in the process (Mitchell et al, November, 2000: 47; McLeish had the 'strong backing of Gordon Brown and Labour's leadership in London' — Mitchell, November 2001: 3). He also appeared to learn from McLeish's mistakes by exposing the skeletons in his closet at the early stages of the next Labour leader campaign before being elected unopposed (see Mitchell, November 2001: 3–5 for the background to McLeish's resignation). McConnell then served as First Minister for over five years, and proved Mitchell (November 2001: 7) wrong in the process ('the politics of Scottish devolution may be about to become more interesting'), perhaps with the exception of an initial show of strength—his first Cabinet included only one person from the old Cabinet (Wendy Alexander, who resigned in May 2002—see Mitchell, February 2002: 41-2; Mitchell, November 2002: 33) and brief attention to 'irregularities in the finances of Jack McConnell's constituency party' (Mitchell, November 2002: 32).

McConnell resigned soon after Labour was defeated in the 2007 Scottish Parliament election following its traditionally-poor campaign (which McConnell did not really lead—Lynch, April 2007: 81; September 2007: 70). He was replaced by Wendy Alexander, who ran unopposed and consequently replaced her leadership tour with a 'listening and learning' (from Labour officials) tour (Lynch, September 2007: 71). Alexander took the unusual step of apologising for Labour's loss in Scotland at a UK Labour conference (Lynch, January 2008: 95). She then became embroiled quickly in scandal related to the source of donations to her campaign. Although she initially decided to 'tough it out with bullish statements claiming she would be cleared of any wrongdoing' (Lynch, January 2008: 96; Bort, January 2008: 30-1) and was not charged by the police or Electoral Commission with any wrongdoing, she was given a one-day ban by the Standards Committee and resigned quickly after (Lynch, May 2008: 77; September 2008: 83).

The SNP

The May (2000: 19) monitor reports (accurate) speculation that Alex Salmond was preparing to leave and that he would most likely be replaced by his ally John Swinney. One reason given is that he had been leader for almost ten years and that victory in the 2003 election would 'condemn him to remain leader for at least another four years' (August 2000: 17). Another is that 'Salmond's strengths are more suited to the Commons than the Scottish Parliament' (Mitchell, February 2001: 53; while this seems dated, it is still true if we take it to refer to his period in *opposition* in the Scottish Parliament). Swinney served as leader until 2004, when he resigned after a quite-poor 2003 election followed by poor results in the 2004 European elections. Swinney is still regarded as a leader of sorts, taking the lead on most financial matters. Further, it was under Swinney's leadership that key SNP policies developed, most notably when the SNP decided in 2002 to pursue a new strategy on economic policy, selling to businesses the idea of lower corporation taxes under a fiscally autonomous Scotland, and selling to unions the idea of an alternative to public-private partnerships (Mitchell, May 2002: 58; see chapter 9 on PPP). Swinney was also responsible for the reform of the SNP's constitution in 2004 (Mitchell, February 2004: 39; Mitchell, May 2004: 55). He was replaced by

Salmond who, in the classic guise of a politician who had to be persuaded by his friends and colleagues to run (Mitchell, August 2004: 43–5), became leader again in 2004. Deputy leader Nicola Sturgeon led the Scottish Parliament group until 2007 (both won their internal elections comfortably — Mitchell, November 2004: 40). Salmond then reinforced his image as a gambler by choosing to contest the Liberal Democrat-held Gordon seat as part of a strategy of securing 20 constituency seats in 2007 (they secured 21, and 47 overall) (Lynch, May 2006: 67; he also placed a 3-way bet by securing selection at the top of the North East regional list).

The Liberal Democrats

Coverage of Jim Wallace's leadership of the Liberal Democrats perhaps reveals the same initial problems faced by Nick Clegg, Wallace's UK equivalent, from 2010. Wallace faced a lot of early criticism in relation to poor by-election results and his main problem was 'how to maintain a distinct identity for his party while being part of a coalition government. This problem is exacerbated by Labour's determination that it should take credit for all that is achieved while the Liberal Democrats are pushed to the fore when things go wrong ... Wallace faces the problem of being head of a government in which he has little or no control over the main party to the coalition' (May 2000: 20). These concerns faded after the 2001 UK General Election when the Liberal Democrats saw their share of the vote rise to 16.3% to make them the third most successful party 'for the first time ever in a Scottish general election' (McGarvey, August 2001: 43). Indeed, during the campaign, the Liberal Democrats were much more able to claim credit for, and exaggerate, successes in Scotland, while they were much less subject to attack than Labour (McGarvey, August 2001: 43; Mitchell, February 2002: 43). Further, Wallace's decision to resign after the 2005 UK General Election coincided with a rise in Liberal Democrat vote to 22.6%, the second highest after Labour (Lynch, January 2006: 109). However, there is still a residual sense, expressed well by Ross Finnie, that the Liberal Democrats struggled to maintain a distinct identity (Lynch, September 2008: 91).

Wallace was replaced by Nicol Stephen. While Stephen was less forthright than his competitor Mike Rumbles about leaving the Scottish Executive coalition and exploring other options (such as a coalition with the SNP in 2007), his appointment marked the beginning of a new phase in which the coalition was operating well but also preparing to dissolve in the lead up to the 2007 elections (Lynch, January 2006: 110). This phase began properly in the run up to the Dunfermline and West

Fife by-election, won by Liberal Democrat Willie Rennie (who now leads the LibDems in the Scottish Parliament after becoming an MSP in 2011), partly on the back of criticism of the Scottish Executive's handling of the future of the Forth Road bridge (Lynch, May 2006: 65–6). It was followed by key points of Labour-Liberal Democrat tension, most notably on the issue of new nuclear power stations in Scotland, which the latter opposed (Lynch, May 2006: 67–8; Cairney, May 2006: 73; September 2006: 77). Stephen was pivotal in the decision to reject a coalition government with the SNP in 2007, before becoming one of the few people to really resign to spend more time with his family (Bort, September 2008: 26–7) – a decision that exposed the gulf in resources of a government and opposition party leader (Lynch, September 2008: 89). Nicol was replaced by Tavish Scott (August 2008), who served until shortly after their disastrous showing in the 2011 election.

The Conservatives

Perhaps ironically, the May (2000: 20) monitor has far greater confidence in the fortunes of Conservative leader David McLetchie, an effective leader who had few expectations to manage (given the low electoral popularity of the Conservatives in the run up to devolution). By 2001 a divided and critical parliamentary group left his position 'precarious', but he was bolstered by his strong parliamentary performances, most notably in the run up to McLeish's resignation (Mitchell, November 2001: 56; February 2002: 44). McLetchie resigned in 2005 following embarrassing revelations about his taxi expenses (Lynch, January 2006: 112). He was replaced by Annabelle Goldie, who was elected unopposed following a dream-team ticket with Murdo Fraser as deputy leader (Lynch, January 2006: 112). Goldie's leadership was particularly important from 2007. The Conservatives were partly responsible for the stability of minority SNP Government, providing regular support in exchange for some policy concessions (see chapter 3; Lynch, September 2007: 74; Lynch, January 2008: 93–4 discusses the SNP's removal of a bar on coalition with the Conservatives in local authorities; for SNP-Green cooperation see Lynch, May 2006: 65) at a time when the UK party was often presented as 'anti-Scottish – especially because of the support they receive from the more nationalistic sections of the English press' (Lynch, January 2008: 97; see also Lynch, May 2008: 80). However, Goldie shared the fate of all three main party leaders after the 2011 Scottish Parliament election and will be replaced by the end of 2011.

Party Leadership and Party Devolution

All three UK parties faced the need to balance being 'seen to be in tune with London while being sufficiently independent of it' (May 2000: 20). That sense was strongest among Labour (the Scottish leader leads the parliamentary party only) and least worrying among the 'federal' Liberal Democrats (the Scottish leader leads the whole party in Scotland), with the Conservatives representing a party that has adapted well to devolution in Scotland but not the UK (see McGarvey, August 2001: 44 and Mitchell, November 2001: 57 on Scots Tories' antipathy towards leadership candidates Iain Duncan-Smith and Kenneth Clarke because of their attitudes to devolution and Scotland's funding settlement). Indeed, the 2011 leadership race proved to be controversial when candidate Murdo Fraser proposed a new name for the Scottish party and a looser coalition between the Scottish branch and London.

Their uneasy positions as part of UK parties are perhaps demonstrated best in a discussion of constitutional debates (see chapter 10). Both UK and Scottish Labour attitudes tended towards a rejection of further devolution (Wright, August 2001: 25) and few Labour leaders have spoken out against this line until recently. Indeed, as late as 2008, Labour leader Wendy Alexander lost a lot of credibility when her challenge to the SNP to bring on an early referendum on independence was not supported by Prime Minister Gordon Brown, and this may have contributed to her resignation (Bort, May 2008: 29–30; Bort, September 2008: 24–5). That episode prompted Alexander's potential successors to champion, 'a more robust and a more Scottish approach to relations with the UK party' (Jeffery, September 2008: 4). The leadership debate included a discussion of the prospect of the Labour leader in Scotland emulating the Liberal Democrat position and taking on cross-Scotland leadership—something that has yet to happen (Lynch, September 2008: 86). Instead, Alexander was later succeeded as leader by Iain Gray, 'seen to be London's candidate' (Lynch, September 2008: 85) and the same discussion resurfaced following Gray's resignation in 2011 (Maddox, 2011). In short, Labour is the party least likely to accept further party or political devolution (Bort, September 2008: 32–4).

The Scottish Conservatives were reported to have been banned from discussing constitutional change during the Calman review 'for fear of exposing splits, embarrassing David Cameron and tying his hands when in office', reminding us that 'Labour is not the only party with often-problematic organisational devolution' (Cairney, January 2009: 32). However, they have at least adapted to their position, becoming more open to the idea of further devolution if supported by the Scottish electorate (Wright, August 2001: 25). For example, recent statements by David Cameron that he would 'govern the Scots with respect' were preceded in 2004 (when Michael Howard was leader) by vague claims that the Scottish Conservative leader would always be welcome to attend Michael Howard's UK Cabinet (Wright, May 2004: 34–5) and by assurances by the Shadow Chancellor that the Conservatives were open to the idea of fiscal autonomy (Wright, August 2004: 28). In the Conservative's case, it has often been the Scottish leader that is most likely to reject further devolution, with David McLetchie often stating that he would still vote 'no, no' in a devolution referendum (Mitchell, February 2002: 44). The position of the Liberal Democrats is perhaps ironic—Nick Clegg's leadership campaign had little 'resonance North of the Border' (Lynch, January, 2008: 97), but his decision to enter a coalition with the Conservatives in 2010 made the Scottish party electorally toxic in 2011.

Leadership and New Politics

The issue of leadership also sums up the low likelihood of new politics in the Scottish Parliament. For example, from 2000, there was a degree of media speculation about the prospect of a new government-opposition relationship following the election of two new leaders. First Minister Henry McLeish and SNP leader John Swinney were not as 'socialised into the ways of the Commons' as their predecessors and they previously enjoyed a good relationship when they both held the Enterprise and Lifelong Learning portfolios. Further, Swinney represented the 'pragmatist', not 'fundamentalist', side of the SNP, which views devolution as a positive development and a 'step towards independence', rather than an unwelcome dilution of, and potential obstacle to, the SNP's aims (the distinction was used in the 1980s by Mitchell, to highlight a more important cleavage than left/right within the SNP, but it is becoming less important as devolution progresses and 'fundamentalist' MSPs engage fully with the Scottish Parliament—see Mitchell, August 2004: 44; 54, note 95). The size of Swinney's victory, and those of his pragmatic colleagues, also suggests that the 'core hardliners ... are weaker in today's SNP than probably at any time in the party's history' (Mitchell et al, November 2000: 42). Still, both McLeish and Swinney were quick to engage in confrontations as party leaders, suggesting that 'confrontational styles seem a function of the intense electoral competition between Labour and SNP' (Mitchell et al, November 2000: 41). Swinney's relationship with McConnell was even more 'theatrical' (Mitchell, February 2002: 42). Since then, there has rarely been a government-opposition relationship that goes beyond the theatrical, leaving the field wide open for Annabelle Goldie (as a non-threatening figure, given the parliamentary arithmetic) to appear highly reasonable merely by asking sensible questions in a normal voice. Indeed, partisanship seemed to rise after the formation of an SNP government in 2007, and the final monitor is perhaps the best example of a report dominated by partisan tensions (see Cairney, September 2009: 40-1; see also Bort, January 2008: 28 on Wendy Alexander struggling to keep up that tradition).

Conclusion

Scottish Parliament elections may not be 'second order', but there are clear differences in the way that people vote in Scottish Parliament and UK General Elections. Labour still dominates General Elections in Scotland (regardless of its performance overall in the UK) but its grip on Scottish Parliament elections has been falling since devolution. It was the main party in 1999 and 2003, forming a coalition government with the Liberal Democrats, but it lost the election in 2007 by a whisker before being subject to an embarrassing defeat to the SNP in 2011. The SNP has become the strongest electoral force in the Scottish Parliament's history while securing only about 10% of Westminster seats in Scotland. This is the main lesson from Scottish electoral politics. While 1999 and 2003 gave some hint of a rise in the importance of small parties, and the Scottish Parliament has a multi-party system in which at least 4 parties often determine the make-up of the Scottish Government, it is a Parliament increasingly linked to the fortunes of the two main parties. In this sense it is not as different from Westminster as we may have expected. Indeed, in 2011, it looks more like Westminster than Westminster!

As chapter 3 makes clear, the new electoral system has not produced a cultural shift in Scottish politics. Holyrood still resembles Westminster in this sense. The electoral imperative is primary and party competition is constant. The competition between Labour and the SNP has historically been fierce—a process that is magnified by their competition to determine the form of constitutional change—and cross-chamber cooperation often seems less likely than between Labour and the Conservatives in Westminster. It may make sense to talk of a political class in Scotland and the UK, in which elected representatives have increasingly similar backgrounds and are surrounded by a very small world and pool of recruitment, but this does not always translate to an equivalent sense of cooperation.

The monitors do not discuss these issues systematically, perhaps because they are so true as to be taken for granted. Instead, the major themes relate to the selection of candidates, the role of leadership, the multi-level nature of party competition and how all three relate to new politics. In each case they demonstrate a tension between the pursuit of new politics and the pursuit of party coherence. The selection of candidates suggests that the successful adoption of new politics principles, most notably in relation to gender equity, requires a strong centralisation of the party. For example, the party with the best record on candidate recruitment (Labour) is also the party with the least popular system of party centralisation. The performance of leaders also reflects the difficulty of rejecting the performance side of politics. While it would be difficult to separate the manifestos of at least three of the four main parties, you would not know it from parliamentary behaviour. Instead, they tend to exaggerate their differences – a process that undermines their ability to cooperate in any meaningful way. Further, most Scottish leaders (Labour, Conservative, Liberal Democrat – in that order) are subject to the constraints of a multi-level system in which there are pressures associated with different forms of party competition; they are only responsible for certain policy decisions and may be subject to internal party constraints regarding the issues on which they can cooperate meaningfully. Overall, new politics makes way for electoral competition and partisanship. This is the context for chapter 3, in which we find that coalition government undermined cross-party cooperation, while the SNP was able to maintain a minority government despite a remarkably low level of cross-party consensus.

The Scottish Parliament and Scottish Government Does Minority Government Make a Difference?

This chapter explores the difference that minority government makes when compared to coalition government, focusing primarily on the relationship between the Scottish Parliament and Government. Chapter 1 demonstrates that the Parliament does not have the resources to do much more than perform a traditional parliamentary role, monitoring government departments and scrutinising legislation proposed by the Scottish Government. Chapter 2 identifies the continued importance of political parties and the government-versus-opposition culture inherited from Westminster. This chapter builds on these insights to show that the image of a 'consensus democracy' (Lijphart, 1999) is often misleading in Scotland. The first eight years of devolution were marked by a form of majoritarian (coalition) government that would not seem out of place in the UK. Labour and the Liberal Democrats formed a governing majority able, through a strong party whip, to command a majority in plenary and all committees. They used that power to pursue a demanding legislative programme, demonstrating that the government produces the vast majority of legislation and that the Parliament struggles to do more than scrutinise policy in these circumstances. The only significant 'brake' to that process was the negotiation required between the coalition parties within government. However, even then, the production of successive 'partnership agreements' in 1999 and 2003 gave a good idea of the legislative programmes in each four-year term.

The advent of minority government was accompanied by renewed calls for the spirit of 'new politics'. The image that springs to mind regards cooperation and negotiation between parties: the minority government needs the support of other parties to pass legislation and to stay in government for a full term; opposition parties trade that support for policy influence. This practice did not progress in the way that it does in countries, like Denmark, with a long term history of cooperation. The minority government lasted a full four-year term, but largely because no party wanted to be responsible for an extra election. There was some evidence of cooperation on a small number of bills and, more systematically, between the SNP and Conservative parties. However, the Scottish Parliament plenary was used largely as an adversarial forum and committees were not particularly effective. Instead, the main parties generally disengaged from Parliament. Labour and the Liberal Democrats rarely engaged constructively with the SNP government and did not seem to value the role of committee work in opposition. While the SNP was not able to pursue legislation in a small number of areas (independence, council tax reform, aspects of alcohol policy), it was still able to pass and amend the majority of bills and pursue many of its objectives without passing new primary legislation.

Consequently, the imbalance of power between executive and legislature did not disappear in 2007 when the SNP formed a minority government. Rather, it demonstrated that governments could further most public policy without recourse to the Scottish Parliament and that the gulf in resources (including the number of people available to analyse policy issues and decisions) between the Government and Parliament helped undermine effective scrutiny. Further, there were no internal 'brakes' to policy because the SNP formed a rather cohesive single party government. This is the context for majority government in 2011. The SNP now enjoys the parliamentary majority enjoyed by the Scottish Executive coalition, and the coherence the SNP enjoyed as a single party minority government. However, while it can now pass legislation in a less encumbered way, we should not expect a radical difference in the executive-legislative relationship, because an imbalance of power already existed.

Coalition Government from 1999–2007

The use of mixed member proportional representation for Scottish Parliament elections suggests that parties will rarely gain majority control. Yet, devolution in 1999 produced the closest thing to majority government: two four-year parliamentary sessions of coalition government formed by the largest party, Scottish Labour, and its junior partner, the Scottish Liberal Democrats. In 1999, Labour won 56 seats and the Liberal Democrats 17, producing a majority—73 (57%) of 129 seats (minus one seat held by Liberal Democrat Presiding Officer David Steel). This was followed in 2003 by a reduced but still significant majority—67 (52%) seats produced by Labour's 50 and the Liberal Democrats' 17 (the Presiding Officer was the SNP's George Reid). The Scottish Executive coalition also commanded a majority in every Scottish Parliament committee. This control of the parliamentary arithmetic, combined with a strong party whip (particularly within Labour), produced a form of majoritarian government that would not seem out of place in the UK.

The first eight years of devolution proved that new powers and institutions were not effective on their own. Rather, the implementation of new politics also required a cultural change among MSPs and political parties (Cairney, 2006). We know this now because no profound cultural change took place. Rather, we witnessed a curious mix of 'consensus democracy' institutions operated by politicians in the Westminster tradition. Although the parties were not particularly divided on ideological lines (Bennie and Clark, 2003), they reproduced a form of government-versus-opposition politics that Westminster parties would be proud of. In particular, the Labour-SNP relationship in the Scottish Parliament reflected a 'reactionary mentality' in which 'some Labour MPs were so paranoid about the Nationalists that any idea emanating from the SNP was immediately rejected because of its source' (Dennis Canavan MSP in Arter, 2004: 83). Similarly, the opposition parties were quick to exploit government weaknesses on issues such as 'Lobbygate' (see chapter 8), the cost of the Scottish Parliament building, and Scottish Executive coalition tensions regarding flagship policies such as free personal care and the abolition of student fees (McGarvey and Cairney, 2008: 40; 122; 205; 242).

The Scottish Parliament was driven primarily by parties rather than 'independent-minded MSPs' (Mitchell, 2008: 77). Most importantly, the coalition formed between Labour and the Liberal Democrats only provided 'superficial evidence of "new politics"' and undermined the more meaningful political style envisaged by its architects: 'a minority single-party Labour cabinet obliged to work in the Scandinavian manner with the opposition parties to get legislation through, would have vested parliament with significant policy influence and constituted 'new politics' in a real sense' (Arter, 2004: 83). Instead, the parties formed a governing majority. This gave Labour the sense of control that they feared would be lost if they were forced to cooperate on a regular basis with the SNP: 'We have to have a settled programme rather than a programme where we could be ambushed every time' (Maureen Macmillan, Labour MSP, in Arter, 2004: 83). Further, the parties produced partnership agreements that tied both to a detailed programme of legislation and towards supporting the Scottish Executive line (and collective cabinet responsibility) throughout.

The effect of the strong party role was impressive. The coalition controlled the voting process in both committees and plenary, with Labour demonstrating a particularly strong whip in both parliamentary sessions—caused in part because their MSPs were screened rigorously before their selection (chapter 2; McGarvey and Cairney, 2008: 85; Mitchell, 2008: 77) and because Labour ministers held regular meetings with Labour MSPs before any committee meeting in which a significant vote or decision was likely to take place (although this can occasionally be used to exert committee power—see Cairney, 2007a: 79). There were similarly few instances of Liberal Democrat dissent, and none which threatened the coalition's *Partnership Agreement*. The parties were also able to dictate which of their members became conveners of committees (although the numbers of conveners are allocated proportionately) and even which MSPs sat on particular committees. As a result, the independent role of committees was undermined as MSPs were appointed and then whipped, while committee turnover was too high to allow a meaningful level of MSP subject expertise (McGarvey and Cairney, 2008: 99; Scottish Council Foundation, 2002; Arter, 2003: 31-2).

The experience from 1999–2007 suggests that it would be wrong to equate the formal capacity of legislatures with their power or influence over policy outcomes (Arter, 2006; Cairney, 2006; McGarvey and Cairney, 2008). From 1999–2007, the Scottish Executive coalition dominated the legislative process, passing so many bills that they undermined the ability of Parliament to set the policy agenda through inquiries. It presided over a punishing legislative schedule, producing the sense in which committees became part of a 'legislative sausage machine' rather than powerful bodies able to set the agenda through the inquiry process (Arter, 2002: 105). While there is *some* evidence of parliamentary influence during the scrutiny of government legislation (Shephard and Cairney, 2005; Cairney, 2006), the Scottish Executive produced and amended the majority of bills (McGarvey and Cairney, 2008: 106), reinforcing the rule of thumb by Olson (in Arter, 2006: 250) that executives initiate 90% of legislation and get 90% of what they want. There was also a trend from 2003 towards increased Scottish

Executive dominance, perhaps following the honeymoon period of the first session (and despite the new makeup of the Parliament in which more small parties were represented).

This unequal executive-legislature relationship is reflected in the early reports (see also Jervis and Plowden, 2001: 9–10). On the one hand, the first report (November 1999: 5) suggests that 'there has been a heavy commitment to ensuring that everyone understands the importance of these committees', and Leicester (2000: 21) points to the need (not felt in the old Scottish Office) for ministers to engage seriously with the chamber as 'a vital arena in which to build or damage a political reputation'. On the other, Leicester (2000; 21; see also May 2000: 3; Shephard, February 2001: 17) identifies, almost immediately, 'a growing concern that there are insufficient staff and resources' in committees, particularly since MSPs sat on more than one committee and the skills of committee staff varied. Further, since few committees found an ability to set their own agenda (or initiate legislation), MSPs turned to cross-party groups less likely to be whipped (although see Shephard, August 2004: 8). This produced an additional workload on top of the punishing constituency/regional role and a strong impression of overload (Leicester, 2000: 22) which, coupled with high committee turnover and a new role for substitutes, undermined the ability of MSPs to become experts in their subject areas (Shephard, February 2001: 19; Cairney, January 2006: 25). The problem prompted the Parliamentary Bureau (which determines parliamentary business; it was controlled by Labour and the Liberal Democrats) to discuss an early restructuring of committees to ensure that they could deal with the imbalances of Scottish Executive policy priorities (the Justice Committee was under particular strain). Yet, problems of overload were still pronounced at the end of parliamentary sessions when some committees were obliged to process a large number of bills before the election recess (Cairney, September 2007: 14).

Problems of overload were often reinforced by the lack of information necessary to provide effective scrutiny. In the case of finance, the Financial Issues Advisory Group (FIAG, the sister of the Consultative Steering Group) was strong on the need for the Scottish Parliament to have reliable financial information to help the Parliament hold the Executive to account and therefore allow 'the people of Scotland [to] have a say in how money is spent' (February 2000: 15). Further, the first budget bill was preceded by a 'seemingly open consultation process' explaining how budgets have been allocated in the past and, according to Donald Dewar, giving '"people from across the whole spectrum of Scottish society a say in how the resources at the

Executive's disposal should be spent"' (May 2000: 11). Yet, the reports are sceptical about the effect this has on budgets, particularly since spending demands have to be met by reducing spending elsewhere. The May (2000: 12) report highlights the importance of incrementalism, particularly when existing recipients of resources resist change, and argues that even one of the most pressing issues (tuition fees) combined with a 'carefully considered and costed report' (the Cubie Report) resulted in finding the money from within the same department, suggesting that it would be difficult for the Finance Committee to influence anything but modest changes within existing and discrete budgets. The Finance Committee may have the potential to be the most powerful, but 'it has yet to make that influence felt' (May, 2000: 12).

Similarly, while the committee established its *right* to produce an 'alternative set of proposals' (effectively an 'alternative budget' – November 2000: 36), there is no evidence to suggest that it ever demonstrated that ability (indeed, Bell August 2003: 32 argues that a significant alternative supported by Parliament would oblige the Executive to resign). Instead, much of its time was devoted to trying, generally unsuccessfully, to get reliable figures from the Scottish Executive (Bell, August 2001: 36; Cairney, January 2006: 23). In some cases this issue is caused by the problems tracking money when it is spent locally in a discretionary way (Bell, August 2001: 35–6). In others, the problem is caused by incomplete information, or information which lacks comparisons with previous years (Bell, August 2001: 36). Further, the time for detailed scrutiny is curtailed once every four years by the 'electoral period of "purdah"' (Bell, August 2003: 32; Winetrobe, June 2003: 3; there is also a purdah of sorts during UK general elections, restricting the Scottish Executive to publicising 'worthy but dull' public policy announcements and parliamentary debates the month before – Winetrobe, August 2001: 8–10).

In the case of the European Committee, MSPs were effectively kept in the dark because Scottish Executive discussions with the UK government (regarding the UK line in the EU) were kept confidential. Thus, its attempts to emulate Westminster and adopt a 'scrutiny reserve', in which a final position could not be made without parliamentary approval, were never successful (Wright, February 2002: 32). Instead, it began 'scrutinising the implementation of EU policies', conducting 'inquiries into issues that are of strategic interest' and making sure that Scottish ministers gave evidence at the start of each EU presidency (Wright, May 2002: 45–6; see Wright, August 2002: 30; Wright, November 2002: 25; Wright, November 2003: 36–7; Wright, May 2004: 44; Wright, August 2004: 34–5 and Wright, November 2004:

22 on its continued lack of influence despite its membership of the Network of Regional Parliamentary European Committees). For example, in 2007 it produced a strategic report, calling for earlier Scottish Executive engagement in the 'upstream' phase of policy development to address the problems with its obligations when EU policy comes 'downstream' (Cairney, April 2007: 8). In one case, both committees suffered the same problem, when the Finance and European committees could not convince the Scottish Secretary to attend their meetings to explain how EU structural funds would work. While this became a matter for the Presiding Officer (November 2000: 36–7), the issue was never resolved.

The reports quickly suggest that any initial hopes for non-executive legislation soon faded and 'Parliament has had very little time to consider anything else but Executive bills' (Shephard August 2001: 13). Shephard (November 2001: 17–18; August, 2002: 8–9; June 2003: 6) notes that Executive Bills receive priority over Members' Bills, reflecting (from 1999–2007) the dominance of the coalition-controlled Parliamentary Bureau and a concern expressed by the Procedures Committee that the Parliament is becoming 'a "conveyor belt for passing legislation" ... at the expense of quality scrutiny and influence' (Shephard, June 2003: 9). This view was reinforced by various 'legacy' reports of committees bemoaning the lack of time for inquiries because of the amount of legislation (Cairney, April 2007: 12–14; note the Conservative claim that Scottish Executive ministers admitted to suffering from 'legislationitis' — Cairney, January 2007: 22).

Members' Bills were used increasingly to set the agenda only (Shephard, November 2003: 7; Shephard, February 2004; Cairney, May 2006: 25; April 2007: 14). Further, this ability was constrained, following changes to the standing orders that undermined the ability of opposition and small parties to have bill proposals accepted (Shephard, August 2004: 7). Indeed, the strain on the Scottish Parliament's Non-Executive Bills Unit (NEBU) was used by the Procedures Committee and four main parties to justify reforming the rules on member's bills to make it harder to introduce them (Shephard, 2004: 7), producing some suspicion that this was designed to stop the smaller parties such as the SSP setting the agenda (Cairney, January 2006: 30; September 2006: 25; April 2007: 15; but note that there is still an issue of capacity — Maddox, 2009)

The coalition's control of the parliamentary arithmetic also undermined the independence of committees. It was used to pass a motion limiting the ability of committees to exercise their evidence-gathering powers, producing a Westminster-style relationship associated with the term 'MacOsmotherly Rules' to ensure that civil service advice to ministers remains confidential ('Osmotherly Rules' refers to guidance to UK civil servants on how to give evidence to select committees—see Mitchell, 2001: 59; MacMillan, November, 2000: 13; Shephard, February 2001: 18; Winetrobe, February 2002: 9; see also Cairney, April 2007: 17 on non-disclosure during the McKie inquiry). There is little evidence of effective parliamentary scrutiny of the Scottish Executive's governance functions and 'it has no formal say either on the division of governmental business into particular portfolios, or the allocation of ministers to those portfolios' (Winetrobe, May 2001: 9–11). The introduction by First Minister Jack McConnell of Ministerial Party Aides (MSPs who support particular ministers and sit on committees) could also be interpreted as a further move to maintain a consistent party line in Parliament (Winetrobe, May 2002: 7; Mitchell et al, 2003: 130; see also Winetrobe, November 2002; 6; the Scottish Executive also failed to inform Parliament of two appointments in 2003, 'undermining its own open government policies' and obscuring 'their participation in plenary and committee proceedings' —Winetrobe, May 2004: 3). This, combined with the lack of career advancement opportunities outside of the Scottish Executive, unlike in Westminster where backbenchers can pursue senior committee roles, makes it difficult to find evidence of a strong independent parliament.

Mitchell (2004: 35–36) argues that the 'myth of a strong legislature' was entertained by the Scottish Executive when it suited its interests, such as when it wanted to shuffle off responsibility for the cost of the Scottish Parliament building. Overall, the 'committees have worked well but there is a tendency towards self-satisfied myth-making and an exaggeration of success which has crowded out appreciation of failings' (Mitchell, 2005: 27). Much of this 'success' often merely relates to its ability to get better information from the Scottish Executive (see for example Cairney, January 2006: 23; January 2007: 26). There may also be a tendency to conflate the value of the Scottish Parliament with the opportunities afforded by *devolution*—such as when Shephard (August, 2001: 13–14) lauds the ability of the Parliament to process legislation that Westminster would not have had the time or the inclination for (before stating in November, 2001: 19 that there is minimal power-sharing between Executive and Parliament). In effect, we are left with a party-dominated Parliament that enjoys sporadic wins in the context of a fairly powerless position (for examples of its wins see: the election of the Deputy Presiding Officer—Mitchell, February 2002; 4; amendments regarding smacking children, Shephard, November 2002: 7; Winetrobe, November 2002: 34; fire service reform, Shephard, February 2003: 9;

and, the rejection of part 3 of the Protection of Vulnerable Groups (Scotland) Bill due to insufficient consultation, Cairney, January 2007: 27–8; Shephard, April 2005: 6).

Overall, the Scottish Parliament and its committees enjoyed neither the resources with which to scrutinise government policy effectively nor the stability nor independence necessary to assert their new powers. Further, although members and committees have the ability to initiate legislation, the same rules apply: members are constrained by party affiliation and limited resources, while committees rarely find the time or inclination to legislate (Bort, January 2006: 42–3). After a honeymoon period in the first parliamentary session, the Scottish Parliament produced non-executive legislation comparable in number and scope with Westminster (McGarvey and Cairney, 2008: 103). From 1999–2003, 50 Scottish Executive, 1 committee and 8 member's bills were passed while from 2003–7 the split was 53, 1, and 3. From 1999–2003 166 inquiries were conducted (Arter, 2004: 77), but this fell to 99 in 2003–07 (of which 11 were short or one-day inquiries). In short, 'while the Scottish Parliament's powers are extensive in comparison to most West European legislatures, it is much more difficult to demonstrate the effects of their powers in relation to the Government in the first two parliamentary sessions' (McGarvey and Cairney, 2008: 108). The evidence of new politics and the effects of the new institutions were thin on the ground.

Minority Government from 2007–11

In this context, it is understandable that May 2007 was seen by many as a new beginning. Newly-elected Presiding Officer Alex Fergusson used his acceptance speech to call for the return of new politics (Scottish Parliament Official Report 14.5.07 col. 13). However, the first thing to note is that minority government was not the SNP's first choice. Instead, it followed the combination of unusual parliamentary arithmetic and an inability of the SNP and Liberal Democrats to agree on the terms of a coalition.

In 2007 the potential for coalition was not straightforward. The SNP won 47 seats compared to Labour's 46 but, given the nature of the overall result (the Conservatives won 17, Liberal Democrats 16, Green 2 and Margo MacDonald 1) it could not form a majority coalition with one other party. Although there was some scope for cooperation between the SNP and the Greens (based on the same attitude to Scottish independence and an SNP commitment to certain environmental issues), its potential links to the other parties were problematic. Formal coalition between the SNP and Liberal Democrats proved impossible when the latter insisted that the former drop its plans for an independence referendum (Lynch, September 2007: 66; 72). Further, a formal coalition with the Conservatives would be politically damaging for the SNP in the short term (the Conservatives are still tainted by 18 years of unpopular government in Scotland from 1979–97; the SNP is to some extent a left-wing social democratic party) and the long term (the SNP may campaign for independence by highlighting the re-emergence of a 'democratic deficit' in Scotland and minimal support for a Conservative government ruling Scotland).

Therefore, the SNP was initially reluctant, but effectively obliged, to form a single party minority. The rhetoric on the scope for 'new politics' under minority government was only spoken loudly *after* the options for coalition had been exhausted. The SNP subsequently made a 'virtue out of necessity' (Mitchell, 2008: 79) but was uncertain about its ability to make legislative progress (or at least present an image of governing competence—Paun, 2009) and was not confident about its ability, or the ability of any minority government, to stay in office for the four-year period. This reflects two main factors. First, despite Strøm's (1990) best efforts,[4] it reflects a strong 'conventional view' of minority government that 'associates it with instability, inefficiency, incoherence and a lack of accountability' (Mitchell, 2008: 73). There is a strong, longstanding culture or set of assumptions held by most parties in Scotland in favour of majority government (although there is some evidence that Labour studied minority government in 2006 and perhaps favoured it from 2007—Lynch, January 2007: 69). Minority equates with instability not opportunity; potential opposition and disarray, not opportunities for new politics. There is also the occasional charge, regarding the SNP's independence agenda, that minority government is unrepresentative (McIver and Gay, 2008). Second, the 'conventional view' has been reinforced in the UK by the very limited, unhappy experience of minority Westminster government in the mid and late 1970s (Mitchell, 2008: 74; Cairney, 2009).

In other words, the omens did not look good: minority government appeared to be a necessity rather than a choice. Scottish politics lacked a factor key to minority government success: a feeling that it is a desirable way to engage in politics. In this light, we witnessed a remarkable turnaround of the image of minority government in Scotland (for an 'insider view', see Harvie, 2008). It is striking how quickly minority government became the norm in Scotland in the sense

---

[4] Strøm (1990: 237) argues that minority governments are common, not aberrations, and that they may result from rational strategic calculations rather than 'as a consequence of political instability, conflict and malaise'.

that, while the SNP Government was challenged regularly on its policies and governing record, its right to govern was not. Most importantly, the SNP Government served for a full four year term despite minimal evidence of the behaviour and attitudes we might associate with new politics. In fact, if anything, partisan tensions increased from 2007.

For example, one of the longest running sores in the 2007–11 session regarded the use by opposition MSPs of points of order to question the veracity of ministerial statements. While we may accept and even enjoy a degree of partisanship during the theatre of First Minister's Questions, this was taken to the extreme by allegations that ministers were making untruthful and misleading statements to Parliament (Cairney, 2009b). This prompted two key responses (as well as a revision to the Scottish Ministerial Code). First, Alex Salmond took the unprecedented step of referring complaints about his conduct to the new independent advisory panel consisting of the two former Presiding Officers David Steel and George Reid (which ruled in all three cases that he did not mislead Parliament—Cairney, May 2009: 32–3; Cairney, September 2009: 41; Scottish Government, 2010). Second, Alex Fergusson reiterated a belief, held variously by all Presiding Officers (and reflected in Standing Orders), that he should not become the arbiter of the truthfulness of comments made by any MSP in Parliament. Instead, he asked the Standards committee to investigate the use of points of order. In turn, the committee endorsed Fergusson's view, proposed new guidance on the party political use of points of order, and called for a joint protocol between the Scottish Government and Parliament on their respective roles (Cairney, May 2009: 32).

The perceived need to introduce new mechanisms in this way presents a counterintuitive conclusion: that partisanship increased and cooperation decreased during minority government. Yet, it did not seriously undermine the SNP's position, largely because: the opposition parties did not want to be held responsible for holding an extra election (a successful vote of no confidence would oblige the government to resign and prompt an election if a new First Minister could not be found in 28 days); few parties could afford to finance an extra election; and, the opposition parties could not hope to improve their number of seats, since Alex Salmond and the SNP were generally popular throughout.

The maintenance of these arrangements reinforced the imbalance of power between Government and Parliament, in four main ways. First, the SNP Government was able to distance itself from the Scottish Parliament by pursuing many of its policy aims without recourse to legislation (Cairney, September 2007b: 83; September 2008: 94). The Scottish Government has the vast majority of policy capacity and many of its policy aims (on intergovernmental relations, the civil service, capital finance projects, public service targets, curriculum reform, prescription charges) were pursued without using legislation, while others could be pursued using legislation that exists (i.e. with secondary legislation and regulations much less subject to parliamentary scrutiny) (Cairney, September 2007: 82). Further, small committee size and MSP turnover still undermine the abilities of committees to scrutinize government policy and the huge gulf in resources remains (Cairney, January 2008: 17). The best example regards the Scottish Government's concordat with COSLA to grant local authorities more discretion in the use of their budgets, and more leeway when monitoring local outcomes (chapter 6) — a decision that undermined the ability of the Scottish Parliament to monitor local authorities through the Scottish Government.

Second, the Scottish Parliament produced minimal legislation and proved unable to go beyond the level of scrutiny and agenda setting that it achieved from 1999–2007. Most notably, from 2007–9, the Scottish Parliament did not use the opportunity to assert its position at a time of low legislative output. A key outcome of the 1999–2007 sessions was a widespread sense that too much legislation had been produced and that a new government should slow down (Cairney, September 2007: 24; 83; Mitchell, in correspondence). The 'legacy' reports produced by committees in 2007 suggested that they were unable to perform their scrutiny and inquiry functions properly because there was too much legislation to consider (McGarvey and Cairney, 2008: 102). Minority government had an initial effect. The SNP Government, already committed in its manifesto to a reduction in legislative volume (and faced with a tight budget that precluded expensive policy innovation), found that it did not have the votes to pass legislative measures that it would certainly have introduced if it enjoyed a majority (including a referendum bill in 2010). Consequently, from 2007–9, legislative demands on the Scottish Parliament were not high. The SNP's first legislative programme was dubbed by opposition parties as 'legislation lite' (Cairney, September 2007: 83), while Labour's business manager, Michael McMahon, labelled Alex Salmond as a 'work-shy First Minister leading a group of idle ministers' because the Scottish Government had passed seven pieces of legislation in two years (Peterkin, 2009; note that opposition party criticism of the legislative programme has always been an annual event).

Yet, the Parliament did not fill the legislative gap. There has not been a perceptible rise in successful legislation initiated by committees or MSPs since 2007 (committees passed 2 bills and members passed 7 from 2007–11, compared to 3 and 8 from 1999–2003 and 1 and 3 from 2003–7). While there was some talk by Labour regarding their alternative legislative programme (Cairney, September 2008: 97; May 2009: 31), this never took off (and it seemed to consist of four member's bills — Holyrood.com, 2008). While committees had more time to set the policy agenda through inquiries, few used their time effectively (compare with the second session committees which had begun to identify useful cross-party issues — Cairney, September 2006: 20–1; January 2006: 27–30; April, 2007: 15). Few found enough common ground to pursue a long-term inquiry in any meaningful way, while others merely exploited the chance to make party political points with short, headline grabbing, inquiries (Cairney, January 2008: 16 discusses the inquiry into Donald Trump's development in the Menie estate; see also Cairney, May 2008: 17–18; September 2008: 20–1; for more recent evidence that committees were able to find areas of common interest, see Cairney, September 2008: 21; January 2009: 37–8; September 2009: 45–8).

Third, the Scottish Government produced most policy and passed and amended most legislation. Overall, it produced 42 bills in four years (compared to 50 and 53 in previous sessions). Its small number of high-profile manifesto successes includes a bill to abolish the graduate endowment and, less importantly, to abolish bridge tolls. Its ability to pass so many other bills reflects the fact that a large proportion of government business in Parliament is rather innocuous legislation that would have been passed by any party. There is little incentive for the opposition parties to oppose the principles of, for example, a bill reforming flooding policy. The SNP also inherited many bills from its predecessor government (on issues such as the need to prepare for the Commonwealth Games, reform the judiciary and courts, reform public health law, and revise the law on sexual offences).

The tangible effect of the opposition parties on Scottish Government legislation is unclear. While we could reasonably expect more government defeats and amendments coming from opposition parties, the effect on the substance of legislation does not seem particularly significant. For example, 98.7% of Scottish Government amendments to its own legislation were passed successfully from 2007–11 (figures from Steven MacGregor; see MacGregor, 2010) compared to 99.4% from 1999–2003 (Cairney, 2006: 186). The SNP Government lost more votes than its predecessors, but its legislative programme remained unharmed and very few bills were amended against the SNP's wishes. To a large extent, the SNP was helped by support from the Conservative party, with the two parties voting together 72% of the time, reflecting almost 100% Conservative support for the majority of SNP bills (MacGregor, 2010). In some cases, in the absence of Conservative support, the SNP was able to use support from other parties (e.g. on tobacco control policy—an agenda furthered by the previous Scottish Executive). In one other, it benefited from parliamentary rules that effectively limited the extent to which the Scottish Parliament could amend a bill. The opposition parties could not amend the Education (Additional Support for Learning) Bill as much as they hoped, because the Scottish Government had not passed a Financial Resolution—effectively prompting the Presiding Officer to reject amendments which involved significant additional costs (references to this constraint can be found in the stage 2 debate—Scottish Parliament Education, Lifelong Learning and Culture Committee Official Report 25.3.09 Col.2165—and the stage 3 debate—Scottish Parliament Official Report, 20.5.09 Cols. 17576–644).

Although there may be some evidence that civil servants were more likely to anticipate the reactions of opposition parties when developing policy (Paun, 2009: 52), there is less to suggest that this affected policy substantively. Indeed, civil servants appeared to be committed to implementing SNP policy and, in some cases, defending that policy and the Scottish Government's record in public (Paun, 2009: 52; Cairney, September 2009: 53). Further, the process is nothing like coalition government in which civil servants had to clear policy with two parties (Paun, 2009: 52; Cairney, 2011a). Therefore, if anything, the Scottish Parliament has become an occasionally effective policy-stifling forum, acting as a deterrent to some policy initiation and slowing down the legislative sausage machine, without using the extra time to any great effect.

Fourth, a lot of opposition party activity was geared towards the production of non-legislative motions. The Scottish Government's initial reaction prompted some concern that it was subverting the role of Parliament by ignoring its wishes (Davidson, 2008). The first example followed the motion passed by the opposition parties in favour of continued funding for the Edinburgh Airport Rail Link and Edinburgh tram project. Both John Swinney and Alex Salmond were accused of bending the will of Parliament, with Swinney citing irresolvable problems in EARL and Salmond quoting Donald Dewar to suggest that he was not bound by parliamentary motions (Cairney, September 2007; 22; Mitchell, 2008: 80). However, even in this case there is evidence of a negotiated position (the trams project did go ahead) and ministers generally seek to avoid unnecessary confrontations, particularly since too many confrontations produce opposition party pressure for ministers to resign (see the case of Kenny MacAskill and court reform—Cairney, May 2009: 52). Instead, SNP whips and business managers sought to avoid confrontations by negotiating the wording of motions with their counterparts in other parties (Cairney, May 2008: 18; January 2009: 35–6) and acting on many motions (Cairney, January 2008: 21).

The best example may be the Scottish Government's decision to drop plans for a flagship bill introducing a local income tax, although many other factors were in play (for example, the UK Government refused to modify the rules on council tax benefit—Cairney, 2012a; chapter 9). Parliamentary opposition, along with the uncertainty over funding, was cited by Finance Secretary John Swinney as the reason to withdraw the policy (Scott, May 2009: 75). Yet, few motions forced the hands of the Scottish Government in that way. Far more motions either demonstrated a lack of united opposition or merely (in examples such as police numbers or rural schools) sought to 'reinforce existing Scottish Government policies and place them higher on its agenda' (Cairney, May 2009: 38). This agenda-setting role is also a feature of the better committee inquiries (Cairney, September 2009: 45–8; 57).

Overall, this outcome is not surprising because, despite the range of Scottish Parliament 'powers', it was not designed to be a policymaking body. Rather, the institution represents an attempt to improve on the scrutiny powers of Westminster without marking a profound change in the executive-legislative relationship. Committees have the power to hold ministers and civil servants to account, to make sure they consult properly (i.e. they do not undertake large consultations themselves) and to initiate legislation as a last resort if MSPs believe that government policy is inadequate. They are also instructed by the CSG to let the government govern, arguably encouraged to play a minimal pre-legislative role and, particularly in the case of the budget, not well equipped to develop alternative legislation (see Cairney, September 2009: 47–8 for a discussion of the Finance Committee inquiry and new Financial Scrutiny Unit). Further, the Scottish Parliament's lack of a 'scrutiny reserve' for EU issues, combined with issues such as the release of the Lockerbie bomber, suggests that it often has no role to play before Scottish ministerial decisions are made (Cairney, September 2009: 40–1). The resources of committees and opposition parties are too thin on the ground to provide anything more than scrutiny and criticism (and there appears to be no appetite to boost the resources of committees). It would therefore take much more than minority government to solve the wider problem of parliamentary constraint.

Scottish Parliament committees did not provide the 'motor of a new politics', particularly since Labour's front bench did not sit on them and Labour did not fully engage with them (in part because the former Scottish Executive does not want to scrutinise its own policies). Rather, key debates were played out and negotiations were conducted in plenary. Indeed, there seemed to be a *rise* in the propensity to overturn decisions reached in committee in plenary from 2007–11. In the 1999–2003 session the key indicator of respect for committee decisions was the non-Executive amendment of Executive legislation—less than 80% of these were reversed by a Scottish Executive (which had the majority to reverse them all), in part because committee assertiveness was linked to at least one vote by an MSP from a Scottish Executive party (Cairney, 2006: 203). From 2007–11, the parliamentary arithmetic was such that a Scottish Government bill may have been amended against its wishes at stage 2 merely because the Scottish Government and its supporting party did not have enough votes, only for this to be reversed in plenary at stage 3 when they did (see, for example, *The Herald*, 2009 on children's hearings). Or, in the case of the Graduate Endowment Abolition (Scotland) Bill, the whole bill may be rejected in committee only to be approved in plenary (Cairney, January 2008: 23). In many cases this is linked to the post-2007 abandonment by conveners of the status quo convention (in which conveners, when asked to provide a casting vote, would generally vote against an amendment to maintain existing policy). Instead, many used their casting vote strategically, undermining the convention that committee decisions are respected in plenary.

Minority Government and the Annual Budgets

The budget bill process took on a new significance under minority government. It became the most important legislative test because there was an obligation for a majority of the Scottish Parliament to agree to the bill each year. Effectively, for minority government to continue, the Scottish Government must seek agreement for its budget and a proportion of the opposition parties must find a way to reach a negotiated settlement. This process showed the best and worst aspects of minority government. First, it is certainly more significant than under coalition or majority government (it was a routine process from 1999–2007). Yet, there are still similarities: only government ministers may amend the bill; and, committees still tend to focus on limited aspects of the budget, reflecting a lack of information and resources with which to conduct effective scrutiny.

Second, there have been concessions, but their overall importance is debatable; they did not contradict SNP policy but perhaps forced it to make choices among competing priorities. In the first budget, the Conservatives secured a greater commitment to fund new police officers and to revisit drugs policy (with the hope that the SNP would move further from harm reduction to abstention—chapter 8), independent Margo MacDonald secured special funding status for Edinburgh and the Greens secured a commitment to the 'carbon assessment' of spending plans (Cairney, May 2008: 16). In the second, the Conservatives secured a reduction in business rates, Labour secured funding for modern apprenticeships and the Liberal Democrats secured a vague commitment for the SNP to involve Parliament more in budget planning and engage with the Calman Commission on fiscal autonomy (the Greens lost a larger commitment to fund home insulation when their votes were no longer required). In the third, the Conservatives secured an independent review of Scottish Government spending in preparation for expected cuts following the economic crisis, the Liberal Democrats secured £20m for college places and £10m to the Scottish Investment Bank, and the Greens secured £12m towards home insulation and boiler schemes. In the fourth, the Conservatives secured modest spending increases on housing and business, while the other parties secured new targets on employment apprenticeships and college bursaries (BBC News, 2011). Overall, the concessions represent a small fraction of the overall budget (for example, Bell's 2011 calculation is a change of 0.04% in the 2008/9 budget).

Third, few parties took a consistent negotiating position. The Conservative party was the only consistent actor, seeking concessions in exchange for support. The Greens surprised many by voting against the second bill despite securing concessions. The Liberal Democrats opposed the first two bills (only to support the second bill when revised marginally) and abstained in the third. Labour abstained in year one for fear of causing the bill to fall, opposed in year two— contributing unwittingly to the bill's failure on the assumption that the SNP had secured Green support[5] (followed by support for the second bill when assured on modern apprenticeships)—and opposed in years three (citing the loss of the Glasgow Airport Rail link) and four (citing a mere 0.1% movement towards Labour concessions—see Scottish

[5] A similar example of Labour and Liberal Democrat bafflement and miscalculation can be found in the failure of the Creative Scotland Bill (Cairney, September 2008: 15).

Parliament Official Report 9.2.11) when it was clear that it was safe to do so.

Finally, the failure of the second budget bill did not deserve the incredible amount of Scottish and UK attention it attracted. Rather, the process showed that the parties could work together very effectively when faced with an apparent crisis, and a new bill (almost identical to the defeated one) was passed the following week. The budget crisis showed that there was little appetite among the opposition parties for an impromptu election, particularly when Alex Salmond remained popular.

Conclusion

The Scottish Parliament is not a policymaking body. Instead, it is a scrutinising, revising and legitimising chamber with limited powers to scrutinise and revise. This point is most apparent under majority single party and coalition government, but is still the case under minority government. While the advent of minority government was accompanied by renewed calls for new politics in the spirit originally envisaged, it actually represented the last nail in its coffin. The Parliament has been a peripheral part of the Scottish policy process for the majority of its 12 year existence and majority government will only accelerate its declining importance.

In the first eight years, the Labour and Liberal Democrat coalition performed the role of a majority government, controlling the vote in plenary and committees and passing so much legislation that most committees devoted most of their activities to scrutiny (instead of agenda setting inquiries). There was little evidence of 'power sharing' and much more evidence of a concentration of power in the government combined with an adversarial atmosphere that we associated so much with 'old Westminster'. We might have expected a big difference in the latter four years, with the Scottish Government finally having to negotiate with opposition parties in the Parliament to secure its policy aims. Yet, with the exception of some high profile government retreats (on the independence referendum, local taxation reform and minimum alcohol pricing—all of which are set to return), there was a muted parliamentary effect. The Scottish Government produced and amended the vast majority of the legislation and found that they could pursue many of their aims without recourse to Parliament. Committees were no more effective. Indeed, at times, they seemed less effective because the main opposition parties seemed disinterested in committee business, party politics got in the way of business-like cooperation, or simply because they did not have the resources or authority to find out how local and health authorities were spending public money.

In this light, it is time to stop kidding ourselves about 'new politics' for three main reasons. First, what we have, and have had for some time, is government and opposition. Second, the term breeds complacency. It makes it look like Scotland solved electoral and intuitional design before 1999 and that it is superior to its London counterpart. Instead, Westminster is also changing as an institution, while Holyrood's institution has not changed parliamentary behaviour. Third, 'new politics' is a heavy chain around the neck of Scottish politics, producing unrealistic expectations and therefore skewed evaluations of the success of new political practices. In the absence of such expectations, we may come to different conclusions about the first eight years of coalition government which provided *some* examples of new parliamentary influence, the ability of committees to be 'businesslike' and the ability of Scottish Executive ministers to negotiate and compromise rather than dominate Parliament. Similarly, we should be careful not to judge the experience of minority government too harshly. Although 'new politics' as originally envisaged has not materialised, the arrangements proved to be relatively stable, allowing the SNP Government to demonstrate an impressive degree of policy coherence and governing competence. The main caveat is that the minority years were marked by high SNP popularity, suggesting that it would not be in the interests of the opposition parties to destabilise minority government – particularly since they may be held responsible and would need to fund an extra, expensive, election campaign. It is therefore difficult to attribute the new system to a powerful new norm when an explanation based on party self-interest is just as convincing.

Equally unclear is the effect that minority government has on public policy. Eight years of coalition government largely produced a policy agenda driven by the government. Four years of minority government has produced a new relationship between the Scottish Government and Parliament, but this is not based on the eagerness on either side to mark a profound shift in responsibility for policy formulation and implementation. The initial drop in legislative activity from the Scottish Government was not met with an equivalent rise from Parliament. Committees did not produce more agenda setting inquiries. Rather, the Parliament became a forum for limited policy concessions based largely on the (usually uncontroversial) Government legislative agenda. The opposition parties also have a very limited ability to monitor Government policy activity that is not brought to parliament for regular approval. We may find evidence of parliamentary power in other areas—such as in the anticipated reactions of the SNP when deciding which bills to pursue and when civil servants, developing policy, pay heed to what they perceive to be the parliament's (as well as the minister's) 'mind'. However, this is an area of public policy that has not been researched in great depth either in Scotland or in the comparative literature.

From the evidence that we have, it is difficult to identify enough policy influence for opposition parties to give them an incentive to eschew public office when it is available. This is not really an issue for the Conservatives who are not likely to be offered the chance to form a government and will therefore benefit more from minority government. However, the lack of policy influence enjoyed by the Liberal Democrats since 2007 seems to diminish the probability that it will accept minority government in the future (assuming that it recovers some of its vote and majority SNP governments do not become the norm). Strøm (1990) argues that minority governments are most likely in political systems, such as Scotland's, which possess strong parliaments. The argument is that a strong parliament gives an opposition party the chance to have policy influence. The party is therefore content to negotiate policy concessions, from a minority government that often needs its support, and wait until the next election produces a better result. Yet, the Scottish experience shows us that relatively high parliamentary power, when compared to other legislatures, does not translate into policy outcomes. In the absence of such a policymaking role the opposition parties may have little incentive to support minority government. Conversely, the SNP's experience may have convinced both major parties that they do not need to form a coalition government to satisfy their policy objectives.

Chapter 4

From Scottish Executive to Scottish Government

Chapter 3 argues that the Scottish Parliament is not a powerful policymaking body. Rather, there is an imbalance of power towards the government. However, we should not overestimate the coherence of the large number of actors, organisations and institutions which may be covered by the term 'government', particularly in a multi-level system where power is shared with supra-national (EU) and national (UK) governments (chapter 5) and devolved to local governments and other bodies (chapter 6). This chapter considers the extent to which we can identify a locus of power within the Scottish Executive or Government ('Executive' refers to 1999–2007 and 'Government' to 2007 onwards). It suggests that, in the early years of devolution, the Scottish Executive took some time to develop as a collective entity: for ministers to appreciate and learn their new role; and, for the civil service to move from its old Scottish Office focus on implementing UK policy to its new focus on policy formulation. Further, this took place in the context of coalition and a need for party cooperation within government, of which few UK actors had any significant experience.

In this context, the aim of this chapter is to consider how the monitors identify the locus of power within government. First, it examines the idea of strength and stability. It draws on Cairney's (2011a) comparison of coalition and minority government to argue that the Scottish Executive effectively traded higher strength and stability in the Scottish Parliament for lower strength and stability in government. Conversely, the single party SNP minority government may have been more vulnerable in Parliament but more effective within government. In other words, we may find, when we examine the monitoring reports' focus on issues such as collective cabinet responsibility and the 'core executive' that there were more problems from 1999–2007 compared to 2007 and beyond. Second, it considers the role of the civil service and the relationships that they formed with pressure participants such as interest groups. The monitors cover the idea that civil servants compete with ministers for power within government (particularly in the early years when actors were learning their roles), various attempts to reform how the civil service operates (largely by moving staff out of Edinburgh), and issues, such as freedom of information, that capture the sense in which the civil service was adapting to its new role. However, it finds little room for a discussion of 'territorial policy communities', or the relationships that develop between ministers, civil servants and interest groups when they are all involved in policymaking over the longer term. This chapter introduces the literature on group-government relations in Scotland and considers how to integrate that material with the wealth of information provided by the monitors.

Strength and Stability

As chapter 3 suggests, the largest parties in UK and devolved elections generally prefer coalition to minority government because it offers strength and stability in Parliament. Strength in this sense means an ability to 'dominate Parliament and its legislative process', while stability refers to the fact that coalition governments have longer lives than their minority counterparts because they are less vulnerable to votes of no confidence in Parliament (Cairney, 2011a: 261; Muller and Strøm, 2003: 1 suggest that the average tenure of a coalition majority government is 17–18 months, compared to 13–14 months for a minority government and 30 for single party majority). Coalition government gave Labour 'the sense of control that they feared would be lost if they formed a minority government and were forced to cooperate on a regular basis with other parties' (2011a: 262). However, strength within government is a different matter. Most importantly, the coalition parties were obliged to consult and cooperate with each other on a regular basis, rather than pass policy unencumbered. Indeed, three of the highest profile pieces of legislation passed from 1999-2007 — to introduce the single transferable vote in local elections, introduce 'free personal care' and reform student tuition fees — may not have been produced if Labour had not entered into coalition with the Liberal Democrats. Further, that process of negotiation between separate parties had the potential to produce governing instability if one party was willing to 'break ranks' and join forces with opposition parties to pursue their policy aims (2011a: 263). To some extent we may welcome this set up if it leads to greater policy coordination and 'joined-up government' as the two parties produce an overall plan for government (set out in successive 'Partnership Agreements'). However, Cairney (2011a: 264) suggests that the new arrangements often had the opposite effect, by exacerbating 'the sense of diminished individual ministerial responsibility that we now find in the era of multi-level governance'.

Conversely, the SNP minority government was less able to dominate the legislative process and more vulnerable to defeats and motions of no confidence in Parliament (although note that zero motions of no confidence were considered formally from 2007–11). Yet, it appeared to enjoy greater strength and stability within government. As a single party, it was unencumbered by the need to cooperate, and coordinate policy, with other parties within government. Further, it operated with a streamlined cabinet[6] that showed the potential to engage in meaningful cabinet decision making, with few signs of internal division and instability.

Coalition Government 1999–2007

We can find some concern about the stability of coalition government, particularly in the first session when the Liberal Democrats were portrayed as 'a party of local heroes in Scotland, with little ideological coherence' and with members more likely to display 'independence or recalcitrance' during negotiations on key policies such as free personal care and tuition fees (Mitchell, February 2001: 4) (see chapter 8 for the policy background). Labour 'could be excused for thinking that instead of being in coalition with one other party [it] is in coalition with a loose coalition of seventeen other MSPs' (February 2001: 4). Indeed, Saren and Brown (February 2001: 12) suggest that by initially 'failing to commit to free personal care, Labour Ministers provoked a serious public row with their coalition partner'; it 'feared that the Liberal Democrat MSPs would join forces' with opposition parties until a 'last minute deal was struck behind the scenes' (although compare with the discussion of tuition fees—'even the usual Lib Dem MSP dissenters appeared to agree that this was as much as they were going to get'— February 2000: 26).

Similar concerns were expressed about the durability of the 2nd term coalition, perhaps in part because the Liberal Democrats seemed to get a worse deal in 2003 (in 1999 they were much better prepared than Labour for coalition negotiations—McGarvey and Cairney, 2008: 111). This time, they focused on: the Liberal Democrats' '"Faustain pact" of support for Labour's hard line on law and order (especially the

---

[6] Coalition governments had more Cabinet ministers than single-party governments would choose (Winetrobe, June 2003: 3; Winetrobe, August 2003: 6).

provisions of the Anti-Social Behaviour Bill) in return for PR for local government'; their reduced incentive to remain in coalition after the introduction of STV for local elections (before the 2005 UK General election); and, recurring tensions on issues such as constitutional change (Winetrobe, May 2004: 3–4). Yet, the coalition remained intact for eight years.

Indeed, in the first few years, we can link most examples of weakness and instability to developments *within* the Labour Party. The early monitors suggest that, as it adjusted to its new role, the Labour-led Executive has 'hardly given the impression of being a force to be reckoned with' (November, 1999: 3; Winetrobe, August 2001: 11; Winetrobe, May 2002: 6). This problem was compounded by various examples of Labour Cabinet in-fighting. For example, several ministers briefed against the Scottish Executive line on the repeal of 'section 28' (which prohibited the 'promotion' of homosexuality in schools — chapter 7). There were also public spats between individual ministers, such as when health minister Susan Deacon and finance minister Jack McConnell clashed on the issue of NHS underspends being 'redirected' (August 2000: 2–3; 25). Such instances reinforce the UK or Whitehall image of ministers being responsible primarily for defending their departments within government rather than acting as part of a collective body.

Labour-related problems were also compounded by early crises. For example, the Scottish Qualifications Authority (SQA) affair, in which Scottish school students did not receive accurate results of their exams in time, put early pressure on Education Minister Sam Galbraith to resign (August 2000: 3; see MacMillan, November 2000: 53–4; Saren and Brown, February 2001: 62; and Winetrobe, May 2001: 53 on the aftermath, including the mass resignation of the SQA board and the appointment of Jack McConnell as education minister). Then, 'lobbygate' drew attention to claims made to undercover journalists by John Reid's son that he could guarantee privileged access to Scottish ministers (chapter 8). More importantly, the death of Donald Dewar produced an unanticipated problem — the need to replace the First Minister in 28 days, to satisfy the rules laid down in the Scotland Act, rather than the period normally taken by the party to elect a leader (November 2000: 4).

Dewar was replaced by Henry McLeish, who had a knack for hitting the headlines for the wrong reasons, either when he made remarks off the cuff (note the term 'McLeishies') or appeared to be making policy 'on the hoof' (Mitchell, November 2001: 6; Mitchell, February 2002: 3). His style occasionally became useful, such as when intervening to change Scottish Executive policy on free personal care (MacMillan, November, 2000: 7). However, he struggled to maintain backbench Labour support and his bad luck reached its peak in 2001 when he became obliged to resign following, first, revelations that he breached parliamentary rules on expenses and, second, his poor attempts to explain his behaviour (Mitchell, November 2001: 3–5; Winetrobe, November 2001: 8; Winetrobe, August 2002: 7; note that a further 'Officegate' scandal did not affect his successor in the same way — Winetrobe, November 2002: 6). Further, the departures of Dewar and McLeish in the space of one year contributed to high Labour ministerial turnover caused by reshuffles following the elections of new First Ministers (November 2000: 6; Winetrobe, February 2002: 5; Winetrobe, May 2002: 5).

If anything, Liberal Democrat ministers provided a much-needed sense of stability during the turbulence of Labour turnover (Winetrobe, May 2002: 6) and there is evidence of an impressive degree of cross-party consensus within Cabinet (few, if any, decisions went to vote — Winetrobe, August 2003: 6). Indeed, the majority of public policy was driven by successive partnership agreements between Labour and Liberal Democrats which generally tied the hands of each party's MSPs (or produced rebellions too small to change results — Winetrobe, May 2001: 7) and produced the avalanche of legislation discussed in chapter 3 (Saren and Brown, February 2001: 8; Winetrobe, February 2003: 6–7).

The Core Executive?

Overall, these early examples do not give us a clear idea about where power lies within the new Scottish Executive. Instead, we find a combination of individuals jockeying for position and a series of crises which undermine the idea of one or a group of people being in charge. For example, Mitchell (February 2002: 3) describes McLeish's term as 'in office but not in power'. In other words, the early reports betray a feeling that it is difficult to identify a 'core executive'[7] in Scotland for four main reasons.

First, in the early years of devolution, it still seemed unclear how autonomous the Scottish Executive was from the UK Government,

---

[7] The 'core executive' is a rather woolly term which refers to a set of people and organisations at the heart of government. In the UK it includes the Prime Minister and related offices (the Prime Minister's office, the Cabinet office and perhaps Cabinet and Cabinet committees) and usually includes the Chancellor of the Exchequer since the Treasury is generally considered to be the most powerful department within the UK system (and most other systems). In Scotland it was often difficult to find an equivalent Scottish Treasury — see chapter 9.

particularly since Labour effectively controlled both governments (see chapter 5). An early suggestion in the monitors was that, when push came to shove (such as when Jim Wallace deputised for an unwell Donald Dewar), the UK government could intervene to maintain a degree of Labour control (May 2000: 2). This issue arose periodically, with sporadic reports of ministerial recalcitrance in relation to the First Minister, in part based on their relationships with senior UK Government figures (see for example Winetrobe, May 2001: 8 on Wendy Alexander).

Second, the reports suggest that the role of the Scottish Executive's finance department is nothing like a Scottish equivalent of the Treasury (November 2000: 34). While much of this can be explained by the continued role of the UK Treasury in the big economic decisions affecting Scotland, it is furthered by the fact that the Scottish Executive did not have a finance department with the capacity to centralise power. Nor did the Scottish Executive have a powerful unit built around the First Minister (see chapter 9).

Third, the reports bemoan the lack of central leadership and coordination in the early years of devolution. For example, Mitchell (February 2001: 5) argues that weak leadership from McLeish exacerbated the introduction of a range of expensive policy commitments with no sense of 'effective central financial control'. Further, the SQA affair undermined the idea that the Scottish Executive enjoyed a form of intentional joined-up government when the responsibilities of ministers crossed departmental boundaries. Instead, it reinforced the impression of 'ministers without ministries' inherited from the Scottish Office days when there were fewer ministers than departments (Parry and Jones, 2000: 54; Keating, 2005a: 98). Initially, two ministers appeared to be responsible for the SQA (Sam Galbraith, Education Minister and Henry McLeish, Minister of Enterprise and Lifelong Learning, the sponsoring department) — although Galbraith effectively took most of the blame when reshuffled by new First Minster Henry McLeish (Curtice, November 2000: 20-1; see also MacMillan's November 2000: 13 coverage of the parliamentary inquiry which demonstrates the lack of direct civil service accountability to Parliament). Wendy Alexander's eventual transformation into 'minister for everything' further undermined the image of coherent government. The move towards giving Alexander a wide range of responsibilities may seem like joined up government in action. Instead, it relates more to cabinet politics: Alexander defended her turf to ensure that lifelong learning was not lost from her portfolio; Jack McConnell added transport either to keep her happy as a minister or 'to overburden her so as to keep her sidelined' (Winetrobe, February 2002: 5–7; Winetrobe, May 2002: 5; Alexander resigned in May 2002).

Fourth, it was often difficult to tell where the Scottish Executive ended and other organisations began. The best example is the role of the Lord Advocate, not only as a member of the Scottish Executive cabinet but also 'Scotland's chief prosecutor' (February, 2000: 3). During Lord Hardie's brief tenure (he resigned in February 2000), the potential conflict between the party political role and the impartial prosecutorial role was often exploited by opposition parties, a situation made worse following an ECHR ruling that temporary sheriffs were 'not sufficiently independent of him'. Issues regarding the conflict between roles were partly diffused when his successor, Colin Boyd, remained in Cabinet but lost his 'voting rights' (November 2000: 6). However, Boyd returned as a full Cabinet member in 2003 (Winetrobe, August 2003: 4) and tensions resurfaced in 2006 when Boyd became not only the chief prosecutor of Shirley McKie but also part of the Scottish Executive that settled out of court with her (see Cairney, May 2006: 14; Cairney, September 2006: 12; see also Cairney, May 2008: 14; Curtice, May 2006: 40). Scottish Executive ministers praised Boyd's propensity to 'jealously safeguard the Lord Advocate's independent prosecutorial role' when commenting on his decision to resign. However, his replacement Elish Angiolini was the first non-advocate to take the post, raising further issues of role confusion because the status of advocate was traditionally seen as a 'symbol of independence from government' (Cairney, January 2007: 17–18). Therefore, the issue did not go away until the SNP Government redefined the Lord Advocate role as 'apolitical and professional': 'the government would retain Elish Angiolini (despite her appointment by the previous government) but would remove the automatic inclusion of the Lord Advocate in Cabinet meetings' (Cairney, September 2007: 16 — see also the SNP's criticism of the UK Attorney General role during the Iraq War; and Cairney, January 2008: 14–15; Cairney, September 2008: 13 on the continued links between law and politics; Angiolini was replaced by Frank Mullholland in 2011).

Collective Cabinet Responsibility

The issue of collective cabinet responsibility sums up well the initial uncertainty and lack of clear leadership within the Scottish Executive when the rules took some time to clarify. In theory, the convention inherited from Westminster and Whitehall is that, when a decision has been reached by Cabinet, all members are obliged to defend it publicly. As Winetrobe (November 2002: 4) suggests, this was a particular concern for the Scottish Executive keen to 'provide disciplines on the two groups of ministers' (although it is unlikely that a Labour First Minister would discipline a Liberal Democrat minister). In practice there are often grey areas and the convention's limits take time to define and enforce. Assessments by the head of government on any alleged departure from the convention are, 'usually made on pragmatic, political grounds, depending on factors such as the strength of the "dissident" ministers and their relationship with the head of government, the views of the parliamentary party, as well as media and public reaction' (Winetrobe, November 2002: 4).

The first major test in Scotland was not clear cut because the cabinet member was addressing a constituency matter on an issue that had an indirect link to government policy, and he expressed concern publicly but sided with the Scottish Executive when voting in the Scottish Parliament. Culture Minister Mike Watson expressed opposition to the hospital reorganisation plans of Greater Glasgow Health Board (which had been approved by the Scottish Executive), but also voted with the Scottish Executive on an opposition debate. Ministerial Parliamentary Aide Janis Hughes abstained on one motion but then supported the amended motion. In contrast, MPA Ken Macintosh voted against the Scottish Executive and resigned. Thus, the parliamentary vote appears to be the line in the sand for both MSP and Scottish Executive (although note that Watson did not form part of the 2003 Cabinet—Winetrobe, June 2003: 6).

This conclusion was reinforced during the firefighter dispute, when Education Minister Cathy Jamieson came 'under scrutiny' but was not dismissed for not being 'on message' (Winetrobe, February 2003: 4). Further, Elaine Murray and Malcolm Chisholm were not asked to resign when they effectively criticised the Iraq War—on the grounds that it is a reserved issue linked to UK Government policy and the votes related to party, not Scottish Executive, amendments (Winetrobe, June 2003: 5; it was also not covered by the Partnership Agreement, allowing Labour and the Liberal Democrats to disagree publicly). Chisholm also kept his job after he criticised UK Government policy on dawn raids on failed asylum seekers (chapter 5). However, he then felt obliged to resign when voting with the SNP on a motion critical of UK Government policy on Trident. Given that 'the motion had no formal weight and there was no need for a Scottish Executive position on the issue', we can only wonder if his non-resignation would have led to his dismissal (Cairney, January 2007: 17).

Junior Finance Minister Tavish Scott (Liberal Democrat) remained safe despite previously resigning a different post over fisheries policy and then 'appearing to come out publicly against membership of the [EU] Common Fisheries Policy, contrary to the conventions of collective ministerial responsibility' (although the same justification, based on fisheries as a reserved issue and no parliamentary vote, would apply) (Winetrobe, February 2004: 3). The case of Paul Martin, an MPA to the Law Officers, further tested the boundaries of CCR when, as a member of the Local Government and Transport Committee, he 'dissented on the decision to support the Bill's general principles and abstained on the key Stage 1 plenary vote on the Bill' (Winetrobe, May 2004: 3).

Notably, this issue received much more attention than cabinet reshuffles (except during periods of First Ministerial change). The monitors discuss the effectiveness and popularity of ministers occasionally, but there is generally little to report (Winetrobe, August 2004: 4; Winetrobe, November 2004: 3) and very little sense of the Westminster and Whitehall-based excitement or the fixation on ministerial status. This is perhaps because Scottish ministers were relatively anonymous (a partial reverse of the relative visibility of MSPs compared to MPs) or viewed by political commentators as mediocre (Winetrobe, November 2004: 3; chapter 7). Labour ministers were much more likely to be reshuffled than their Liberal Democrat counterparts, who were selected by their own parliamentary colleagues (Ross Finnie stayed in the same post for eight years). The only cross-over came when the coalition selected ministerial portfolios. However, much of this negotiation took place at the beginning of the parliamentary sessions (for example, Labour requested the Justice portfolio from 2003) and there was little room for manoeuvre between sessions (Cairney, January 2006: 12).

The Scottish Government 2007–11

The first SNP Government attempted to solve the problem of power diffusion, and the lack of a core executive, by moving a huge range of policy responsibilities to the finance department under the direct control of the Finance Secretary John Swinney and two supporting ministers (McGarvey and Cairney, 2008: 111; 120). This move was helped significantly by the absence of coalition government, which would have prompted a degree of negotiation on departments and their portfolios. Instead, the SNP was able to announce a very 'quick win' by 'slimming down' the Scottish Cabinet to six 'Cabinet Secretaries' (plus 10 deputies and the law officers). It was promoted by the SNP as 'a first blow in his administration's efficient government agenda' (Cairney, September 2007: 13; the move also reflected

Permanent Secretary John Elvidge's move to develop the 'Scottish model' of policymaking with fewer departmental boundaries – see Elvidge, 2011). It also produced greater potential for the Scottish Cabinet to become – at least compared to the UK's 20-plus Cabinet (which relies much more on an extensive series of sub-committees) – a decision-making body, albeit one weighted heavily in favour of one department. The SNP also simplified the Scottish Government's use of targetry, identifying 45 key indicators (on its *Scotland Performs* webpage) and encouraging civil servants to 'focus on achieving them rather than (according to the caricature of officials) pursuing their own indicators of prestige by trying to maximise the budgets of their departments' (Cairney, September 2008: 15).

This move is set within the context of a policy management style geared towards setting strategic priorities. As chapter 6 discusses, it has professed a desire to decentralise policymaking; to set a strategic direction for government and give a greater degree of freedom for civil servants, local authorities and (when elected) health boards to carry it out. Further, Alex Salmond generally gave the impression of a First Minister, rather like Jack McConnell, with no inclination to interfere in the running of individual departments (a frequent throwaway line is that Alex Salmond was happy to lead the country while John Swinney and Nicola Sturgeon ran the government). Rather, Salmond has been keen to develop a 'statesman' image, calling for a new relationship with the UK Government and EU, promoting the Scottish brand aboard and, for most of the first SNP term, leading the agenda on the 'National Conversation' (Cairney, September 2007: 18; chapter 10).

Criticisms of ministerial ineffectiveness did not stop with the election of the SNP, particularly since the characterisation of ministers as weak and indecisive is a key electoral tool of opposition parties. The earliest and most significant example was Education Secretary Fiona Hyslop who came under pressure from opposition parties decrying her lack of leadership on the new *Curriculum For Excellence* (perhaps ironically, since it was designed by the previous Scottish Executive to give teachers and schools greater autonomy in the delivery of education) and blaming her for the problems the SNP faced in fulfilling its manifesto promise to abolish student debt (Cairney, January 2009: 35; 53–5). Hyslop then lost her job following media and parliamentary pressure on the issue of class size targets (see also chapter 6).[8]

---

[8] For a list of newspaper coverage on class sizes and Hyslop, see http://paulcairney.blog spot.com/2011/05/class-sizes.html

Hyslop was the only Cabinet Secretary to be replaced (by Mike Russell, current Education Secretary) from 2007–11, and her experience contrasts to some extent with that of Justice Secretary Kenny MacAskill, who was often under more pressure to resign, but also backed more strongly by Salmond. MacAskill was the focal point for the SNP's controversial alcohol policy, court reforms and its push to minimise short-term jail sentences. He was criticised heavily for missing a key petition-inspired debate on knife crime in the Scottish Parliament (he was in Canada to promote Homecoming) and took some of the blame for high profile prison breaks (Cairney, January 2009: 51; Cairney, May 2009: 52). Most notably, his decision to release the Lockerbie bomber put him under intense domestic and international pressure. Nicola Sturgeon also came under pressure over her role in addressing the C difficile outbreak at the Vale of Leven hospital (Cairney, September 2008: 14; Cairney, January 2009: 47–8; Cairney, May 2009: 39). Yet, these examples did little to undermine the idea of central government leadership. Rather, Alex Salmond pursued an almost blanket policy of support for ministers (such as when he threatened to resign if the Scottish Parliament passed a motion of no confidence in MacAskill — Cairney, May 2009: 52) and has resisted most calls for Cabinet reshuffles. The only further example from 2007–11 related to a reshuffle of deputy ministers combined with the shift of Mike Russell to Minister for Culture, External Affairs and the Constitution, accentuating his new constitutional remit and signalling a push towards the independence referendum bill in 2010 (Cairney, May 2009: 51–2). Russell then moved to education to replace Hyslop when the independence referendum agenda waned.

The Scottish Ministerial Code

The *Scottish Ministerial Code* received considerable scrutiny under SNP government following eight years of relative anonymity — a process that said as much about the SNP's minority position in Parliament as it did about Scottish Government. The Code was initially an imported then tartanised version (taking into account the recommendations of the CSG) of its UK equivalent (McGarvey and Cairney, 2008: 14), which has received fairly minimal revisions at the beginning of each parliamentary session. It covers issues such as collective ministerial responsibility, truthful conduct within Parliament and to the public, ministerial responsibilities regarding civil servants, the receipt of gifts and paid service, the boundaries between ministerial and constituency roles and the (discouraged) use of public resources for party political ends (Scottish Government, 2009: 6). Ministers are also governed by the

Code of Conduct for MSPs (2009: 7). Perhaps the most notable aspect of the Code is that ministers are generally responsible for regulating their own behaviour. Further, while MSPs and the civil service may highlight issues of concern, the 'the ultimate judge of the standards of behaviour expected of a Minister and the appropriate consequences of a breach of those standards' is the First Minister (2009: 7).

Over the years, issues regarding the Code have included: the procedures to release embargoed information to the media before it is relayed to Parliament (Winetrobe, February 2003: 6); its relationship to the *Guide to Collective Decision Making* and the requirement in a coalition government that 'the partnership party with fewer MSPs shall have a share of Ministerial appointments at least equal to its share of partnership MSPs' (Winetrobe, August 2003: 4); the Code's revision to cover MPAs (and the lack of ministerial adherence to it — Winetrobe, May 2004: 3); and the receipt of gifts (Schlesinger, April 2005: 13). In other words, with the exception of the issue of collective cabinet responsibility, the operation and adequacy of the Code has generally received minimal attention.

This changed quickly following the election of the minority SNP Government and the development of a new form of partisanship within the Scottish Parliament (chapter 3). Attention to ministerial ethics began with media accounts of various practices by Scottish ministers, including Alex Salmond's decision to remain an MP (producing *Daily Record* headlines on the theme 'two cheque Eck' — Cairney, September 2007: 17); and, the ability of the SNP to charge more for companies to hear ministerial speeches, which prompted some opposition MSPs to call for parliamentary or independent scrutiny of the Code. This was rebuffed by Alex Salmond who replied that the same MSPs had not raised the issue when in government and that Donald Dewar himself had rejected this approach (Cairney, January 2008: 14, footnote 18; for Dewar's speech on 'lobbygate' and the Code see Scottish Parliament Official Report 30.9.99 cols.937–49). However, the issue became a regular focus for Labour and Liberal Democrat MSPs (and, to a lesser extent, Conservative MSPs), who raised attention to a series of issues, including: the involvement of Alex Salmond (wearing his constituency MP/MSP hat) and John Swinney in Donald Trump's planning application; and, Nicola Sturgeon's role in the 'go ape' planning proposal and alleged ministerial influence on SEPA when considering a planning proposal in Aviemore (Cairney, May 2008: 11–12; Cairney, January 2008: 16). This attention put pressure on the SNP to produce a revised Code and address the fact that First Ministerial conduct was not dealt with fully by the Code (since, according to the Code, the First Minister decides if ministers are acting appropriately).

The Scottish Government revised the Code in 2008 (Cairney, September 2008: 10). It maintained the principles of the original (particularly regarding the need for ministers to regulate their own behaviour), but added sections to reflect parliamentary pressure and to put the SNP's stamp on government. To reflect the former, there is a new mechanism to refer issues of (primarily First) ministerial conduct to an independent panel, and a section recommending that the First Minister makes clear when s/he is acting as a constituency MSP giving an opinion rather than the First Minister giving a directive (section 8.8 of the Code). To signal an SNP approach, there is a rejection of the need to consult UK departments before agreeing to TV interviews, a signal that the Scottish Government (and not just the Presiding Officer) will decide if legislation is within the competence of the Scottish Parliament and a signal that the use of MPAs will not continue—although the distinctiveness of 'Parliamentary Liaison Officers' (who may sit on committees related to their minister's brief) is not clear. There is also a shift in the use of Law Officer advice, to signal further distance between formal-legal and ministerial-legal advice (2.30); routine queries are dealt with by the Scottish Government Legal Directorate and advice from the Law Officers only given when 'expressly sought' (2.27).

A further section seeks to clarify collective responsibility, suggesting that ministers may object in private to policies affecting their constituency before a decision has been made, but they must defend the decision after it has been made (2.5). If unable to do so, the implication is that the minister should resign or expect to be removed (2.8). In Cabinet they should act in their ministerial, not constituency, capacity (2.9) (see Cairney, September 2008: 10). There are also moves to tighten up the rules on special advisers, the recording of meetings with interest groups and the rules on quango appointments. Yet, the new Code did not stop a significant concerted attempt to use points of order to suggest that ministers were making misleading statements to Parliament (Cairney, January 2009: 30), prompting Alex Salmond to refer complaints about his conduct to the new independent advisory panel (chapter 3).

The Scottish Executive Civil Service 1999–2007

The monitors cover the idea that civil servants compete with ministers for power within government, although attention to that issue has always been sporadic (the same can be said for special advisers).[9] It surfaced in 2004 following claims by Brian Wilson, former Scottish Office minister, that civil servants are 'more firmly in control of policy than they were prior to devolution' (Wright, August 2004: 28). The role of the 'senior leadership team' in the Scottish Executive came under close scrutiny following the publication of its (externally commissioned) *Taking Stock* report in 2006, particularly when Head of the Environment and Rural Affairs Department Richard Wakeford (already stung by criticisms regarding his commute by air to work) criticised the *Scotsman* for claiming that the report was 'damning' and that several departmental heads had been removed from the 'top table' as a result (Cairney, January 2007: 19). Most importantly, the treatment by senior civil servants of departments as their 'fiefdoms' also came under scrutiny by departing minister Tom McCabe in 2007 (Cairney, January 2008: 11) — a statement reminiscent of claims made by former UK Labour ministers such as Tony Benn and Richard Crossman.

Relocation of the Civil Service

Yet, quarterly reports are not well placed to give wide accounts of the locus of power within political systems. Instead, they are often useful to track specific initiatives such as the Scottish Executive's policy of relocating civil service staff from Edinburgh. The Scottish agenda largely followed on from the Lyons Review, which built on previous UK reviews designed initially to reduce the need for civil servants to travel to London or maintain large mortgages to live there (see Gay, 2006: 4). Subsequent reviews were often based on supplementary motives, such as to reduce the costs of public administration (London government property prices and the London allowance), relieve congestion and create jobs in 'depressed areas' (2006: 5). The Thatcher government partly reversed this policy and sought, instead, to reduce civil service numbers. Labour resurrected the policy from 2003, with the Lyons review making clear that the policy required continuous leadership and political weight behind it: it is a long term project with

---

[9] Most attention to SPADs regards their personal conduct or health, not their access to or use of power (February 2000: 1-2; May 2000: 2). The August 2000: 5 report notes the first appointment of an adviser to an individual minister rather than the policy unit. While MacMillan (November 2000: 6) notes that McLeish was more comfortable with the idea of special advisers than Dewar, Winetrobe (May 2002: 9) highlights the extent to which the roles were qualified publicly under McConnell, particularly given the image of advisers provided by Alistair Campbell and Jo Moore in Whitehall (and subsequent Phillis review into government communications — Winetrobe, November 2003: 6). Overall, advisers are more likely to attract attention based on their costs rather than their influence (Winetrobe, August 2003: 7).

up-front costs that would take some time to recoup; and, those cost reductions may come largely from reductions in civil service pay to reflect the lower costs of living in some areas (2006: 9). The Lyons review accelerated the UK Government's civil service dispersal agenda (occasionally moving civil servants to Scotland – Bell, May 2004: 51–2; Winetrobe, May 2004: 4; Winetrobe, August 2004: 5; Winetrobe, April 2005: 4; Cairney, January 2006: 15; Cairney, September 2007: 19; Cairney, January 2008: 13) and prompted similar moves in Scotland.

The approach in Scotland was often portrayed as problematic. While some opposition from relocated staff and Edinburgh-based MSPs was to be expected (Winetrobe, June 2003: 5; Winetrobe, August 2003: 6; Winetrobe, November 2003: 5; Winetrobe, February 2004: 3–4; Winetrobe, May 2004: 4; Winetrobe, April 2005: 4), the image of the policy was often dented by reports of the move's costs and decisions to move staff only as far as Glasgow in some cases (Cairney, January 2006: 15; the Scottish Executive also had trouble when trying to oblige quasi-governmental bodies like the Mental Welfare Commission to relocate – Cairney, January 2007: 21). It was criticised by the Parliament's Finance Committee which highlighted the uneven nature of relocations to some 'areas of deprivation' rather than others (Winetrobe, August 2004: 5).

The efficiency of the moves were also questioned by Audit Scotland, which reported that 933 (56%) of the 1653 jobs moved from Edinburgh have gone to Glasgow and that the impact ranged between a £33000 per job saving to a £45000 per job cost (Cairney, January 2007: 22). This prompted the Audit Committee (with two MSPs from Edinburgh constituencies) to further investigate the policy. It found that while the policy's principle was sound, its implementation was not. For example, the decision to consider relocation when a public body's lease was up may be practical but does not produce strategic decisions (Cairney, April 2007: 9). Jack McConnell's rather distinctive argument, that the relocation of public sector jobs helped Edinburgh by boosting the private sector, did not win the day (Cairney, September 2006: 13; although the SNP made similar noises on public sector employment – Cairney, January 2007: 20). The lengths that the Scottish Executive went to move people out often suggested a greater commitment to the policy itself than its long term success (see for example, Cairney 2007: 9). To all intents and purposes, a clear commitment to the policy was dropped when Labour left office. While the SNP Government supported the principle of relocation, it was 'less convinced of the practical benefits' (Cairney, September 2007: 19) and more convinced of the 'significant cost to business continuity and to staff' (Cairney, May 2008: 14).

Open Government and Freedom of Information

Freedom of information was also an issue that received regular attention, partly because it goes to the heart of the role of civil servants and their relationships with ministers (although the policy advice given by civil servants to ministers is still generally out of bounds, to allow the former to be frank) (Winetrobe, May 2001: 51; May 2002: 8; November 2003: 5; August 2004: 6). FOI is also linked strongly to transparency, an issue central to the devolution rhetoric and pursued by Liberal Democrat leader Jim Wallace when Justice Minister. Wallace appeared to ensure, in Scottish legislation, a more open system of FOI than UK ministers in equivalent UK legislation (Cairney, January 2006: 17; compare with criticisms in Winetrobe, November 2001: 64–5). Yet, much comes down to the implementation (note the new context, with Wallace no longer Justice Minister), or a combination of: the willingness of public bodies to cooperate; the intensity of media attention (often focused on the issue of MSP and Scottish Executive expenses — Winetrobe, April 2005: 4; Cairney, January 2007: 24); the robustness of the Scottish Information Commissioner; and, the level of public awareness of the new rules on FOI. That willingness to cooperate appeared to be undermined by a public sector perception that FOI had produced greater-than-expected costs (either financial, or the opportunity costs related to what civil servants could be doing instead). The Scottish Executive view, quite early on, was that many requests were 'frivolous' and it consulted quickly on the issue of legislative 'fine tuning' (Cairney, January 2006: 17). It explored the stipulation that FOI requests costing more than £600 (including ministerial and civil service time) can be rejected (Cairney, January 2007; 23). Labour MSPs helped portray some newspapers as 'verging close to abuse of the Act by the number and content of their requests' (Cairney, May 2006: 18). The Scottish Executive also showed an initial propensity to appeal decisions made by Scottish Information Commissioner Kevin Dunion. However, the outcome of its review was a statement of satisfaction with the process and no plans to change the fee structure (Cairney, April 2007: 10; although a bill amending FOI legislation was introduced in 2011).

According to Dunion, there is growing evidence of a 'shift towards a culture of more transparency and accountability' (Cairney, September 2006: 15; Cairney, January 2007: 23). Scotland's FOI law is 'one of the strongest in the world' and its provisions conform to key UN Human Rights Commission principles, 'such as maximum disclosure rights; rapid and fair processing of requests; costs should not deter applicants and that there is a right of review, by way of free appeal to me' (Dunion in Cairney, April 2007: 10). There is also '"clear blue water" ... emerging between the Scottish and UK FOI procedures' given the 'general culture of secrecy in the UK' (Dunion in Cairney, May 2009: 72-3). Initially, Dunion found that 'most Scots did not know much about the new FOI legislation', prompting him to initiate new advertising campaigns (Winetrobe, November 2004: 7; April 2005: 4). Dunion also sought to publicise potentially high profile decisions relating to: the private sector contract to escort prisoners from court to jail (Winetrobe, April 2005: 4); regional childhood leukaemia statistics (to examine the effect of the Sellafield Nuclear plant in Cumbria—Cairney, January 2007: 23; Cairney, September 2008: 15-6); morbidity rates for surgeons (Cairney, January 2006: 18); correspondence between the Scottish Executive and Home Office on the Dungavel detention centre; and, the 'naming and shaming' of firms reported to the Trading Standards Authority (Cairney, January 2007: 23; although the Commissioner has no power to oblige the publication of the so-called 'secret guidelines' on fiscal fines to minimise the number of minor criminal cases going to court—Cairney, September 2008: 12).

Awareness rose from 47% in 2005 to 74% in 2008 (although it was relatively low among the young and old—Cairney, May 2008: 15), while 'public belief that government is becoming more open and accountable' rose from 34% in 2005 to 67% in 2007. Further, the high number of referrals of cases to the Commissioner (much higher per capita than in England) may suggest that awareness of FOI is high and public authorities are content to refer issues for an external decision (Cairney, April 2007: 10; although there are still signs of sensitive information 'management'—Cairney, January 2008: 15). Dunion also kept up the agenda to oblige the Scottish Executive to widen the net of FOI (Winetrobe, April 2005: 5; Cairney, May 2009: 73). Of particular concern was the extension of FOI to housing associations and private companies providing public services (prompting Dunion to oblige NHS Lothian to reveal its PFI contract—Cairney, January 2008: 15; Cairney, May 2008: 15; Cairney, September 2008: 12) followed, in 2010, by Dunion's disappointment that the Scottish Government had not decided to include 'private prisons, local authority leisure trusts and the Association of Chief Police Officers in Scotland' (Scottish Information Commissioner, 2010: 22). Recent decisions have also continued the ability of FOI requests to inform policy scrutiny, with recent decisions on the release of information on Shirley McKie (above) and progress on Scottish Government commitments to increase and then maintain police officer numbers (Scottish Information Commissioner, 2010: 16; 18).

Territorial Policy Communities and the Scottish Policy Style

Devolution in Scotland produced the potential for major changes not only to public policy (chapter 8) but also policy*making*. For example, the Scottish Constitutional Convention (1995) expressed vague hopes for a move away from consultation with the 'usual suspects', or the most powerful interest groups, whose close relationships with governments come at the expense of other participants (Cairney, Halpin and Jordan, 2009; see also Woods, 2002: 6 on new First Minister Jack McConnell's instruction to ministers: 'go out there and talk to people on the front line, the public service leaders and the public, and listen to them – not just listen to the interest groups that may come to Edinburgh to lobby'). Such hopes are always likely to remain unfulfilled because there is a 'logic of consultation' that ties civil servants to the most interested, active, knowledgeable and representative groups. The size of the state is such that no single policymaker could realistically control the whole process. Rather, policymaking is broken into smaller, more manageable units – or sectors and subsectors. Ministers and senior civil servants devolve most policymaking issues to relatively junior civil servants within those subsectors. Civil servants tend not to be trained experts in their field and they rely on others, such as interest groups, to maintain their policy capacity. They need information and advice to produce good policy, and groups trade their information and advice for access to policymakers. Consequently, the 'usual suspects' are consulted most often because they are in the best position to trade their resources for access (2009; Richardson and Jordan, 1979; Jordan and Maloney, 1997; Cairney, 2008; 2011b; 2012b).

Further, groups tend to devote their efforts to areas in which they are most interested and/or they feel they can maximise their influence. While they might use the Scottish Parliament to 'hedge their bets' or seek a second chance at influence (perhaps particularly during terms of minority government), the 'usual suspects' generally recognise that the government is the main hub for their activities. Indeed, as in many political systems, the pressure participants in most contact with the Scottish Parliament tend to be government related: government agencies, quangos and local and health authorities (Cairney et al, 2009) – hence the use of the term 'pressure participants', by Jordan et al (2004), partly to show us that terms such as 'pressure groups' or 'interest groups' can often be misleading because the organisations most likely to lobby governments and parliaments most are businesses, universities and other levels or types of government. Further, while some groups may be interested in the wider policy field, groups with limited resources tend to focus on their core areas (such as when teaching unions focus primarily on school education).

Thus, after a 'honeymoon period', or period of adjustment to devolution, in which groups lobbied the Scottish Parliament and formed rather wide networks with other groups, they soon moved towards their 'core business' (Cairney et al, 2009). To some extent, we can link this process of change to the idea of consultation fatigue. The Scottish Executive came under some rather ill-informed criticism for appearing to consult too frequently with pressure participants and the public. It first felt the need to explain its consultation rate in 2005 when it was announced that over 900 consultations had taken place since 1999 (Winetrobe, April 2005: 4) and then came under criticism when the number reached 1000. Yet, the figure is misleading and hides some laudable practices of multiple consultations on the principles and then the details of policy (Cairney, January 2006: 18; which help the Scottish Executive look better than the UK Government at 'listening to people's views before it takes decisions' — Curtice, January 2006: 48; Curtice, May 2006: 35). Indeed, this is a practice that shows us the pre- and post-devolution differences in consultation. While we should not exaggerate the differences in consultation practice between the Scottish and UK governments as a whole, we should note the difference in the numbers of consultation documents issued by the old Scottish Office (approximately 20 per year) and the new Scottish Executive or Government (approximately 100, including consultations on the implications of EU and UK policies).

Indeed, there are *some* signs of a distinctive 'Scottish policy style', involving new ways in which the Scottish Government makes policy following consultation and negotiation with pressure participants such as interest groups, local government organisations and unions. Most notably, devolution has prompted many participants to change their *organisations* (devolving lobbying functions to Scottish branches) and/or lobbying *strategies* (shifting their attention from the UK to the Scottish Government). Keating et al (2009: 54) suggest that devolved policymaking arrangements are particularly significant in Scotland, compared to Wales and Northern Ireland, because the Scottish Parliament was granted the most powers within the UK political system. Their main suggestion is that, in Scotland, we should expect:

1. Relatively high levels of interest group devolution (or the proliferation of new Scottish groups) as groups are obliged to lobby Scottish political institutions.

2. 'Cognitive change', in which policy problems are defined from a territorial perspective and groups follow, and seek to influence, a devolved policy agenda.

3. A new group-government dynamic, in which groups might coalesce around a common lobbying strategy, or perhaps find that they are now competitors in their new environment.

4. A series of 'historic legacies' based on how groups initially viewed devolution.

They find, following an extensive process of interviews with pressure participants,[10] that point 1 in particular is borne out. While many UK groups had regional arms, and many Scottish-specific groups existed before devolution (partly reflecting the value of lobbying the old Scottish Office), there has been a significant shift of group attention to reflect the new devolved arrangements. UK groups have devolved further resources to their Scottish offices to reflect the devolution of power and their new lobbying demands (50% of groups lobbying in Scotland fall into this category—Keating, 2005a: 65). However, we should not overestimate the shift, since organisational devolution has varied (often according to the level of devolution in their areas—e.g. trade union devolution is often limited, reflecting the reservation of employment law) and some groups have provided few additional resources (such as one additional member of staff).

Further, groups increasingly follow a devolved policy agenda. The broadest, albeit indirect, marker of this change is the attitude of Scottish branches to their UK counterparts, with many bemoaning the lack of UK-based understanding of the devolved policy context (in fact, this perception of being ignored can be found across Scotland—within government, groups and even academia!). They also face a new organisational task, with the old focus on policy implementation (or joining with a coalition of groups and the Scottish Office to lobby the UK Government) replaced by the need to fill Scottish Government demands for policy ideas—a process that may be more competitive in the absence of a Scotland-wide lobby. The evidence suggests that some groups addressed that task more quickly than others. Most notably,

---

[10] See Keating et al (2009: 54). We have conducted 300-400 interviews in the UK since devolution, including 100-200 interviews in Scotland. This includes 40-50 interviews with education-specific pressure participants, primarily in two phases (2006 and 2011), to inform the discussion in chapters 6 and 8.

business groups opposed to devolution (and linked in the minds of many to Conservative party rule up to 1997) were relatively slow to adapt, while the voluntary sector quickly established links that it began to develop with the Labour Government from 1997 (Keating et al, 2009: 55). There were also some group-government links already in place, reflecting extensive levels of administrative devolution in areas such as education and health.

Interviews with participants suggest that the overall picture is positive: new 'territorial policy communities' have developed, reflecting the generally open and consultative approach of the Scottish Government and the increased willingness and ability of groups to engage constructively in policymaking in Scotland (Keating and Stevenson, 2001; Keating, 2005; 2010; Cairney, 2008; 2009a; McGarvey and Cairney, 2008: 236; the same impression can be found in the first monitor—November 1999: 28). Most groups feel that they have the chance to take at least some part in policymaking and enjoy regular dialogue with civil servants and (less frequently) ministers who are a 'phone call away'. Many (but, of course, fewer) also discuss the chance to influence the terms of reference of wider consultations by, for example, becoming part of working groups. Many also describe a fairly small world and the 'usual story of everybody knowing everybody else' (Keating et al, 2009: 57).

Most contrast this with their perception of the UK policy process which they believe to be more top-down, less reliant on professional or policy networks and perhaps even more competitive between groups (Cairney, 2008). In other words, their satisfaction cannot just be explained by the fact that Edinburgh is easier to get to than London. Yet, while we can call this the 'Scottish' or 'devolved' policy style (since it is also apparent in Wales), and perhaps link it to the pre-devolution rhetoric of 'new politics', there at least three key *practical* (i.e. not cultural) reasons for close group-government relations in Scotland.

First, compared to the UK, Scotland is small and Scottish Government responsibilities are limited. Scotland's size allows relatively close personal relationships to develop between key actors, and perhaps for closer links to develop across departmental 'silos'. Indeed, Jervis and Plowden (2000: 9) describe 'policy villages' with 'tight political and professional networks' with the potential to produce 'quicker and easier agreement over policy and strategy' and better implementation because Scotland's small scale 'would make it easier to work across departmental boundaries'.

Second, the capacity of the Scottish Government is relatively low, prompting civil servants to rely more (for information, advice and support) on experts outside government and the actors responsible for policy implementation (Keating, 2010: 202–3). Both factors combine to explain the Scottish Government's governance style. This refers to a relative ability or willingness of the Scottish Government, when compared to the UK, to devolve the delivery of policy to other organisations in a meaningful way. In other words, implementing bodies are given considerable discretion and/or pressure participants are well represented in working groups set up to manage implementation. This may be more possible in Scotland compared to England in which policies travel further distances and the UK government attempts to control far more organisations with less scope for personal relationships (resulting in a relative desire in England to set quantitative targets for service delivery organisations). While this difference has been a feature of Scottish-UK Government comparisons since devolution, the 'bottom-up' not 'top-down' approach to policy implementation is also associated closely with the post-2007 SNP government and, in particular, its relationship with local authorities (chapter 6).

Third, devolution went hand in hand with a significant increase in UK public expenditure (chapter 9). Its main effect was that there were comparatively few major policy disagreements. Departments or groups were competing with each other for resources, but that competition was not fierce because most policy programmes appeared to be relatively well funded. It is only now that we see the potential for strained relationships between government and groups, and competition between different groups or interests, when tougher policy choices have to be made. While we might expect the decade of good relationships to stand the Scottish Government in good stead, we may also recognise that the economic crisis takes us into new territory and that good relations may have been built on good policy conditions. Much depends on how we explain the first decade of group-government relations: does it reflect a particularly Scottish culture of cooperation and the pursuit of consensus (summed up by the term 'new politics'), or does it reflect the once favourable, but now undermined, conditions that were conducive to a particular style at a particular time?

Any general picture of group-government relations also masks mixed outcomes, reflecting a certain degree of unpredictability in political systems. For example, government ministers do not always consult before making decisions, and they do not always try to reach policy consensus when they have a clear idea of what they want and how they want to achieve it (chapter 8; Cairney, May 2006: 71–2).

Therefore, we should not go too far with this picture of consensus and influence derived from interviews, particularly since interviewees in Scotland may base their impressions on their previous experiences as Scottish groups trying to influence UK institutions rather than the experiences of their UK counterparts (Cairney, 2008: 358).

Scottish groups also qualify their own experiences. Many acknowledge the difference between being consulted regularly and *influencing* policy choices—particularly when ministers have already formed views on the subject (see also November 1999: 28). Further, many distinguish between their influence at the point of Scottish Government choice and the eventual policy outcome. Ministerial attention tends to lurch from issue to issue because they have to react to events and do not have the resources to address all of the problems for which they are responsible. While much of the effect of these lurches of attention are addressed by relative constants in the system (such as the role of civil servants and their relationships with groups), there is still the potential for long periods of stability and policy continuity to be 'punctuated' by short bursts of instability and policy change (Baumgartner and Jones, 1993; 2009). Consequently, policy relationships tend to vary according to policy issue and over time (John, 1998; 2011).

In short, the Scottish Policy Style may be important, but we should not exaggerate its distinctiveness or link it uncritically to the vague notion of new politics. Indeed, Scottish groups often appear to be *more disappointed* with policy outcomes than their UK counterparts (see Cairney, 2009b). One explanation is the irony of the new system— groups who buy into the idea of 'new politics' and meaningful government engagement are likely to be more disappointed than the more experienced or jaded campaigners. Or, there is often a significant difference between the initial policy choice (policy formulation) and the final outcome (policy implementation). This has particular relevance to the devolved context often characterised by a 'bottom up' approach to implementation in which flexibility is built into the initial policy and there is less of a sense of top-down control that we associate with the UK government. Further, some groups are less supportive of this approach than others. In particular, groups with limited resources may be the least supportive of flexible delivery arrangements because they only have the ability to influence the initial policy choice. The more that governments make policy commitments that lack detailed restrictions, and leave the final outcome to the organisations that deliver policy, the less they see their initial influence continued during implementation (2009b: 366). This devolution of power, to local authorities, has become a key element of SNP Government strategy, which may exacerbate tensions between groups and government (and further undermine the role and status of the Scottish Parliament).

Conclusion

The Scottish Executive took some time to develop as a collective entity in the early years of devolution. While it was relatively clear that the Executive, not Parliament, would produce most policy and amend most legislation, it was less clear *how* it would perform that role. The coalition government quickly produced a partnership agreement, but took some time to establish a partnership able to withstand the strains of party cooperation and tensions still to be resolved *within* those parties. The Labour Party's role in Scotland took time to develop, with the death of Dewar and resignation of McLeish, and with the apparent willingness of the UK ministers to intervene during periods of uncertainty, contributing to a sense of governing instability. Perhaps ironically, given their initial image, the Liberal Democrats provided some much-needed balance. Indeed, the coalition government proved to be remarkably stable, lasting two four year sessions. However, stability does not necessarily produce governing strength. It is difficult to identify a strong core in the Scottish Executive, in part because of early problems of leadership (and an apparent lack of enforced Collective Cabinet Responsibility) but also, more generally, because the 'core executive' did not appear to have the necessary levers to control ministers and civil servants. We can identify similar issues in the UK, but the added element in Scotland is the lack of a Scottish Treasury able to direct departmental activity through the use of targets linked to performance measures and money.

The Scottish Government experience from 2007 is different in some ways. It was more vulnerable in Parliament, but also more able to present an image of governing competence. The small size of the cabinet allowed it to operate as a relatively cohesive unit, at least when compared to the Scottish Executive or UK Government. There is also more evidence of a Scottish Treasury, if only because so many responsibilities came under the purview of John '37 jobs' Swinney. The SNP also suffered fewer problems related to cabinet decision-making (rather, Salmond spent more time defending ministers in Parliament). Most notably, its approach has been to set strategic objectives for other organisations to carry out. As chapter 6 discusses, the largest effect of this move may have been on the role of local government and, consequently, the pressure participants that seek to influence national and local policy.

There is a similar sense of transition within the civil service, moving from its old Scottish Office focus on implementing UK policy to its new focus on the need to engage with interest groups and other organisations to formulate policy. It is difficult to identify a devolution-specific agenda in relation to the civil service. Its role was not considered in great detail before devolution and the most notable developments in the Scottish Executive, at least in terms of monitor attention, relate to the problematic policy of civil service relocation and the development of a new culture of openness and freedom of information. There are sporadic reports relating to civil service power and departmental 'fiefdoms', but this is nothing new. Rather, it relates primarily to the logic of government in which responsibilities are subdivided into departments and units, or policy sectors and subsectors. In this context, it is natural for civil servants to act somewhat protectively towards certain aspects of policy for which they are involved over long periods, particularly when they develop relationships with pressure participants — and particularly when those relationships endure much longer than governments and individual ministers. The thing that *is* new relates to the shift of group attention to the Scottish arena and the need for groups to respond to issues that may arise at different times, and in a different way, according to Scottish ministerial attention and priorities. Territorial policy communities have developed, often around distinctly Scottish policy conditions and institutions, and in the context of a decision making environment that is often characterised by greater personal contact between senior policymakers and groups. As chapter 6 discusses, Scottish policy communities may also be marked by an increasing tendency for the Scottish Government to leave the implementation of policy to local authorities. Given with the new economic context, in which participants may now compete more fiercely for scarce resources, we may find that the relationships developed in the first ten years of devolution may be subject to new pressures.

Chapter 5

Intergovernmental Relations

Scotland, the UK and the EU

In this chapter, 'intergovernmental relations' (or 'IGR in Scotland') refers to the relationships that have formed between the Scottish and UK executives (ministers and civil servants) since devolution. This chapter also covers Scottish involvement in Europe and the EU because most of that activity relates to the Scottish Executive's (1999–07) or Scottish Government's (2007 onwards) relationships with the UK government, as Scotland seeks (or, if we are being provocative, *seeks permission*) to be involved in European and foreign affairs. Three things are most worthy of note. First, IGR in Scotland seems relatively informal when compared to most political systems. This relationship is most noticeable from 1999–07, when the UK and Scottish executives shared the same governing party (a UK Labour majority government and a Scottish Labour-led coalition with the Liberal Democrats). Second, the first term of SNP government (2007–11) was marked by a significant degree of continuity. While there were more high profile disputes from 2007, we did not see a radical shift of relationships. Nor did we see a major shift in 2010 when a Conservative-Liberal Democrat coalition government replaced Labour in the UK.

Third, however, we should not exaggerate the level of agreement between executives during these periods. While it was broadly sensible for executives to resolve intergovernmental matters quietly and generally behind closed doors, politics is not always driven by what we (as observers) consider to be sensible. Further, the relationship also reflected an imbalance of power towards the UK government. In this context, the value of the monitors is that they outline, in considerable detail, the tensions that existed in the early years of devolution as both executives adapted to their new roles. This process was complicated by the changing status of Scottish Labour within the UK Labour Party (a relatively centrist party structure when compared to the federal Liberal Democrats) and the formation of a coalition government in Scotland which required cooperation with the Liberal Democrats. That tension, when UK ministers were at their most involved and interested in devolution, was replaced by a form of *neglect*, in which UK ministers (and often civil servants) disengaged from devolution from the early 2000s.[11] In other words, we should not equate the lack of visible disputes, or limited recourse to formal dispute resolution mechanisms, with a high degree of consensus. Similarly, heightened UK Labour Government attention to Scotland from 2007 was not driven solely by its desire to foster good working relationships with the SNP-led Scottish Government. Rather, Labour recognised a threat to its position and sought to counter SNP electoral popularity more directly than it did when Scottish Labour was in government. It is perhaps only from 2010, when a Conservative-Liberal Democrat coalition government sought to appear, in the words of Prime Minister David Cameron, to 'govern Scots with respect', that the UK Government has appeared so publicly respectful of the Scottish Government's position. However, again, this stance is taken within the context of a UK-led policy process, particularly in an era of spending cuts over which the Scottish Government has limited control. Further, the election of a majority SNP Government in 2011 may signal the beginning of a new relationship in which the UK Government has to make harder choices when faced with more demands for constitutional change.

This chapter explores the potential for a contradiction between the broad picture of IGR in Scotland, in which the process appears to be smooth and informal, and the more detailed picture in which we find a significant number of disagreements and (often very personal) power struggles. First, it outlines a broad picture of informality and situates Scotland within a comparative context. Second, it explains why these informal relationships developed and why they did not change dramatically under the SNP. Third, it qualifies that picture by focusing on particular examples of tension, such as the roles of the civil service and the Secretary of State for Scotland and various attempts by Scottish executives to take a more active role in EU and foreign affairs. Finally, it considers the modern era of IGR in which eight years of predominantly Labour party links have been replaced by links between

---

[11] See Bulpitt (1983; and Bradbury, 2006) for the idea that UK Government ('the centre') neglect allowed actors in the 'periphery' (such as local authorities and devolved administrations) a form of qualified autonomy.

the SNP and a Conservative-led coalition. We consider the existence of rather smooth relations up to 2011 with the potential for new tensions following the SNP's game-changing election victory in 2011.

Scotland and the UK in Comparative Context

A significant part of the UK-focused IGR literature is devoted to characterising the nature of the modern UK (is it a unitary, union or quasi-federal state?), considering how comparable its arrangements are to federal states, and examining how much power is retained and devolved by the UK government (Mitchell, 2003; Watts, 2007; Horgan, 2004; Agranoff, 2004). In these terms, the UK is difficult to characterise (Cairney, 2006; McGarvey and Cairney, 2008: 157–8). In a broad sense, it shares a key characteristic with federal states: an often-unclear division of responsibilities when governments pursue the dual aims of devolving decisions and maintaining central control (Keating, 2005: 18). It devolves a set of legal, executive and fiscal powers to allow the Scottish Parliament a meaningful level of autonomy, but these responsibilities are often not clear cut. Table 7.1 indicates this division between policy areas reserved by the UK Government (under schedule 5 of the Scotland Act 1998) and devolved to the Scottish Government.

Table 5.1 Reserved and Devolved Policy Areas

Policy Areas Reserved	Blurry Boundaries: (1) UK- Scotland	Policy Areas Devolved
International relations	Industrial Policy	Health
Defence, National security	Higher Education	Education and training
Fiscal and monetary policy	Fuel Poverty	Economic development
Immigration and nationality	Child Poverty	Local government
Drugs and firearms	Dawn Raids	Law and home affairs
Regulation of Elections	Smoking Ban	Police and prisons
Employment	Malawi	Fire and ambulance services
Company law	NHS Compensation	Social work
Consumer Protection	New Nuclear Plants	Housing and planning
Social Security	Effect of Scottish Policies on Social Security	Transport
Regulation of professions The civil service	Cross-cutting themes: New Deal, SureStart	Environment
Energy, nuclear safety	2007 Election review	Agriculture
Air transport, road safety	(2) Scotland- Europe	Fisheries
Gambling	Common Agricultural Policy	Forestry
Equality	Common Fisheries Policy	Sport
Human reproductive rights	EU Environment Directives	The arts
Broadcasting, Copyright	Medical Contracts	Devolved research, statistics

Source: adapted from Keating (2005: 22); Cairney (2006a: 431–2);
McGarvey and Cairney (2008: 2; 160–3)

The left and right columns give the impression that there is a clear line between responsibilities, but the middle column highlights examples of issues that span the reserved/devolved boundary (see McGarvey and Cairney, 2008: 163 and Keating, 2010: 36–7). In particular, crime and justice are complicated by entangled responsibilities—for example, issues regarding the classification of illegal drugs and the regulation of firearms are reserved, but the criminal justice system and the police forces are devolved responsibilities. The UK and Scottish governments also need to maintain some degree of policy uniformity to avoid legal loopholes (on issues such as the sex offences register, cross-border investigation of crimes, and prisoner transfer) and to allow UK bodies to operate in Scotland (Cairney and Keating, 2004: 119). Further, the UK Government is responsible for policy relating to the policing of immigration and asylum applicants, with high profile examples of 'dawn raids' (when unsuccessful applicants are taken into custody in the early hours of the morning, before being deported) demonstrating that the Home Office can still direct the Scottish police force (Cairney, January 2006: 19). Other examples include: industrial policy, in which economic policy meets economic development; fuel and child poverty, in which the Scottish Government may have the power to insulate homes and distribute health and education services, but not to amend taxes and social security benefits (Cairney, January 2007: 76–7; September 2008: 108; May 2009: 70–1); the fire service strike, which highlighted a 'devolved service ... subject to UK-wide service regulation, including pay and conditions agreements' (Winetrobe, February 2003: 45); UK Government moves to help people with mental health problems keep their jobs (Cairney, September 2009: 56); and, the smoking in ban in Scotland, which was partly inspired by legislation passed in Ireland to protect bar workers (health and safety is a reserved issue), was justified on public health grounds (devolved), but required changes to employment law to cover aspects such as smoking in work vehicles (see chapter 8 on tobacco policy).

Higher education has some reserved (the research excellence framework, research councils) and devolved (Universities, tuition fees) responsibilities. It also shows that Scottish issues are more or less influenced by UK policies which have a knock-on effect on the Scottish budget (chapter 9). In particular, the decision to introduce larger top-up fees in England from 2012–13 (up to £9000 per year), combined with a major reduction in direct government funding for English Universities, produces a reduced Scottish Government budget and the need either to follow the English lead (which the SNP has so far refused to do), reduce University funding and/or find the money to fund Universities from another part of the Scottish budget (see Keating et al, 2012).

Devolution has also taken place in the context of the increasing 'Europeanization' of policy. While issues such as agricultural and environmental policies have been devolved, most major decisions in these areas are made at the EU level. Further, the UK generally places EU affairs in the realm of 'international relations' and, as the member state, negotiates the UK's policy input and performs a monitoring role in regard to Scotland's implementation of EU policy (Keating, 2010: 39). EU directives and regulations also have some occasional indirect consequences, such as when the Working Time Directive placed limits on the number of hours that doctors could remain on call (and influenced the negotiations, between governments and unions, of medical contracts). Overall, as in most federal and devolved systems, the supranational-national-regional (or federal-state-local) division of responsibilities produces many blurry boundaries. The EU-UK-Scotland set-up produces some complicated relationships, while UK decisions often produce externalities or spillovers that the Scottish Government has to address (Keating et al, 2012).

The UK is also federal-like because it maintains Scottish representation at the UK level, largely through the Secretary of State for Scotland (generally a member of the UK Cabinet, supported by the Scotland Office), and provides an 'umpire' (such as the Joint Ministerial Committee or, potentially, the court system) to rule in disputes between devolved and UK governments. However, the UK lacks the supreme constitution which allows states within a federal system to protect themselves from unilateral change from central government. In that crucial sense, the UK appears to be a unitary (not a federal) state; the devolved territories have subordinate status within the UK rather than the power to veto constitutional changes (Bolleyer et al, 2012). Indeed, the Scottish Parliament was created when Westminster passed the Scotland Act 1998, which is subject to amendment by the UK Government and Parliament—although this is generally done in consultation with the Scottish Government (or Parliament—chapter 10). However, it is often described as a 'union state' because the terms of the Union protect, to a large extent, a range of Scottish institutions and practices (Mitchell, 2003; 2009; Rokkan and Urwin, 1983; Keating, 2012). The UK also has a non-federal approach to the size of devolved territories, with devolution granted only to 16 per cent of the population (Scotland, Wales and Northern Ireland)—an imbalance that has few equivalents (Watts, 2007; although 'asymmetrical concessions to individual territories' are a feature in other systems, Keating, 2012).

Scotland is more comparable with other systems when we compare specific institutions. For example, it shares with other parliamentary systems (such as Canada and Australia) a tendency to resolve intergovernmental issues through executives rather than parliaments. It also shares with many systems a tendency to use the courts as a last resort to resolve disputes, although the UK's lack of court involvement is particularly striking (Watts, 2007). The role of political parties is more difficult to compare. The influence of national parties varies considerably, from Germany which has a strong national influence (parties are integrated, with clear formal links used to coordinate policy across levels of government) to Canada which has a devolved party structure, producing different party systems and territorially specific party competition at the sub-national level (Horgan, 2004). Scotland has its own party system to some extent (see chapter 2). The role of parties in relation to IGR was most relevant from 1999–2007. The Labour party was in government in both arenas and its structure is relatively centrist when compared to the Liberal Democrats' federal constitution. For example, the leader of Scottish Labour leads its MSPs only, while the Liberal Democrat leader is responsible for policy in Scotland as a whole (both have annual conferences and policy forums, but these have become stage managed publicity events rather than serious decision making venues — Keating, 2010; McGarvey and Cairney, 2008). Further, Labour's Scottish leadership (with the exception of Henry McLeish) was generally keen to maintain a rather uniform UK party line to reduce the SNP's ability to exploit divisions (Keating, 2010: 62; 2012).

The UK's Informal Style: 1999–2007

Bolleyer et al (2012) identify a simple distinction between federal systems, with relatively formal relationships, and non-federal systems, in which the use of formal dispute resolution mechanisms is relatively infrequent. The relationships between the UK and devolved governments confirm the latter picture: they are relatively informal and the frequency of interaction is relatively low (Horgan, 2004; Trench, 2004; Keating, 2005 and 2011; Page, 2005; Cairney, 2006; McGarvey and Cairney, 2008). The level of informality was particularly marked from 1999–2007 (Cairney, 2012a). Mechanisms for negotiation and dispute resolution existed but were used rarely. The role of the courts was minimal (Winetrobe, February 2003: 39).[12] There were no references of

---

[12] Instead, the courts were used by *private* interests to challenge, for example, the fox hunting bill (Winetrobe, August 2004: 39-42) and the Parliament's handling of 'lobbygate' (Leicester, 2000: 27; chapter 8). This came on top of an increasingly significant European dimension regarding the justice process (2000: 28) and human rights, taking in issues

Scottish bills to judicial review; the Scottish Executive was more likely to 'remove offending sections' than face delay (Page, 2005). The role of Holyrood-Westminster relations was limited, and the Scottish Parliament was restricted to the passing of 'Sewel' motions — or 'legislative consent motions' (LCMs) — passed by the Scottish Parliament giving consent for Westminster to pass legislation on devolved policy areas (Cairney, 2006; Cairney and Keating, 2004).[13]

There was a clear bias towards informality between executives. Although the UK and Scottish government produced a *Memorandum of Understanding* (MoU) to guide the conduct of governments, and individual concordats to encourage cooperation between government departments, the day-to-day business was conducted through civil servants with minimal reference to them. As Horgan (2004: 122) suggests, there was an 'informal flavour' to formal concordats since — as in Canada and Australia — they are not legally binding. Rather, they represent a, 'statement of political intent ... binding in honour only' (Cm 5240, 2001: 5). The MoU's main function is to promote good communication between executives, particularly when one knows that forthcoming policies will affect the other. This emphasis is furthered in the individual concordats which devote most of their discussions to the need for communication, confidentiality and forward notice (the 'no surprises' approach). For some of the civil servants that produced them, they represented 'common sense' with little need to refer to them (Sir Muir Russell, former Permanent Secretary, Scottish Office and Scottish Executive, in Commission on Scottish Devolution, 2008a: 2; see also Jack McConnell, former First Minister, Commission on Scottish Devolution, 2008b: 13).

The Joint Ministerial Committee (JMC) was designed to represent the main source of formal intergovernmental contact. It allows the UK government to call a meeting with the devolved governments to coordinate working arrangements, discuss the impact of devolved policy on reserved areas and vice versa, share experience and consider disputes. However, it met infrequently when Labour was in office (Trench, 2004; the JMC plenary did not meet from 2003–7; the JMC Europe met much more frequently). In part, this is because the JMC is a consultative rather than an executive body, with issues to be referred to

---

such as 'slopping out' (Winetrobe, May 2004: 53; Winetrobe, April 2005: 36; Trench, May 2009: 88) and compulsory detention related to mental health (Winetrobe, August 2001: 38; Winetrobe, November 2001: 51-3).

[13] Named after Lord Sewel, the Scottish Office minister responsible for ensuring the progress of the Scotland Bill through the House of Lords in 1998, but then renamed 'Legislative Consent Motions' (LCMs) by the Procedures Committee in 2005.

it on the rare occasions that discussions between executives break down. Such was the bias against taking issues to the JMC that its members found little to discuss (Jack McConnell, Commission on Scottish Devolution, 2008b: 12; Jim Wallace, former Deputy First Minister, Commission on Scottish Devolution, 2008c: 9). Instead, bilateral working relationships between government departments became the norm, while matters of concern were discussed through political parties (and Scottish and UK Labour ministers in particular). The existence of coalition in government in Scotland complicated matters to some extent, and the most high profile instance in which an issue 'broke free' from the quiet world of IGR related to a policy (free personal care for older people) linked closely to Liberal Democrat aims (there were also tensions on PR in local elections, below). Yet, there was no systematic pattern of disputes and little demand for high profile resolution. Indeed, the formal system of IGR is described by Mitchell (2010) as an afterthought and was treated as such.

The UK's Informal Style: 2007–11

The post-2007 period has been marked by some differences but also a striking level of continuity in UK-Scottish relations (Cairney, 2012a). The SNP had already stated that it would not continue with the existing arrangements. Instead, it would: push for an independent civil service; discourage Sewel motions; call for a reinstatement of regular JMC plenary meetings; challenge UK policies (such as nuclear power); and publicly 'stick up for Scotland's interests' (McGarvey and Cairney, 2008: 162). The ascension of a Scot, Gordon Brown, to Prime Minister also prompted an increase in UK media and (particularly Conservative) party attention to the idea that Scotland had a privileged role in the Union, perhaps prompting Brown to take a robust UK line on Scottish demands (and pursue, briefly, an agenda on Britishness) (Cairney, 2012a).

Overall, the vast majority of IGR is devoted to the resolution of day-to-day issues that arise from blurry boundaries. In other words, unlike in Spain or Canada, the UK Government rarely intervenes directly or competes to change policy in the same area (Keating, 2012). It has also made few direct attempts to oblige the Scottish Government to follow its policy lead (although this practice was much more significant from 1999–2007 — below). Indeed, IGR networks are not even used regularly to foster policy learning and diffusion. Instead, most policy transfer, if it occurs, can be linked to 'externalities' caused by UK government decisions, ad hoc agreements or arrangements between departments, and very rare instances in which the UK follows a devolved government lead (Keating et al, 2012). The UK and devolved governments did produce a revised *Memorandum of Understanding*, which included a new 'Protocol For Avoidance And Resolution Of Disputes', before the 2010 UK general election (Cabinet Office, 2010; Cm 7864, 2010). However, it largely represented a logical progression from the MoU that was produced in 2001 and rarely referred to by executives (Trench, 2010b).

Why Did These Relationships Develop and Endure?

Cairney (2012a) outlines three main explanations for the development and maintenance of these relationships. First, there may be a 'logic of informal IGR' which resembles the 'logic of consultation' (Jordan and Maloney, 1997) when governments engage with pressure participants such as interest groups. The general 'logic of accommodation' refers to the benefits—including the maximisation of government knowledge and the 'ownership' of policy by those who may influence its implementation—of reaching a consensus or practical understanding with consultees ('stakeholders'). It suggests that top-down policy making by the UK Government is politically expensive and few governments are willing or able to bear the costs. Instead, both governments sought ways to cooperate for mutual gain. For example, they maintained the 'Barnett formula' which produces automatic changes to the Scottish budget and reduces the need for regular negotiations (chapter 9), passed a large number of Sewel motions, and maintained productive links through the Labour party and UK civil service. While the election of an SNP Government produced some change in that relationship, it proved remarkably willing to exploit many of the same channels of influence and pursue an, 'insider strategy which includes an acceptance of the "rules of the game", or a willingness to engage in self-regulating activities (the value of which some of the party rank-and-file may not appreciate) in the short term, to allow it to benefit in the long-term' (Cairney, 2012a).

Second, the balance of power is tipped towards the UK Government and, in particular, the Treasury which decides how much money is raised and spent in Scotland. As Keating (2005: 120; 2010: 151) suggests, the UK 'centre' is faced with small devolved governments which do not match the powers of federated or devolved authorities in countries such as Germany, Spain, Belgium or Canada. Scotland, Wales and Northern Ireland are not part of a collection of powerful regions. The asymmetry of power has three main effects. First, the devolved governments do not have a mechanism with which to oblige the UK government to consult, and there has been a tendency for UK ministers to disengage from the formal IGR process. Second, civil servants in Whitehall often forget about Scotland and neglect to consult, then make statements on UK policy without a Scottish qualification. Third, Scottish actors are reluctant to challenge the authority of the UK government (Cairney, 2012a). This was particularly the case from 1999–2007, when Labour ministers were generally careful about making challenges that would embarrass the UK Government and give the SNP the chance to exploit divisions. Further, Bolleyer et al (2012) draw on Héritier and Lehmkuhl's (2008) idea of 'shadow of hierarchy' (when the central level clearly has the final say) to show that Scottish Labour was bound by *two* hierarchical relationships (government and party). However, the SNP did not pursue the opposite strategy when in Government. Instead, it combined the occasional challenge to UK authority with a fairly stoical approach to its position, to maintain its strong image of governing competence (which might be undermined if it constantly refers to the limits to its powers—Cairney, 2012a).

Third, the SNP formed a minority government in its first four years of office. The main consequence is that it struggled to secure parliamentary support for policies that may have caused a higher level of intergovernmental tension. Most importantly, it could not secure support for a bill introducing a referendum on independence (chapter 10). Nor did it have the support to replace council tax with a local income tax. The latter move would have prompted considerable intergovernmental discussion because the Scottish Government would effectively require UK government support. It would have produced the loss of a UK (council tax) benefit that the Scottish Parliament does not have the power to change; Treasury rules dictate that the Scottish government has no claim on any money that might be saved from (reserved) UK expenditure as a consequence of devolved policy decisions, and the UK government did not appear willing to negotiate (Cairney, 2012a).

Overall, the 2007–11 period produced a notable degree of continuity. UK and Scottish ministers developed fairly cordial relationships and the SNP operated rather quietly within a UK intergovernmental framework. The logic of informality is strong and governments from most parties have much to gain from these arrangements. In contrast, the substantive payoffs from challenging the UK position are unclear. The Scottish government does not have any formal powers or a written constitution on which to draw and is unlikely to win high profile disputes with the UK government. While the SNP government may have preferred to supplement its informal relationships with a select number of high-profile disputes of its own making, it was often blocked by the Unionist parties within the Scottish Parliament. The UK government has also avoided pushing other potentially divisive issues towards the need for intergovernmental resolution.

How Were These Relationships Reported in the Devolution Monitors?

The same basic argument can be derived from the monitors: relationships were generally informal and this reflected the logic of informal IGR, the asymmetry of power and the complications of inter-party relationships within Scotland (note that the monitors initially had a section called 'Devolution disputes and litigation', but it withered on the vine when there was little to report). For example, they report on the role of Sewel motions but generally consider them to be innocuous and for the convenience of both parties. However, the monitors pay most attention to the asymmetry of power and the tensions between governments, particularly when: the role of the civil service changed over time; the respective roles of the Scottish Secretary and First Minister developed; the UK neglected to consult with the Scottish Executive; and, the Scottish Executive sought, often in vain, to develop its role in European and foreign affairs.

Legislative Consent (Sewel) Motions

Tensions on intergovernmental issues have generally been more likely to arise between the Scottish Parliament and Executive rather than between executives,[14] particularly when MSPs accuse the Scottish Executive of political cowardice by using uncertainty over devolved competence to pass the issue to Westminster (for example, when it seemed content to let the UK Government take the lead on GM crops — Wright, May 2004: 35–6; Wright, May 2002: 36–8; Winetrobe, November 2003: 52; May 2004: 59). Early academic discussions of Sewel motions tended to remark on at least two perceived problems: they were used much more than expected and, their use suggests that the Scottish Executive was passing back control to the UK Government (see Winetrobe 2005, who also criticises the lack of parliamentary involvement in the process). This is reflected in early monitors that (a)

---

[14] There are also occasional problems between ministers and civil servants, such as when Permanent Secretary Sir Muir Russell appeared not to consult Jack McConnell on new civil service appointments (an issue that is reserved, and ultimate power resides with the Prime Minister, but Scottish ministers are practically in control of senior Scottish appointments — Wright, August 2002: 26).

report pre-devolution assurances by Donald Dewar that the possibility of Westminster 'legislating across devolved areas' is 'not one we anticipate or expect' but (b) suggest that 'Sewel is proving addictive' (Wright, November 2001: 38). Wright (February 2002: 28; June 2003: 45) also warns that if the Sewel motion 'is used too frequently it calls into question the worth of having a Scottish legislature'.

However, the fact that the monitor took so long to report on the use of Sewel perhaps suggests that, until then, the process was fairly routine and dealing with innocuous issues (see Cairney, 2006; Cairney and Keating, 2004; McGarvey and Cairney, 2008). Or, as Conservative MSP Bill Aitken (in Cairney, September 2007: 24) puts it: 'The majority of them are not controversial and are agreed on the nod'. Thus, attention only became raised at the first hint of political cowardice, following the Scottish Executive decision to allow Westminster to legislate on the age of homosexual consent (Wright, November 2001: 38; Cairney and Keating, 2004). It was then raised intermittently: when discussed by the Lords Select Committee on the Constitution (Wright, November 2002: 20) and the Procedures committee in 2003 (Wright, June 2003: 44–5); when the issue of civil partnerships raised the further prospect of political cowardice (Wright, November 2003: 30–1); when the debate between the SNP and the Scottish Executive spilled out into the media (Wright, May 2004: 29–30); and, when discussed in relation to a UK-Scottish Executive protocol regarding the practice of the Scottish Parliament granting devolved powers to UK ministers (Wright, August 2004: 27). The issue appeared to come to a head in late 2004 when the Queen's speech highlighted the amount of UK legislation affecting Scotland and opposition party resistance became more frequent (Wright, April 2005: 20–1).

In 2005 the Procedures committee conducted an inquiry into the process, exploring the original expectations of the need for Sewel motions, the reasons behind their continued use and the scope for more formal procedures to address the perception that the Executive was ignoring the Parliament. The decision not to examine the *numbers* of motions passed or their *substance* proved frustrating to opposition members (Wright, April 2005: 21–4) and the timing of the inquiry (in the run up to a General Election) also made proceedings more politically charged. However, the final report succeeded in defusing much of the tension associated with Sewel, by requiring the Scottish Executive to engage in a formal process of consent by committees before a vote in plenary (Cairney, January 2006: 24; see also Trench, January 2007: 46 on the Scottish Affairs Committee report; see chapter

10 on the Calman Commission's recommendation to formalise the relationship between Holyrood and Westminster).

From 2007 there was an SNP effect, with the Scottish Government more likely to seek ways to legislate in the Scottish Parliament rather than propose a Sewel motion. However, the change was small and it rarely provoked a UK Government response (Cairney, September 2007: 25). The SNP used Sewel motions for the sake of expediency and passed 8.5 per year from 2007–11 compared to 9.5 from 1999–2007. Thus, several opposition MSPs 'could not help themselves when pointing out the irony of the SNP using a procedure it had so often opposed in principle' (Cairney, January 2008: 25). For example, Labour MSP George Foulkes could not resist stating: 'It is an interesting paradox that there have been more bills at Westminster affecting Scotland in the current session than there are bills here' (Scottish Parliament Official Report, 20.2.08 c.6129). Similarly, Johann Lamont (Labour) was keen to remind Parliament about the SNP's opposition to the use of Sewel motions when in opposition: 'On numerous occasions in the past, SNP members voted against entirely rational and logical LCMs on the basis that it was a point of principle for them to do so' (Scottish Parliament Official Report 20.2.08 c. 7140). Similar party-political points about the SNP handing powers back to Westminster (a classic argument used by the SNP when in opposition) prompted Communities and Sport Minister Stewart Maxwell to make a remark which could have been said by any Labour/Liberal Democrat minister from 1999–2007:

> It is suggested that the LCM impacts on the Scottish Parliament's legislative competence or is tantamount to our handing back powers to Westminster. Let me be clear: only through changes to the reservations in the Scotland Act 1998 can powers be handed back to Westminster or the legislative competence of our Parliament altered. Individual motions, such as the one that we are discussing, represent no more than a one-off agreement by the Scottish Parliament for Westminster to legislate on our behalf on a specific aspect of a devolved matter (Scottish Parliament Official Report 19.3.08 c.7106-7; Cairney, May 2008: 22–3).

The UK's Informal Style 1999–2007

The first report outlines the formal IGR mechanisms and highlights the Scottish Secretary/First Minister relationship as the only subject of note (November 1999: 13). For the most part, the UK and Scottish Governments were 'at pains to point out how smoothly the relationship is working' and only sporadic examples of tensions (regarding, for example, the Home Office granting a visa for Mike Tyson's visit to Glasgow) and potential tensions (such as the hyped-up potential of the Treasury to withhold the secondary legislation required to introduce the 'tartan tax') could be found (August 2000: 9; Wright, February 2001: 33–4; see also Jervis and Plowden, 2001: 20–3 on informal IGR in health). The outbreak of foot-and-mouth disease prompted the very early need for a policy response which 'would not only have to be largely coordinated, but to be publicly seen to be so', but few problems were identified (Winetrobe, May 2001: 54). Similarly, the potential tensions involved in the UK Government overseeing rail policy in Scotland (Winetrobe, November 2001: 60; August 2002: 48) were solved by the devolution of that responsibility (Winetrobe, April 2005: 43; Cairney, January 2006: 126; presumably on the basis that the Scottish Executive would not renationalise rail—Curtice, February 2001: 25; Winetrobe, February 2004: 42). In most cases, IGR issues rarely produced publicly visible tensions between executives and/or the Scottish Executive chose not to publicly oppose the UK Government. Most notably, it did not criticise publicly the decision of the Department of Work and Pensions to implementing existing rules removing Attendance Allowance entitlement to those receiving personal care payments, adding at least £20m to the cost of free personal care in Scotland and possibly delaying its implementation (Bell, November 2001: 50; the delay was 'a humiliation for the Executive'—Winetrobe, November, 2001: 47; see also Simeon, 2003; Cairney, 2006: 433; McGarvey and Cairney, 2008: 205).

By 2002, the longer experience of devolution had produced more examples of blurry boundaries between reserved and devolved issues, regarding issues such as the pan-European arrest warrant system (a reserved issue drawing on devolved police forces), the Dungavel detention centre for asylum seekers (immigration is reserved until the applicant is successful and receives devolve services) and the compensation for people who contracted Hepatitis C from contaminated blood (provided by the Scottish NHS). Asylum policy became high profile when an asylum seeker was murdered in Glasow in 2001, but the Scottish Executive was generally (or publicly) content to defer to UK Government policy (despite pressure participant and opposition party criticism and the issue of responsibility for the education of children in asylum centres—Winetrobe, November 2001: 61–3; August 2003: 39; August 2003: 52; August 2004: 49; November 2004: 43; McGarvey, November 2001: 46; Cairney, May 2006: 76; January 2008: 109). Hepatitis C became a cause of relative tension, with the UK Government apparently willing to challenge the Scottish

Executive's right to provide compensation (payments related to injury and illness are reserved), until it came up with a UK-wide compensation scheme (with which Scottish ministers were less happy) (Winetrobe, February 2003: 39–40; February 2004: 42; May 2004: Cairney, 2006: 433; January 2007: 83). The Scottish Executive and UK Government also faced calls for a public inquiry into Hep C in 2006 (Cairney, September 2006: 75). The Scottish Government oversaw its own inquiry on Hep C, partly to put pressure on the UK Government to follow suit (Cairney, May 2008: 87; May 2009: 58).

Nuclear power is an interesting case because the dividing line between reserved and devolved has been subject to debate *within* the UK Government (Wright, May 2002: 36–7). Energy policy, and therefore nuclear power, is reserved, but doubt arises when there is the prospect of a new nuclear power station which requires planning permission in Scotland. Much has been made about the ability of the Scottish Executive or Government, post-devolution, to decide the fate of nuclear power by refusing planning permission. However, planning permission for nuclear power stations has rested with Scottish ministers since the UK Electricity Act 1989. In other words, it is a good example of 'executive devolution' in which the UK Government has the responsibility but devolves it to Scottish ministers. The practice was common before 1999, 'but it has now been enhanced by the Scottish Parliament's legitimacy and the greater powers granted to Scottish ministers since 1999' (Cairney, 2006a: 441). Indeed, the Scottish Government now effectively (in other words, politically rather than legally) has the ability to veto new nuclear power stations. This position was first set out by Tony Blair, who wrote to Alex Salmond (then SNP leader in Westminster) to state that, 'Scottish ministers, answerable to the Scottish Parliament, have the final say over approving or rejecting nuclear power stations in Scotland' (Summers, 2002). The move followed considerable tension within the Scottish Executive coalition (the Liberal Democrats are less keen on new reactors) and pressure on the Scottish Executive within Parliament (Winetrobe, November 2001: 59). It was then reinforced in 2006 (Cairney, May 2006: 73) and, more importantly, in 2008 by the UK Government which chose not to include Scotland in its plans (although UK Minister John Hutton described the Scottish Government's policy as 'a disaster' — Trench, May 2008: 56; Cairney, May 2009: 68; see also Bort, January 2006: 42).

Overall, IGR seemed straightforward, particularly under McConnell's leadership (who was keen to reject the idea of 'turf wars' — Woods, 2002: 7–8). For example, Scottish Secretary Helen

Liddell's speech in 2002 suggested that 'the Government and the Scottish Executive are working seamlessly in partnership' (Wright, August 2002: 25). Similarly, the House of Lords Select Committee on the Constitution (2002 in Wright, February 2002: 25) confirmed that executive-executive contact remained informal, producing the conclusion that 'goodwill appears to have been elevated into a principle of intergovernmental relations' (see also Wright, February 2004: 14 on the resultant lack of parliamentary scrutiny of IGR).

Yet, this goodwill related more to the lack of disputes than a high degree of policy coordination. Indeed, there has been a tendency of Whitehall departments to give little consideration to the effects of their policies on devolved governments (Keating, 2005: 125; 2010: 111). This issue first arose in the reports when Wright (August, 2002: 32) highlighted the lack of Whitehall consultation with the devolved governments on EU matters. It was followed, five years later, by a leaked report (the Aron report, named after the head of the Scottish Executive's office in Brussels) highlighting (according to Trench, April 2007: 66) 'serious problems in liaison with the EU, arising from a failure of the UK Government to take the Scottish Executive's views into account systematically and sometimes at all in formulating the UK 'line' in EU negotiations'. This statement contrasts with the Scottish Executive's official line, suggesting that before EU Council meetings, the 'Executive is fully involved in preparing the UK's position ... there is a comprehensive understanding and appreciation in Whitehall of the Executive's position' (see Wright, May 2004: 43–4). The Aron report suggests that, in some cases, Whitehall departments have deliberately excluded their Scottish counterparts, while in most cases the Executive is just neglected and not consulted at a stage early enough to influence policy (although note that it also argues that the best way for the Scottish Executive to influence Europe is through Whitehall, rather than independently — Cairney, April 2007: 7–8).

Further examples of a lack of consultation include the UK Government decisions to introduce student top-up fees, address the issue of firefighter strikes (Wright, February 2003: 26–7; Mitchell, February 2003: 3; Winetrobe, February 2003: 45; although proposed UK legislation would not cover Scotland — Winetrobe, June 2003: 65), reclassify cannabis (Winetrobe, August 2002: 46–7; although the Scottish Executive could go its own way with enforcement — Winetrobe, November 2003: 54; February 2004: 42; Cairney, May 2008: 89) and introduce the Terrorism Bill — which the UK Government considered to be completely reserved (Trench, January 2006: 85–6; see also p.88 on the

Comprehensive Spending Review and Trench, May 2008: 56 on the EU anti-terror treaty).

By 2004 the JMCs (with the exception of JMC Europe) had 'fallen completely into disuse' (Wright, May 2004: 33; see also Trench, January 2006: 85; Trench, May 2006: 47; and Trench, September 2006; 43; Trench, September 2007: 50; Trench, January 2009: 71 which discuss the more regular British-Irish Council meetings). For Trench (2004: 515-6) it suggests that 'devolution is no longer a prime concern of the Prime Minister and other politicians'. For the former First and Deputy First Minister it suggests that its members found little to discuss (Jack McConnell, Commission on Scottish Devolution, 2008b: 12; Jim Wallace, Commission on Scottish Devolution, 2008c: 9; see also Trench, May 2006: 48 and Trench, January 2007; 44 for Lord Falconer's and Jack McConnell's defences of informal relations). Indeed, McConnell preferred to focus attention on the benefits of a close but informal relationship, particularly when ministers sought opt-outs or special circumstances for UK policies — such as:

- the Fresh Talent Initiative to encourage migration to Scotland by allowing foreign students in Scotland to stay longer after graduation, requiring Home Office flexibility on immigration law (Bell, February 2004: 33; Wright, May 2004: 37-8; Winetrobe, May 2004: 58-9; Wright, April 2005: 30; Winetrobe, April 2005: 41-2; Cairney, January 2006: 122; May 2006: 77; April 2007: 93; see Winetrobe, August 2004: 47; Cairney, January 2006: 122-3 and Lynch January 2006: 94-5; April 2007: 68 on the argument that this was a Scottish pilot designed to be adopted UK-wide and Lynch's September 2006: 48-9; January 2007: 48 argument that it was largely overtaken by migration from the EU accession states; see also Winetrobe, November 2002: 36; June 2003: 65 on Scotland's shrinking population, and possible need for immigration, but also Cairney, January 2006: 122 on reduced fears for Scotland's population);

- the use of identity cards (Wright, April 2004: 24, note that the UK Government eventually dropped this policy before it became a big reserved/devolved issue, while the Scottish Executive consulted on its own voluntary version — Winetrobe, November 2003: 55; February 2004: 42; May 2004: 57; April 2005: 43);

- the conduct of 'dawn raids' and the treatment of families of failed asylum seekers (Cairney, May 2006: 76); and,

- the prospect of a Scottish pilot on airgun law (Cairney, January 2006: 19–20; compare with Bort, January 2006: 41 on the Whitehall 'rebuff' of McConnell; see January 2008: 109; September 2008: 103 on similar moves by the SNP; note that the Calman Commission recommended devolving airgun policy).

Further, the implicit reward for the Scottish Executive's quiet approach on free personal care may have been a substantial additional Treasury payment towards Glasgow's council housing debt (Cairney, 2006: 436; Bell, August 2003: 32).

The UK's Informal Style 2007–11

While, in opposition, the SNP was critical of informality (often linking it to an image of subordination), it frequently took a similar approach when in government (Cairney, September 2008: 105–6). The SNP Government 'surprised many by not being overtly confrontational' and by encouraging its civil service to be, 'open, cooperative and helpful to their counterparts in the UK Government, rather than to maximise points of friction' (Trench, September 2007: 46; Trench, May 2008: 56; although for the occasional 'annoyance or embarrassment in London', see Trench, January 2008: 61 on police pay). It only partly succeeded in its aim to revive the JMC plenary (Trench, September 2007: 45; Trench, January 2008: 61; Trench, May 2008: 57), although the significance of the meetings is difficult to gauge. On the one hand, Trench (September 2008: 66) suggests that the 'fact that a meeting happened at all can be regarded as a form of progress' (see also Trench, May 2009: 85 on the JMC Domestic). On the other, it has struggled to make the links necessary with other devolved governments to act as spur towards a more equal relationship with the UK Government (Trench, September 2007: 49; Trench, January 2008: 66; Trench, May 2008: 57; see also Wright, August 2002: 30–1 who discusses older devolved government relationships and Lynch, September 2007: 53; May 2008: 60–1 who discusses other aims of the relationships, such as to develop common economic and cultural interests). Further, the tendency towards UK neglect of Scotland continued into the new era of SNP Government — including, most notably, the UK Government's lack of consultation with Scotland on its agreement with Libya on prisoner transfer, which affected only one prisoner — the 'Lockerbie bomber' Abdelbaset al-

Megrahi (see Cairney, May 2009: 61–2 on other issues such as drugs classification and firearms).

Of course, there are some SNP differences of approach, but the al-Megrahi issue sums up the complicated strategic position that it faces. It was initially able to criticise the UK Government publicly. Indeed, Alex Salmond led the Scottish Government's forceful and public criticism of Tony Blair on his handling of the issue (Trench, September 2007: 47; Trench, September 2008: 65; Cairney, May 2009: 61). The UK Government, under Gordon Brown, was also criticised more widely in the media for taking such a detached position, when it subsequently left the issue of al-Megrahi's release to Scottish ministers and generally refused to comment (Cairney, September 2009: 2). However, the Scottish Government was not able to engage the UK Government in meaningful discussions or influence its original decision. Further, the final decision demonstrated the ways in which intergovernmental issues could play out in the Scottish Parliament at the SNP's expense. Justice Secretary Kenny MacAskill made the decision to use Scots Law to release al-Megrahi on compassionate grounds (he was diagnosed with terminal cancer) rather than sanction his removal to Libya under the prisoner transfer agreement—a distinction that was partly symbolic because both actions would largely have the same effect (Cairney, September 2009: 2). However, that strategy was fairly unsuccessful in that the Scottish Government's focus on its ability to make its own decisions, and the importance of a distinct Scottish legal system, was soon taken over by widespread criticism of the decision (including the US President and US Senators). It prompted one of the fiercest backlashes from opposition parties in the Scottish Parliament, which focused in particular on Kenny MacAskill's handling of the case (Cairney, September 2009: 2).

A more straightforward and symbolically important issue is the name of the Scottish administration. The SNP succeeded in putting the issue of the Scottish Government's name to bed. While McLeish failed in his bid to rebrand the Scottish Executive (Saren and Brown, February 2001: 7–8; Mitchell et al, 2001: 68–9), this was one of the first things done by the new Scottish Government (Cairney, September 2007: 12; Lynch, September 2007: 54; although note that Jack McConnell's previous informal use of the term 'government' did not cause a stir—Winetrobe, November 2003: 4).

The Changing Civil Service

The role of the civil service may be central to the success of IGR. The UK Government saw the civil service as a key link between it and devolved governments and sought to maintain a unified British service, in part by reserving civil service policy. Consequently, a key theme of the early reports regarded the potential for divided civil service loyalties to UK and Scottish executives or ministers (Wright, August 2002: 26; Wright, November 2002: 20; Winetrobe, April 2005: 3–4; Cairney, January 2008: 10; also note that most, albeit relatively junior, civil servants working in Scotland do so for the UK, not Scottish Government—Winetrobe, February 2004: 3; Cairney, May 2008: 15). However, these concerns were largely unfounded and it soon became clear that Scottish Executive civil servants reported to Scottish ministers. The reservation of civil service matters tended to arise in relation to the conditions of service, such as when the UK Government took the lead on the issue of 'excessive' pensions, linked to the Turner report recommendations to reduce overall pension costs (Cairney, January 2006: 14). Even recruitment processes became quasi-devolved, with the Scottish Executive often able to control its own procedures. Appointments tend to be made by the civil service 'on behalf of the First Minister' (Winetrobe, August 2002: 5; Winetrobe, November 2002: 4; Winetrobe, February 2003: 6; Winetrobe, June 2003: 4; see also Wright, May 2004: 34; Winetrobe, May 2004: 4 on the prospects of job cuts in line with UK initiatives).

The shift of weekly Scottish Cabinet meetings from Tuesday to Wednesday perhaps had the potential to 'symbolise a more autonomous devolved civil service', because it hindered the Scottish Executive Permanent Secretary's ability to maintain links with his Whitehall counterparts (Winetrobe, February 2002: 8). The issue of a further devolved or independent civil service also emerged sporadically (Winetrobe, May 2001: 10–11; Winetrobe, February 2003: 6; Wright, November 2004: 21). In 2003 a survey of some MSPs showed support for further devolution and the Scottish Parliament's Procedures Committee suggested that the reservation of civil service policy 'could restrict the development of novel arrangements between Parliament and officials beyond traditional notions of parliamentary accountability and ministerial responsibility' (Winetrobe, November 2003: 4). In 2004, the Fraser Report on the commissioning and cost of the Scottish Parliament building drew further attention to the civil service role and its accountability to the Scottish Parliament (Winetrobe, February 2004: 4; November 2004: 6). In 2005, John Elvidge appeared relaxed about (but not in favour of) implementing 'any future administration's policy of having a separate Scottish devolved civil service' because he felt that it already enjoyed significant autonomy (Winetrobe, April 2005: 3; Cairney, January 2006: 15; see also the

Scottish Parliament Finance Committee's ambivalence regarding civil service independence—Cairney, 2006: 15).

As Cairney (September 2007: 16) argues, the effect of a shift from devolved to independent civil service may be exaggerated because, 'in practice Scottish ministers have a strong say on senior recruitment; mobility between the services is already low; and Whitehall already forgets to consult with the Scottish Executive (Government) when formulating UK policies'. Thus, any moves towards further autonomy would be formalising relationships that may already exist. As John Elvidge remarked, since informal contact between the Scottish and UK Government has already diminished, further change would be 'breaking quite a slender thread' (Cairney, September 2007: 17). Indeed, that thread quickly became more slender in 2007, following the decision by UK Labour ministers to vet Whitehall documents to be shared with the Scottish Government (although how such a big task was to be implemented is less clear). It followed Alex Salmond's public criticism of Environment Secretary Hilary's Benn's speech on foot-and-mouth compensation to farmers. Scottish ministers had seen a first draft which made a commitment to pay £8.1m compensation to Scottish farmers, but the redraft left this provision out (Cairney, January 2008: 10). The politicisation of senior civil service roles in Scotland also seemed to place greater distance between both executives (Cairney, January 2008: 10–11).

The Secretary of State for Scotland 1999–2007

In 1999, the Scotland Office was a distinct government department formed primarily to act as a conduit, and to smooth relations, between the Scottish Executive and Whitehall. It is therefore ironic that early reports describe a very clear tension between Scottish Secretary John Reid and First Minister Donald Dewar. This perhaps reflects different understandings of the nature and strength of the Scottish Secretary role: 'In a post which, it is widely assumed, will wither over time, he [Reid] immediately raised eyebrows by seeking a large budget to staff the department' (Leicester, 2000: 27). The two roles produced 'bitter turf wars', based in part on personal animosity, between Dewar and Reid that continued under Henry McLeish (particularly since McLeish sought policy divergence and a stronger Scottish role in Europe) until Reid was replaced by Helen Liddell (May 2000: 17; Mitchell et al, 2001: 56; McGarvey, August 2001: 41 reports McLeish's description of Reid as a 'patronising bastard'). Under Reid, the Scotland Office was prepared to intervene in Scottish politics in a way viewed by the Scottish Executive as interference (Leicester, 2000: 27; McGarvey and Cairney,

2008: 159)—a situation made worse by the refusal of Reid to appear before a Scottish Parliament committee (Wright, November, 2000: 26; see also Wright, August 2004: 25; Wright, April 2005: 25–6; note the Calman Commission recommendation to introduce annual Scottish Secretary appearances at the committee convenors' group—Cairney, September 2009: 9). There was also some concern within the Scottish Executive that UK-Scottish relations would be too restricted if the Scottish Secretary become the main channel for Scottish-Whitehall communication (November, 1999: 14). Under Liddell there was still a perception that it was a legitimate Scottish Secretary role to manage, if not the policy process, then at least the internal affairs of the Scottish Cabinet (Mitchell et al, 2001: 56). Saren and Brown (February, 2001: 8) also highlight Liddell's remit, in the wake of McLeish's ascension, 'to keep an eye on the Scottish Executive'.

Over time there was more evidence of a smoother relationship (Wright, February 2003: 24; Liddell described it as 'seamless'—Wright, August 2002: 25) and an alleged feeling by Liddell that there was 'too little for her to do' (Wright, June 2003: 44; although she and her deputy both took a different view in the past—Wright, August 2002: 24; Wright, November 2002: 19). As the confidence of the Scottish Executive grew, 'the perceived necessity (within Whitehall) of the Scotland Office receded' and in June 2003 it became part of the Department for Constitutional Affairs (now the Ministry of Justice) and the Scottish Secretary role became part time, combined with the main brief of another minister (the UK Government had previously rejected the idea of an amalgamated devolution role—Wright, February 2003: 25–6). The first part-time Scottish (and Transport) Secretary, Alistair Darling, also gave his blessing to a new Scottish-UK relationship in which Scottish ministers would be encouraged to deal directly with their UK counterparts: 'they don't need us to hand hold' (Wright, November 2003: 29; Wright, August 2003: 24). From then on, conflicts were rare (Lynch, May 2006: 65; Cairney, May 2006: 73) until the formation of an SNP government—and even then the initial issue was often more about a lack of contact than personal disputes (Trench, January 2008: 61).

The Secretary of State for Scotland and the SNP

From October 2008 the role again became full-time under Jim Murphy, reflecting several concerns. First, the need for more mediation between two different parties (Trench, January 2008: 62 also reports a rise in senior Whitehall staff focused on devolution from 1.5 to 6!). Second, a concern about organisational confusion associated with a part-time

Scottish Secretary and the placement of the Scotland Office within the larger Department for Constitutional Affairs: who would ministers in the Scotland Office report to—Alistair Darling or the DCA Secretary (Wright, August 2003: 24)? Third, Labour felt the need to regain political ground in Scotland. Although Murphy was initially at pains to stress his role as 'Scotland's man in the cabinet rather than the cabinet's man in Scotland' (Trench, January 2009: 71), it is difficult to ignore the party-political overtones of statements about the 'arc of insolvency' (Alex Salmond had labelled independent countries that Scotland should learn from, such as Ireland and Norway, as the 'arc of prosperity'—Cairney, January 2009: 6). Labour also seemed to pursue a strategy of refusing First and Prime Ministerial meetings, to 'equate Salmond on a par with Murphy and therefore less important than Brown' (Cairney, May 2009: 5).

Scotland in Europe and the World 1999–2007

Many policy areas (and agriculture, fishing and environmental in particular) were becoming increasingly Europeanised as they were devolved, suggesting to Bell (May 2001: 44) that, 'the role of the Executive in respect of agriculture is little different from what it was prior to devolution'. Yet, political devolution also produced new expectations in Scotland about its engagement in the EU. Consequently, the European and foreign affairs issue was, at times, an important source of UK-Scottish tension. A continuous theme throughout the reports is Scotland's uneasy engagement with policymaking in Europe. On the one hand, the Scottish Executive created an office in Brussels (Scotland House) to boost Scotland's presence in the EU and make sure it is involved 'as directly and fully as possible in decision making on EU matters which touch on devolved areas' (November 1999: 15; although its lack of staffing soon became an issue—Wright, August 2002: 33; Wright, November 2002: 23, at least until 2005, Lynch, January 2006: 90). Under First Minister McLeish, McConnell's brief included the EU and external affairs and, according to a Scottish Executive press release (in Wright, February 2001: 36), it 'demonstrates that it is a top priority for the Executive to engage constructively and thoroughly with the European Union. With the benefits of devolution we are determined to make a step change in our level of engagement'. More broadly, its strategy has been fairly consistent: to promote Scottish interests internationally, build links with other regions and countries and promote a positive image of Scotland (Wright, May 2004: 42).

On the other hand, the monitors report widespread suspicions (largely promoted by the SNP) that attempts by Scottish ministers to engage in EU discussions, for example as part of a UK delegation, were often rebuffed strongly by their UK counterparts (Mitchell et al, 2001: 55). In 1999 there was no dedicated EU minister or portfolio for Europe in the Scottish Executive, based on the UK Government's argument that EU relations are reserved (see Winetrobe, April 2005: 3 on criticism of this approach by the European Committee). Scottish involvement progressed on a 'case by case basis', with the occasional ability to engage with the UK government to pursue policy issues (for example on unfair trade) perhaps offset by examples of low influence (see August 2000: 10 on Jim Wallace's call for a Human Rights Commission; Wright, August 2002: 31 and Wright, February 2003: 30 on the lack of Scottish Executive influence over the Common Fisheries Policy; and McGarvey, November 2001: 45 on EU rules regarding the Glasgow underground).

Wright (November 2002: 23–5; May 2004: 45) highlights the minimal extent to which the Scottish Executive attends and takes the UK lead formally in EU Council meetings, producing the image of Scottish Executive innovation in 'low politics' but powerlessness on crucial issues such as the Common Fisheries Policy (Wright, February 2004: 25; Wright, May 2004: 45–6; Cairney, January 2006: 125). Winetrobe highlights frustration with Scottish Executive inability to lead EU fishing negotiations and the generally bad deal for the Scottish industry that Scottish ministers could do little about (Winetrobe, November 2002: 34; February 2003: 43; August 2003: 52; February 2004: 41; May 2004: 59; April 2005: 42). Wright (February 2003: 28–31) also suggests that the Scottish Executive did not get far with attempts to seek CFP compensation directly from the EU. Its relative success on the Common Agricultural Policy related not so much to its EU involvement, but rather the scope to implement it differently (Cairney, January 2006: 125).

McConnell suggested, during McLeish's time as First Minister, that Scottish ministers were taking the UK lead on some Council of Ministers meetings when 'away from the table' (Wright, May 2001: 35) and Jim Wallace said they were involved in negotiations on the future of the EU even if not physically present at key meetings (Wright, May 2002: 41). Such comments suggest that Scotland's strategy would mirror its informal approach to IGR, perhaps explaining Wright's (August 2001: 26–7) suggestion that although McConnell was pushing for a 'more direct relationship between Scotland and the EU ... how this was to be realised was rather more ambiguous'. Its most frequent EU involvement relates to the need to implement EU directives.

A second avenue for the Scottish Executive was to develop links with other governments. From 2000, finance minister Jack McConnell took the lead on developing links with international bodies, such as the Congress of Local and Regional Authorities, on the back of his early involvement in securing EU funds (November 2000: 29). McConnell used his role to highlight the potential for the Scottish Executive to form networks with similar nations and regions, given the 'increasing demand for regional identity, regional networks and regional representation within the European framework' (McConnell in Wright, May 2001: 35; although Wright, May 2002: 44 suggests that links with similar nations/regions are used primarily to exchange information on funding and best practice). First Minister McLeish was particularly keen to exploit networks with the 'constitutional regions' or 'ad hoc group of territorial governments each of whom have their own legislative assemblies', and appeared dissatisfied with progress in the Committee of the Regions since it is not a powerful body (and its UK representatives tended to be local councillors until the Scottish Executive decided to also send ministers — Wright, November, 2001: 42; Wright, February 2002: 32). Instead, the Scottish Executive developed links with the Conference of Presidents of Regions with Legislative Powers which discusses ways to demonstrate the difference between regional or local governments with administrative duties only, and governments which 'share the basic tasks of the state itself and must play the main role in adapting European legislation' (Keating, 2010: 160). Deputy First Minister Jim Wallace addressed the conference in 2000 (Wright, February 2001: 35-8).

McLeish went further in 2001 by signing the 'Flanders declaration' which proposed granting regional governments: (a) a more direct role in the 2004 Intergovernmental Conference on the future of the EU; and, (b) an ability to appeal to the European Court of Justice to protect their interests (Wright, August 2001: 27-8; see also Keating, 2010: 111). This position was rebuffed strongly by the UK Government (Wright, August 2001: 27-8). Consequently, McConnell (both before and after becoming FM) was keen to clarify the Executive's position as one of frustration with the EU rather than the UK. He began to express more EU scepticism. He called for a greater use of EU framework legislation, following his growing experience of the need to implement very detailed EU laws without being able to influence or adapt them. He linked the Flanders declaration to concerns about EU, not UK, infringements of devolved competencies. He also called for a 'subsidiarity council' in the EU to ensure 'that bodies such as ... the Scottish Parliament are left free to frame legislation so that it meets our own needs' (August 2002: 28; see also Wright, November, 2001: 41; February 2002: 31; May 2002: 43; August 2003: 27; August 2004: 31). In other words, McConnell's approach was to stress the value of Scotland's position within the Union within the EU, preventing him 'from being accused of formulating a distinctively Scottish foreign policy' (Wright, February 2004: 23–4; see also Wright, May 2004: 39; Wright, August 2004: 32; Wright, April 2005: 27). While this form of 'para-diplomacy', in which 'sub-state actors work in parallel with central governments', was McLeish's main aim (Mitchell et al, 2001: 70), McConnell was perhaps more keen to reduce the ability of the media to misinterpret the Scottish Executive's intentions.

Flanders was followed by the 'Liege Resolution', a more popular (receiving 52 rather than 7 signatories) but also more watered down version calling for regional representation at the Intergovernmental Conference 2004 and highlighting a respect for national constitutions when considering regional redress through the ECJ (Wright, February 2002: 30; note that the subsidiarity council was floated as an alternative to this process—Wright, August 2002: 29; see also p. 29 on the 10-region, or 'sub-member state administrations', declaration on the future governance of the EU). The Scottish Executive signed a similar declaration in Florence in 2002. However, it also sought to qualify its position. The UK's Minister for Europe, Peter Hain, argued that such issues are better resolved by politicians than the courts. This argument was reinforced by the Scottish Executive which suggested that it signed the Liege and Florence declarations because of its provisions as a whole and despite its concerns over the ECJ issue (Wright, June 2003: 46). In any event, the process had 'little effect on the heads of Government' and the Scottish Executive was merely offered the chance to discuss significant Intergovernmental Conference developments at the following JMC Europe (Wright, February 2002: 30; Wright, May 2002: 40; see also Wright, November 2002: 22–3; Wright, February 2003: 28 and Wright, November 2003: 34 on the lack of regional influence in the Convention on the future of the EU; and Wright, February 2004: 26 on the irony that the IGC broke up in disarray anyway).

We can detect similar tensions with Scottish Executive involvement on the wider international stage. FM Henry McLeish was keen to highlight Scotland's role in international affairs, as part of a UK strategy (Wright, May 2001: 34). However, he was characterised by 'key Labour sources' as a 'liability on the international stage ... the Executive has crossed a line in the sand and ... [they] now need reining in' (Wright, August 2001: 23–4; this is confirmed by McLeish in Wright, May 2004: 38–9 and Wright, April 2005: 28–9 but rejected by Robin

Cook in Wright, April 2005: 30). For example, McLeish's efforts to place Scottish diplomats abroad were perhaps misinterpreted as a challenge to the UK Government (Mitchell et al, 2001: 70). Certainly, this policy was quickly reversed when McConnell became First Minister—a sign for Wright (May, 2002: 42) of a desire to show that the Scottish Executive is not stepping on the UK Government's toes (also note that many FCO diplomats are Scottish—Wright, February 2004: 27).

Instead, McConnell and the Scottish Executive restricted formal links to regions and countries with similar policy objectives and complementary economic strengths, and maintained a moderate international profile (Wright, November 2002: 24; Wright, February 2003: 28; Wright, February 2004: 25; Wright, May 2004: 39–42; Wright, November 2004: 22; see also Lynch, January 2006: 93–4; May 2006: 51–2; January 2007: 50; April 2007: 67; September 2006: 47, who describes its partnership approach as 'scattergun'). McConnell's served as a convener of RegLeg, the group of regions with legislative powers, but he was keen to stress its *consultative* purpose, leaving formal involvement with the EU to the less controversial Committee of the Regions (Wright, February 2003: 30; Wright, June 2003: 46; Wright, April 2005: 27–8; Scotland also hosted the G8 summit—Lynch, January 2006: 93—and pursued, successfully, a bid to host the Commonwealth Games in Glasgow in 2014—Lynch, January 2008: 68). McConnell also took a particular interest in international development work in Malawi—an arrangement made possible not so much because Scottish action could be restricted to devolved processes (such as funding NGOs who operate in Malawi—Trench, January 2006: 87–8; Lynch, September 2006: 48) but that the UK Government appears relaxed on Scottish action which supports the UK line on international development (Cairney, January 2006: 127; Lynch, January 2006: 90–3; Cairney, 2006: 441–2; see also Lynch, January 2007: 49; Lynch, April 2007: 68). In other words, McConnell was acutely sensitive to the UK Government's attitude to his activities.[15]

Scotland in Europe and the World from 2007

While Alex Salmond criticised McConnell's approach, the formation of an SNP Government did not instantly produce a sea change in Scottish Government attitudes to foreign affairs. Instead, we find a much stronger rhetoric (backed by detailed proposals published by the

[15] Wright (May, 2004: 41) also points out that Scottish elections are won or lost on domestic affairs and that too much work on external affairs would be electorally risky, particularly when questions were being raised about the cost of the Scottish Parliament building (Bell, August 2003: 32; Bell, May 2004: 52) and the value of devolution.

Scottish Government) but also a significant degree of continuity. For example, the SNP Government was quick to argue that Scotland should take the UK lead in EU affairs in areas such as fishing (Lynch, September, 2007: 52; Lynch, January 2008: 68–9). It also called for IGR reform to address 'Scotland's inferior constitutional status as a region within the UK and EU' (see Lynch, September 2008: 67). Yet, it has generally agreed to follow the longstanding 'rules of the game' in UK-led discussions with the devolved governments on EU affairs. In particular, it has been as unforthcoming to the Scottish Parliament's European and External Relations committee on the details of its negotiations with the UK, despite initially having a minister for Europe (Linda Fabiani) who had been critical of that approach when taken by the Scottish Executive (Cairney, 2012a).

The SNP Government increased its international budget and committed itself to continuing the Scottish Government's work in Malawi (Lynch, September 2007: 53) and China (Lynch, May 2008: 61). Perhaps more controversially (given the UK reaction to McLeish's initiatives), it reinstated the role of a Scottish diplomat in the US (Lynch, January 2008: 69) and used Scotland (formerly Tartan) Week in the US to promote political as well as economic aims (Lynch, May 2008: 60). It also changed the emphasis (perhaps rather than the substance) of its EU and international strategies, making broad references to 'Scotland's reputation as a distinctive global identity, an independent minded and responsible nation at home and abroad and confident of its place in the world' (Lynch, September 2008: 66) and made references to countries linked to the SNP's constitutional agenda – such as the 'Celtic nations' and the Nordic countries associated with Salmond's phrase 'arc of prosperity' (note the previous Scottish Executive's reluctance to seek membership of the Nordic council – Wright, August 2003: 28; Wright, November 2003: 35).

Developments Beyond the Monitor

The election of a majority SNP government in 2011 perhaps marks the beginning of a new era of Scottish politics, but our historical experience can be used to show the potential for significant continuity in intergovernmental relationships (see also Cairney, 2012a). The formation of a Conservative-led coalition government in the UK in 2010 may have prompted a greater incentive for the UK Government to cooperate. Its need to appear legitimate in the eyes of those it governs is a strong driver for a Conservative party that returned only one MP in Scotland in 2010 (its Liberal Democrat partners have 11, compared to Labour's 41 and the SNP's 6). Such concerns contributed to the promotion by the UK government of David Cameron's rather vague suggestion that he would govern the Scots with 'respect'.

The new government certainly prompted some changes and a moderate increase in the use of formal IGR mechanisms. The *Memorandum of Understanding* was used to allow the devolved governments to refer an issue of dispute to the JMC (the refusal of the Treasury, during the term of the previous Labour government, to pay Barnett consequentials on spending for the London Olympics) (Trench, 2010c). The JMC plenary also met very quickly (less than a month) after the 2010 election, was chaired by David Cameron, agreed a 'role' for Scottish ministers in European council negotiations, and produced a schedule of further meetings (Scottish Government, 2010a). However, we can still detect an asymmetry of power combined with a lack of UK attention to devolution. For example, its lack of consultation with the devolved governments on its budget plans (and 'bonfire of the quangos') prompted them to issue two joint statements expressing concern about UK government strategy (Scottish Government, 2011).

The Conservative approach initially produced a generally non-confrontational strategy by the SNP. Most notably, it was highly critical of the Calman Commission's report (chapter 10), but sought to amend rather than reject the Sewel motion on the subsequent Scotland Bill 2011, then voted in support of the original motion once its amendment was defeated. It also passed four Sewel motions to allow the new coalition government to legislate on devolved matters. There have been some disagreements, regarding the Scottish government's access to the fossil fuel levy and the UK government's removal of devolved government access to 'end year flexibility' accounts (plus a spat over the non-issue of the Scottish variable tax rate — Scottish government, 2010b), but not enough to suggest that IGR has changed fundamentally since 2010.

The election of a majority SNP government will certainly have some effect. For example, two of its key policy plans will require some discussion with the UK: the SNP may request the power to tax alcohol to introduce a minimum price; and, a reform of council tax will require a discussion on council tax benefits (but note that the SNP received more opposition on alcohol policy from Scottish parties than the UK Government, partly because both governments are influenced by UK medical and public health groups — Cairney, September 2008: 100; January 2009: 50). Most importantly, the prospect of a referendum on independence will at least require some discussion about how the question should be worded and how the governments should interpret the results. The SNP also has a new incentive to publicise any problems with its relationship with the UK Government. In other words, a UK Conservative government in office during a period of economic retrenchment probably provides the best chance for the SNP Government to demonstrate that it would be better making all of its own decisions, and it would be a surprise if it did not exploit that opportunity. Indeed, the SNP may use any dispute to remind Scottish voters of the legacy of Thatcherism which was associated, particularly in Scotland, with a top-down, impositional style of policy making. Much will depend on the attitude of the UK Government which has, so far, recognised the SNP Government's mandate and sought to engage constructively on key issues such as control over corporation tax, renewable energy funding and the Crown Estate (Maddox, 24.5.11).

Conclusion

The UK intergovernmental style is generally informal. Informality was a particular feature from 1999–2007, when the executives engaged through their civil service networks and shared Labour party contacts. The formation of an SNP government had some effect. There have been more public disputes and the Scottish Government has pursued measures to formalise IGR through venues such as the JMC. Yet, the overall effect has been muted, with the JMC meeting infrequently. Informal and ad hoc relationships between ministers and civil servants in each executive are still the norm. As Cairney (2012a) suggests, these relationships endure for two main reasons: the logic of informality, in which the UK government has minimal incentive to consistently impose policy from the top and the Scottish government has much to gain from pursuing an insider strategy; and, the asymmetry of power which often allows the UK government to neglect the relationship and dissuades Scottish governments from pursuing issues in public.

This juxtaposition of relatively positive and negative reasons for informality is reflected in the substance of the monitors. Although IGR was, for the most part, smooth and informal from 1999–2007, the monitors report tensions regarding the operation of the civil service, the role of the Secretary of State for Scotland in the early years of devolution, the limits to direct Scottish Executive involvement in EU policymaking and foreign affairs, and the tendency for Whitehall actors to ignore their devolved counterparts. Further, there was some sensitivity about policy divergence which had the potential to embarrass UK Government ministers. These are areas with considerable scope for variation, with different First Ministers often taking different attitudes to perceived pressures to conform (also note the comparison to Wales)[16]. The monitors generally portray Henry McLeish as a First Minister keen to push the boundaries (and liable to criticism from UK Labour), replaced by a more conciliatory Jack McConnell. McConnell was then replaced by Alex Salmond who, from 2007–11, was generally less confrontational within intergovernmental circles than we might have expected. Instead, he has sought to 'stand up for Scotland' in more positive ways (such as forming alliances with other devolved governments) and chose his battles quite wisely. The election of a majority SNP Government has changed the conditions for these exchanges, but the knowledge provided by the devolution monitors suggests that there may yet be a substantial degree of continuity regarding IGR in Scotland.

---

[16] The First Minister in the Welsh Assembly Government, Rhodri Morgan, made a famous speech in 2002 describing and promoting the 'clear red water' between policies pursued in Wales and England—see BBC News 11.12.02 "New Labour 'attack' under fire" http://news.bbc.co.uk/1/hi/wales/2565859.stm

Chapter 6

Intergovernmental Relations and Government Beyond the Centre

This chapter discusses the Scottish Government's relationships with local authorities, quasi-non-governmental (quango[17]) and non-governmental bodies and explores the extent to which the SNP government altered those relationships. The monitors largely focus on local government, reflecting its central role in delivering most devolved public policies, its 40% share of the Scottish budget and its employment of over 240,000 staff (McConnell, 2004: 1; McGarvey and Cairney, 2008: 134). The Scottish Executive has traditionally relied heavily on local government not only to deliver policy, but also to give it policy advice, either directly or through key representative bodies such as COSLA (Convention of Scottish Local Authorities). The monitors also cover the Scottish Executive's often highly-public ambivalence towards quangos, relying on them to deliver public services and give policy advice, but aware that they are a soft target because they are unpopular (quangos are often portrayed as unaccountable), and generally convinced that they can do so with fewer bodies at lower cost. The monitors pay relatively low attention to health boards (unless they become part of the bonfire of the quangos), although health policy is considered in more depth in chapter 8 (see the new agenda on health board elections).

---

[17] A quango is a quasi-non-governmental public body, otherwise known as a non-departmental public body, NDPB. Quangos are generally sponsored by government departments and ultimately accountable to Parliament through ministers, but they also operate with a degree of autonomy or 'arms-length' from ministers. Also note the separate Scottish Parliament-commissioned public bodies such as the Children's Commissioner.

While the SNP effect on Scottish-UK Government relations was perhaps less than expected (chapter 5), its effect on central-local relations seems much greater. Indeed, its general approach to the delivery of policy is one of the most distinctive aspects of SNP government. The Scottish Executive has always recognised its interdependence with local government, and its relationship has generally been less fraught than its UK central-local equivalent (McGarvey, 2012). However, 1999–2007 was marked by a relative willingness of the Scottish Executive to use legislation, funding mechanisms and a series of short term targets to control policy outcomes. These measures initially took place in the context of a new era of government in which local authorities were unsure of their place in the new Scottish political system and appeared to feel under threat, particularly when the issue of local government reform was on the agenda.

In contrast, a key plank of SNP policy was to gain the local government support it needed to freeze council tax and portray an image of governing competence. To do so, it reduced 'ring fenced' funding, introduced longer term targets and made a public commitment not to reform or 'micro-manage' local authorities from 2007–11. The reforms largely had the desired effect. Certainly, if we compare the two time periods, we find a reduction in central-local tensions, a central-local agreement to freeze council taxes and, furthering the SNP's image of governing competence, an increasing sense that local authorities are responsible for their own problems. However, we can perhaps also detect a rising tension between the accountability of the Scottish Government and its devolution of power to local authorities (although they also have a local electoral mandate). This issue arose most famously when Education Secretary, Fiona Hyslop, lost her job following media and parliamentary pressure on key SNP targets such as class sizes. However, as chapter 3 suggests, such instances of successful parliamentary pressure are rare, even under minority government. Indeed, post-2007 developments were more likely to expose the lack of parliamentary influence – largely because they did not know how local authorities were spending money and could not oblige the Scottish Government or local government to provide them with enough information to scrutinise their activities well. The post-2007 period has also exacerbated feelings among many pressure participants, such as interest groups and voluntary organisations, that their ability to influence policy diminishes when policy is devolved to local authorities.

This chapter outlines these issues as follows. First, it charts central-local relations from 1999–2007 and compares them with the new era of SNP Government from 2007. It focuses in particular on the issues of partnership working, local government finance and the reform of local democracy. Second, it outlines the relationships between the Scottish Executive and other public bodies, then explores the SNP effect from 2007. Third, it outlines the effects of SNP local government policy on the wider policy process. In particular, it draws on the case study of education, one of the most important responsibilities of local authorities, to show how relationships between the Scottish Government, local authorities and pressure participants have changed since devolution and 2007.

Relations With Local Government 1999–2007

Scottish Parliament and Scottish Executive relations with local government were initially difficult to predict. On the one hand, local authorities and their representatives (primarily COSLA) were key supporters of devolution and played a central role in the post-devolution policy process. They were particularly valuable to government in the early years of devolution, when the Scottish Executive was adapting to its new role and relied on established organisations to compensate for its lack of policy capacity (Keating, 2005; McGarvey and Cairney, 2008: 142). The Scottish Executive has also pursued some measures to increase local government autonomy and tends towards 'suggestion rather than imposition' when engaged in central-local relations (McGarvey and Cairney, 2008: 140). This theme runs throughout the monitors with, for example, McGarvey (February 2002: 36) highlighting a greater commitment to partnerships with local authorities and a reduced focus on top-down regulation in Scotland (see also McGarvey February 2004: 29 and Scott, January 2006: 98 on the Local Government Improvement Service which serves to disseminate 'best practice' across local authorities). This all took place in the context of a continued long term relationship between central and local government in Scotland. While political devolution took place in 1999, administrative devolution was a key feature of the post-war period and many aspects of local government (including compulsory education) were already devolved (McGarvey, 2012). Although the unitary nature of the UK state did not allow for many policy differences before 1999, and Scotland was the first home for one of the most unpopular local government-related policies of all time (the poll tax), the Scottish-local relationship was often better because 'there was enough personal contact to foster something resembling a working relationship' (McGarvey and Cairney, 2008: 138).

On the other hand, there were fears that the Scottish Executive would become a partial replacement for local government, or at least a new and disproportionately powerful partner (a fear exacerbated by the decision of many senior councillors to become MSPs—McGarvey, February 2002: 35). This is reflected in a survey of local government actors by Bennet et al (2002) which reveals a perception, particularly among councillors of opposition parties, that the Executive reduced the importance of local government and that civil servants often still used a 'command model of the world' (2002: 16; McGarvey, August 2002: 34; compare with Jeffery, 2002 which suggests that direct links to ministers helped local authorities get past civil servants and overcome some of that mistrust). The Scottish Executive also controls the main policy levers on the big issues facing local government—such as the legal and financial framework in which local authorities operate (80% of local authority income comes from government), the use of capital finance to build schools (although this is largely controlled by the Treasury), many aspects of education policy (such as the curriculum) and the rules on housing stock transfer (for a critical view of this power, see Gordon, 2002). In short, local government is a creature of Parliament and constrained by the doctrine of *ultra vires*, in which it would be unlawful to carry out activities not explicitly allowed by legislation (see SPICe, 1999).

This is the context in which the monitors began. The first monitor describes the McIntosh Report, commissioned to explore the relationship between the Scottish Parliament, Executive and local authorities as part of a wider review of the democratic role of local authorities. It provided an extensive set of recommendations in June 1999, including the argument that: the Scottish Parliament should set up a 'covenant' with local government and host a regular joint conference based on parity of esteem; the Executive should foster a similar degree of consultation; there should be legislation to give local authorities a power of general competence (to address the inflexibility of the *ultra vires* doctrine); 'local government should always be considered in any review of other bodies delivering public services'; local government finance should be reformed to address issues of complexity and central control; there should be proportional representation (PR) for local elections; there should be a further review of political management within councils (which considers the scope for cabinet models in which leaders would be accountable to full councils or directly elected leaders of councils) to address the issue of party whipping and a lack of transparency; councillors should be drawn from a broader spectrum of society; and, community councils should be better resourced to help them engage more effectively with local authorities (November 1999: 17).

In other words, this is a mix of measures designed to affirm the value of local authorities, but the implicit sense is that the Scottish Executive is in charge and must use its new powers responsibly in partnership with local government. Yet, in the absence of a Scottish Executive commitment to address COSLA's biggest concerns (such as local government finance — February 2000: 13), we may develop the impression of an unbalanced relationship masked by the 'widespread rhetoric of partnerships' (McGarvey, February 2001: 44). This image is reinforced by the Scottish Executive's role in producing performance targets (73) that local authorities were obliged to try to meet (albeit within the context of a less punitive regime than we associate with the UK Government in England) (McGarvey, May 2002: 49–50).

The McIntosh Report set the early agenda for the monitors. In the absence of early guidelines it became clear very quickly that different Scottish Parliament committees dealt with local government differently, with some developing no links at all (February 2000: 13). Thus, it seemed imperative that the Scottish Parliament's work with COSLA to produce a covenant was quick as well as substantive. Yet, instead, COSLA's protocol and guidance from the Presiding Officer focused more on the role of councillors, MSPs, MPs and MEPs when dealing with constituency issues and the overlap of responsibilities which produced the need for some form of coordination (November 2000: 32; note that coordination between *parties* may be more important than between levels of government –Bradbury and Mitchell, 2007). In other words, the wider issue of coordinated meetings and parity of esteem was quickly forgotten. In any event, councils realised quickly that their main relationship would be with the Executive, not Parliament.

The Scottish Executive accepted in principle most of the McIntosh recommendations and established a series of additional working groups: a Community Leadership Forum; a Renewing Local Democracy Working Group [the Kerley Group]; a Leadership Advisory Panel [the MacNish Group]; and, Champions for Change. It agreed to engage in a joint working group with COSLA on issues such as joined-up-government on cross-cutting issues, and flexibility in spending and revenue arrangements. It also produced a consultation paper on the idea of a local authority general competence (November 1999: 17). In June 2000 it announced that local authorities would be given a statutory 'power of community initiative' to 'encourage new ideas and innovation and provide a firm basis for the development of community planning' (August, 2000: 11). This was largely welcomed by COSLA, although it still called for a specific statutory basis for its role in community planning (August 2000: 11). COSLA's call for Best Value (which obliges councils to show that their service provision is better value than any contracted-out alternative)[18] to apply to the public sector as a whole, and not just local authorities, was also met with sympathy in government (although see McGarvey, February 2001: 42 on the Scottish Executive decision to award the trunk road network contract to the private sector). Ministerial consideration of the links between planning and financing local service delivery were made easier when Angus MacKay was appointed as Minister for Finance and Local Government (November, 2000: 30). MacKay appeared to be a key proponent of the local authority role, referring to community, rather than central, planning as a 'flagship policy' (McGarvey, May 2001: 38). In May 2001, McKay signed the 'Partnership Framework' (promised by McIntosh) with COSLA's President Norman Murray, marking an important symbolic commitment to joint working (or at least consultation and information sharing) and making reference to mutual respect and 'distinct and complementary' roles (McGarvey, August 2001: 31–2). In 2003 the Scottish Local Government Act gave a statutory footing to local authority powers on community planning and 'well-being' (McGarvey, February 2003: 35; see Scott, September, 2006: 54 on Audit Scotland's evaluation of the new arrangements). The ascension of Jack McConnell to First Minister was also marked by a (vague) commitment to a 'new beginning' and better central-local relations (McGarvey, May 2002: 49).

Yet, there is often a large gap between the rhetoric of partnerships and the evidence of partnership working (McConnell, 2004: 14; McGarvey and Cairney, 2008: 142). Indeed, only months into McConnell's term, COSLA urged a 'significant change' in their relationship (McGarvey, November 2002: 27). During the 2003 local election campaign, it produced its own manifesto calling for '"constitutional protection" from executive diktats, more financial freedom, new laws to protect council boundaries and services from the whim of ministers, and a power of general competence' (McGarvey, June 2003: 53). Shortly after the 2003 elections, COSLA President Pat Watters 'accused the First Minister of having "a wilful disregard for

---

[18] Best Value was New Labour's alternative to compulsory competitive tendering, allowing for the possibility that local authority provision is better value for money than contracting out — see McGarvey and Cairney (2008: 138; 141)

local government"' and criticised the Scottish Executive's propensity to grant itself new powers in areas such as transport and probation (McGarvey, August 2003: 31). The Scottish Executive had also proved willing to reject the spirit of 'distinct and complementary' roles by intervening directly in 'failing' local authority services such as schools and social work departments (McGarvey, August 2003: 31; McGarvey, August 2004: 36; McGarvey, November 2004: 28). By the end of 2003 the *Herald* was reporting (and exaggerating) a new 'centralising agenda at work, with power being siphoned away from councils to Holyrood, never to return' (McGarvey, November 2003: 39). At COSLA's annual conference in 2004, chief executive Rory Mair called for a 'new relationship' based on 'trust and equal partnership' in contrast to the existing Scottish Executive 'arrogance' and 'frequently over-prescriptive and interventionist' attitude, while President Pat Watters called for constitutional protection to stop the 'threat of being dismantled' from hanging over them (McGarvey, May 2004: 48; Scott, January 2006: 97 also suggests that the threat of local government reorganisation underpinned the push towards 'joining up' local government functions).

There may also be a gap between the rhetoric of 'centralisation' and the actual effects of Scottish Executive policies on local authorities: many Scottish Executive initiatives looked worse than they appeared; and, short term centralist rhetoric often gave way to longer term negotiations. The classic example is an initial attempt by the Scottish Executive to introduce absolute class size targets in schools, followed by its acceptance of average class size targets, with relative numbers to be decided by head teachers (Cairney, January 2008: 84; interview, COSLA, 2006). Similarly, initial top-down pronouncements on social work department reform gave way to the '21st century' review of social work that produced 'general agreement between local government and the Scottish Executive' (Scott, May 2006: 55; Scott, September 2006: 54). While the introduction of legislation to deal with anti-social behaviour was a key plank of Scottish Executive policy in the second parliamentary session (chapter 8), councils were not punished in any way for distributing a minimal amount of anti-social behaviour orders (ASBOs) (Scott, September 2006: 50). While 'free' personal care for older people was its flagship policy in the first session, it took no steps to punish local authorities for any perceived implementation failures (Scott, September 2006: 52; in part because there was minimal evidence of local authority opposition and the policy was generally presented as a success—Scott, April 2007: 70–1). The Scottish Executive's efficiency agenda (McGarvey, August 2004: 37) was mostly about encouraging local authorities to cooperate in ways that would benefit them (although a shift in emphasis may be linked to a change of minister – McGarvey, November 2004: 28). At the very least, the Scottish Executive's rhetoric was very anti-top-down (Cairney, January 2006: 114) and opposition was more likely to come from unions following job losses rather than COSLA (Scott, January 2006: 98; Scott, September 2006: 51).[19]

The proof of the pudding is that the Scottish Executive did *not* reform local government boundaries. Similarly, its use of Best Value to drive improvements in public service delivery did not produce the same movement away from direct service provision as in England. The consequences associated with not meeting government targets were also less punitive (McGarvey and Cairney, 2008: 142). Instead, the Accounts Commission for Scotland conducts audits to assess, 'the extent to which each council is meeting its legal duty to improve service delivery, identifies where this is in doubt and outlines any improvement action that is required' (Scott, January 2006: 100). In many cases, the Accounts Commission effectively sets the agenda for councils in a rather broad way (Scott, May 2006: 56; Scott, April 2007: 71), focussing by 2007 on the issue of council leadership (Scott, September 2007: 61). In other cases, the effect may be more significant, such as: when a critical report of Inverclyde led to the resignation of its chief executive and the appointment of COSLA's Rory Mair as its interim chief executive (Scott, January 2006: 100); when a critical report of West Dunbartonshire prompted its council leader to resign (Scott, January 2007: 57); and, when a critical report of the City of Aberdeen Council contributed to its agreement to seek external help and appoint a new chief executive (Scott, September 2008: 76). Yet, these cases were not

---

[19] In general, the Scottish Executive often maintained a rather fluid approach to its involvement in local government and union issues. For example, it agreed to fund the McCrone deal to increase teacher pay and end a long-running dispute between teaching unions and local government, but did not get involved, despite effectively funding, pay disputes between COSLA and Unison (McGarvey, February 2001: 40-1; McGarvey, November 2003: 40; McGarvey, May 2004: 47; see also Winetrobe, May 2004: on the nursery nurses dispute; the SNP Government also had little formal involvement in such disputes – Scott, January 2009: 65). It signed a protocol with the STUC to ensure that employees affected by PPP would have their employment terms and conditions safeguarded (Bell, February 2003: 36; see also Winetrobe, February 2002: 49 on the Scottish Executive's involvement in strike talks on ferry and railway staff). It avoided direct involvement in equal pay claims for female local government workers, but took the lead on removing the entitlement of those in the local government pension scheme to retire at 65 (then retreated somewhat to phase in the new arrangements by 2020, 4 years later than in England) (Scott, January 2006: 101; Scott, May 2006: 57-8; Scott, September 2006: 53; Scott, January 2007: 57-8; the agreement was finally reached with the SNP Government – Scott, May 2008: 66-7).

accompanied by complaints within local government that the Scottish Executive was overstepping its mark.

Local Government Funding 1999–2007

The McIntosh Report's call for a fundamental review of finance was rejected by the Scottish Executive (against the wishes of COSLA) in favour of the establishment of a joint working group (Strategic Issues Working Group) at 'officer level' (May 2000: 10). The group recommended a series of measures to give local authorities more notice of funding decisions (three years instead of one) and more flexibility when delivering Scottish Executive policies (e.g. with less 'ring fenced' funding—November 2000: 31) and when securing capital funding. While many of these recommendations were accepted by the Scottish Executive, relatively little progress was made on the reduction in ring-fenced budgets (McGarvey, February 2003: 34) or an increase in the proportion of local authority revenue generated by authorities. Thus, COSLA expressed concern over the effects of Scottish Executive policy innovation on local authority budgets (McGarvey, February 2001: 44). In other words, its argument was that the Scottish Executive expected local authorities to stay within its budget estimate when delivering additional Executive policies, and any short-fall would have to be met by an increase in council taxes—a position which shifts the blame, unfairly, to local authorities (McGarvey, May 2001: 39; see also p.40 and McGarvey, November 2003; 38 on the rise in local authority staff to deliver Executive policies; Bell, August 2001: 35; McGarvey, August 2002: 35; McGarvey, June 2003: 53; McGarvey, November 2004: 27).

The Scottish Executive also initiated a narrower look (in partnership with COSLA) at how equitable was the formula used to distribute money to individual local authorities (November 1999: 18; a wider review was conducted by the Scottish Parliament's Local Government Committee). Still, the review proved to be controversial, reminding us that the idea of relations with 'local government' as a whole can be misleading when the most important relationships are often *within* local government or between the Scottish Executive and particular councils (McGarvey, 2012 describes central and local governments as 'loose collections of institutions, politicians, bureaucrats and professions'). As Mitchell et al (2001: 67) put it, the review opened up old disputes associated with the pre-devolution days in which Conservative Scottish Secretaries would favour powerful Labour-led west coast councils (Strathclyde Region and Glasgow district councils in particular) to avoid unnecessary antagonism. When the new Scottish Executive altered the distribution, in its eyes towards a more equitable system, it provoked criticisms from those councils, who suggested that they were being discriminated against. Thus, although the Scottish Executive introduced an overall 'relatively generous' settlement to local authorities, and negotiated the deal with COSLA, it caused significant fallout and contributed to Glasgow City Council (with Scotland's highest council tax) leading the way in voting to leave COSLA, followed by Falkirk, Dundee and Clackmannanshire (2001: 67; McGarvey, February 2001: 41–2; all except Falkirk rejoined in 2003; Falkirk rejoined in 2007). The measure caused a considerable (if temporary) internal crisis and prompted COSLA to undertake a 'fundamental review of its operations' (McGarvey, May 2001: 38; McGarvey, August 2001: 32; see also McGarvey, May 2002: 48 on Glasgow's lobbying on the Scottish Executive's five cities review *Building Better Cities*; for the review itself see McGarvey, February 2003: 34; McGarvey, August 2003: 31).

Over the years we can discern a funding blame game, with annual COSLA announcements that tight funding settlements would cause service cuts and redundancies met with Scottish Executive figures on the rise of council funding since devolution (55% from 1999–2005), its argument that local authorities should be more efficient, its criticism of local authority collection rates and its nod to their financial reserves (McGarvey, April 2005: 32–3; Scott, January 2006: 96–7; Scott, September 2006: 55). Jack McConnell also attempted to divert the blame for council tax rises to councils, arguing that if they rose more than 2.5% that councils 'would have to explain this to voters' (Scott, May 2006: 53). The Scottish Executive initiated in 2004 an Independent Local Government Finance Review Committee (the 'Burt review' group had no local or central government members), but this had as much to do with the Liberal Democrat wish for a local income tax as any Scottish Executive concern about the 50% rise in council taxes from 1996 to 2004 (McGarvey, August 2004: 37; see also Bell, May 2004: 52). In 2005, headline-grabbing above-inflation rises did prompt the Scottish Executive to announce its readiness for a 'root-and-branch' review. Yet, there was still a tendency for the issue of funding shortfalls to become eclipsed by attention to the future of the council tax itself (McGarvey, April 2005: 32–3; Scott, January 2006: 99). The Burt review did not stem the central-local tension. Indeed, 2006 saw COSLA conduct an 'unprecedented campaign' on the 'unfairness of the settlement', highlighting local government's falling share of Scottish public spending when the share taken by quangos was rising, and objecting to the Scottish Executive's 'bully boy tactics' (in part relating to Scottish

Executive demands for efficiency savings—Scott, May 2006: 53; Christie, January 2006: 104; Christie, May 2006: 61).

The appearance of an annual feud ended in December 2006, 6 months before Labour lost the 2007 Scottish Parliament election. Following 'months of negotiation' between COSLA and Tom McCabe, Minister for Finance and Public Sector Reform, McCabe announced a 4.7% rise in local authority funding for 2007–8. This was described by Pat Watters as a '"major win" for local government', marking 'a new, mature relationship between central and local government' (Scott, January 2007: 51; although the money came with strings attached— Christie, January 2007: 62). Subsequently, local authorities increased council taxes at a rate (on average) below inflation (Scott, April 2007: 69–70). However, the Burt review did not help the Scottish Executive build on this new relationship, in part because it recommended a solution that neither Labour nor the Liberal Democrats wanted— replacing the council tax with a local property tax of 0.9% of the market value of homes, with income-poor households able to defer payment (Labour favoured the council tax, Liberal Democrats a local income tax). Indeed, Labour appeared to reject Burt's recommendations before they were published. Perhaps surprisingly, COSLA appeared most open to the proposals. Although it did not welcome the review's downgrading of the importance of a balance of funding between grants and local taxes, it preferred this solution to a local income tax that would remove almost all local authority tax-raising discretion (Scott, January 2007: 52–4).

Local Government Democratic Reform 1999–2007

On the issue of 'renewing democracy', the Scottish Executive decided that there was considerably more opposition to, than demand for, the idea of directly elected council leaders and did not pursue the issue (August, 2000: 11). Following the publication of the MacNish Report, it also showed little desire to impose particular forms of political management on councils (such as the cabinet/executive model put forward by McIntosh), preferring to encourage councils to demonstrate a continuous process of self-review and change (McGarvey, August, 2001: 34; McGarvey and Cairney, 2008: 140; the change is described by MacNish as 'evolution, not revolution'). However, it did commit to legislation giving council employees greater scope to run for election and, following the recommendations of the Kerley Group, to establish a working group chaired by the First Minister to consider its 36 recommendations (August 2000: 13). In other words, this is a working group on the recommendations of a working group considering the recommendations of a commission! The recommendations ranged from measures to widen candidate access — to reduce the age of candidacy from 21 to 18, improve administrative support to councillors, and disseminate the importance of councils to the public — to more controversial issues such as the remuneration of councillors (and the reform of the allowances system in particular), the numbers of councillors in each council and the recommendation to introduce the single transferable vote (STV) in local elections (August 2000: 13; see McGarvey's November 2002: 27 discussion of the National Association of Councillors' argument that better recruitment will only come with 'proper pay, terms and conditions'; see McGarvey, February 2003: 35 on the Audit Committee proposal to lower the voting age to 16).

Not surprisingly, the latter three recommendations proved more difficult to accept than the others. The Liberal Democrats were strongly in favour of proportional representation (PR). Indeed, Mitchell (February 2001: 5; 52) describes PR as the 'one issue on which Liberal Democrats are identified'. Yet, the parliamentary Labour group was burdened by its own ambivalence (McGarvey, November 2002: 27) and the opposition of Labour councillors and party members to PR (McGarvey, May 2001: 41; McGarvey, August 2002: 35; McGarvey, November 2002: 27 and McGarvey, May 2004: 47-8 also report significant COSLA and union opposition). The Scottish Executive decided to 'wait and see', no doubt in the knowledge that it could not avoid the issues indefinitely but it could put them off until the next election (McGarvey, February 2001: 43). Thus, bizarrely, the issue of PR in local government elections was not covered by the Scottish Local Government (Elections) Bill 2001 (McGarvey, November 2001: 46-7). The issue was not resolved until 2003 when STV in local elections became the price Labour paid for coalition with the Liberal Democrats (McGarvey, August 2003: 30).

The Scottish Executive set up three working groups to further the Local Governance (Scotland) Bill: to plan the introduction of STV; to consider the remuneration of councillors; and, to consider how to widen councillor recruitment (McGarvey, November, 2003: 38; note that no decision was made to de-couple local and Scottish Parliament elections until the 2007 election fiasco — Scott, January 2008: 76-7; Scott, May 2009: 76-7). Despite McConnell's initial reluctance, based on a possible public backlash, it introduced a system of severance payments to cushion the blow for Labour (and other) councillors likely to lose their seats following the introduction of STV (McGarvey, November 2002: 27; McGarvey, August 2004: 37; McGarvey, November 2004: 27). It also reformed the terms and conditions of councillor posts to give them a basic wage and pension, but it took some time to reach an agreement because two separate reviews produced contradictory findings (McGarvey, April 2005: 34). In the end, the Scottish Executive accepted in principle the recommendations of the Scottish Local Authorities Remuneration Committee but reduced the highest rates of pay for full-time councillors and limited the severance payments to £20000 rather than the recommended £30000 (to the chagrin of COSLA – Scott, May 2006: 54–5).

The Scottish Executive then announced a rather lacklustre campaign to highlight the importance of voting, and standing for election, in local elections; to 'persuade traditionally under-represented groups to put themselves forward as potential future councillors' (Scott, January 2007: 55). As McGarvey (February 2004: 28) discusses, local councillors are 'overwhelmingly male, middle-aged and white and not particularly representative of the community they serve'. McGarvey also suggests that any changes would likely be 'tinkering' compared to the effects of the 2007 election under STV. STV, coupled with a rise of support for the SNP, 'resulted in a radical change in Scotland's local government landscape with Labour's traditional grip on local government dramatically reduced' (Scott, September 2007: 55). The SNP had the most councillors for the first time and Labour's control of councils fell from 13 to 2 (McGarvey and Cairney, 2008: 73). Yet, there is less evidence of an effect on the social composition of councillors. It certainly had no effect on the gender balance (Siebert, 2009: 177).

Local Government Relations and the SNP

The new Scottish Government's relationship with local authorities is perhaps the clearest SNP effect on IGR. The new 'rainbow coalition' of local authorities, in which all major parties formed coalitions with each other, and COSLA's stated desire to work with the new Government, provided a new context for central-local relations (Scott, September 2007: 57). However, the biggest impetus came from the SNP which saw a range of benefits from a new relationship. Its most specific aim was to maintain enough local authority goodwill to ensure support for its plan to freeze council taxes until it introduced a local income tax. Its income tax plan was outlined in a consultation paper in 2008, but dropped in 2009 because it did not have enough support in Parliament (and there were unresolved issues regarding the loss of council tax benefits – chapter 3). Perhaps ironically, it was dropped despite increased support from the less-Labour-dominated COSLA (and some public support – Scott, May 2008: 62; Scott, September 2008: 74; Scott, January 2009: 62–3; Scott, May 2009: 74–5)

The SNP's wider aim was to present an image of governing competence by fostering consensus with local government and avoiding unnecessary disputes where possible. Its plans had the added benefit of a sense of detachment from unpopular council decisions (such as when Aberdeen City announced spending cuts in 2008 – Trench, September 2008: 78). As the joint statement by Alex Salmond and COSLA President Pat Watters put it, 'local government now had the freedom and flexibility to respond effectively to local priorities but it also had more responsibility' (Scott, September 2008: 72). Finance Secretary John Swinney was quick to embark on a tour of councils (Scott, September 2007: 57) and First Minister Alex Salmond signalled a 'culture change in the relationship between central and local government in Scotland. The days of top-down diktats are over' (Cairney, January 2008: 104).

The Scottish Government oversaw a series of measures to give to local authorities what they most wanted or had been stripped of in previous decades. This includes, most importantly, a new concordat between the Scottish Government and COSLA which refers to 'mutual respect and partnership' and, unlike previous agreements, reinforces the message with a series of tangible commitments, including:

- To reject any consideration of reforming local government structures.

- To move away from centrally driven short-term targets, towards broader and longer term single outcome agreements (SOAs).

- To reduce ring-fenced funding from 22% to 10% and allow local authorities to keep their efficiency savings.

In short, the SNP Government made a commitment to stop 'micromanaging' local government (Scott, January 2008: 70; Cairney, January 2008: 104; Trench, January 2008: 85–6; Scott, May 2008: 64; Scott, September 2008: 71). It then reached a funding settlement (including funding for the controversial Edinburgh tram project that the SNP did not want to fund) that enabled COSLA to recommend a council tax freeze to its members. While there was initial confusion about the level of agreement across the 32 councils (Scott, January 2008: 71–2), the freeze was announced by February (Scott, May 2008: 63). It was ensured in 2009 despite COSLA describing the settlement as 'tight' and a 'standstill at best' (Scott, January 2009: 64; Scott, May 2009: 76). Indeed, the freeze was ensured throughout all of the SNP's 2007–11 term despite annual concerns among local authorities (its manifesto commitment to continue that freeze, based on similar plans to reform council tax, has also been met with concern among some, but not all, local authorities – Currie, 19.4.11).

The Scottish Government also pursued a series of policies that seemed conducive to good central-local relations. For example, it made a commitment to build council houses, end the right-to-buy for new houses and increase social housing provision (Scott, January 2008: 78; September 2008: 73–4; May 2009: 78–9) – measures with strong symbolic value, given the association between the Thatcher government and enforced council house sales from the 1980s. It agreed to abolish the housing and regeneration agency Communities Scotland (an executive agency which had in the past been a quango) as part of a commitment to transfer some of its responsibilities to local government. It signalled legislation to give a 'statutory basis for the presence of local councillors as health board members', as part of its plan to introduce health board elections (Scott, January 2009: 66). It blamed the UK Government, not local authorities, for the funding shortfall for free personal care (Scott, May 2008: 68). It also continued with the fairly popular (at least when compared to CCT) system of Best Value (Scott, September 2007: 62).

While we should not exaggerate the shift of power and responsibility from central to local government under the SNP, its approach certainly prompted opposition parties to criticise what they described as a lack of policy direction or insufficient enforcement. Its decision to finance and encourage, rather than force, local authorities to meet targets on class sizes became a key target for opposition parties (Cairney, January 2008: 104; May, 2008: 90; September 2008: 104; January 2009: 53; May 2009: 66; September 2009: 43; 58–9), particularly when, according to the Conservatives, only one-third of councils included class size targets in their single outcome agreements (Scott, September 2009: 63–4) and it became clear that the legal limit was 30. The class sizes issue contributed to Fiona Hyslop's departure as Education Secretary (MacLeod, 2.11.09; see also footnote 8, page 68 above). However, a disproportionate focus on such issues exaggerates central-local tensions. The monitors report speculation in 2009 that the concordat was 'unravelling' because local authorities were not meeting targets on class sizes and free school meals (Scott, January 2009: 64–5; Scott, May 2009: 77–8). Yet, those concerns proved wide of the mark. Instead, the concordat lasted until 2011 and the experience did not prompt the SNP to reverse its attitude to local authorities. Instead, for example, it is still only *recommending* a class size limit of 18 in primaries 1–3 in the context of its move to reduce the legal maximum in primary 1 to 25 (BBC News 23.9.09; Scottish Government 27.10.10; SNP, 2011: 23).

Such scepticism regarding the SNP's approach to local authorities seems based on a 'top-down' view of the process, rather than the bottom-up approach taken by the Scottish Government (Cairney, 2009d). In other words, the SNP's opposition parties base their criticism on the idea that the Scottish Government is not in control of policy outcomes when it devolves service delivery to such an extent. They then link that lack of control to the role of the Scottish Parliament, which is less able to hold ministers to account and track the success or failure of policies. Yet, the SNP may be more interested in securing a good central-local relationship than controlling policy outcomes because the relationship is linked to its aims on local income tax and a general image of governing competence. In these terms, the SNP policy was a quick success, with COSLA using its first SNP-era conference to laud its new relationship with government (Scott, May 2008: 65). The main threat to this relationship may be tensions over funding rather than parliamentary concerns over accountability.

Relations Beyond Local Government:
Quangos and Public Sector Reform

There were three main foci of attention when the monitor went beyond central-local relations: quangos, public sector reform and public sector capital finance. In each case there is a clear local government element: COSLA's general position is that quangos 'should wherever possible be brought under democratic control' (and one question asked in the first major Scottish review was 'Could the function be put under local authority control?' McGarvey, May 2001: 41); major public sector reforms, and the ideologies that underpin them, cannot take place without considering the role of local government; and, the increased use of public-private partnerships to fund large capital projects have had a major effect on the schools building programme. We discuss quangos in this chapter, before considering public sector reform and public sector capital finance in the wider context of Scottish finance in chapter 9.

Bonfires of the Quangos

As McGarvey and Cairney (2008: 143–4) argue, the need for a 'bonfire of the quangos', in which unelected bodies would be dismantled or subsumed within central government, is a 'recurring soundbite' in UK and Scottish politics. However, few governments introduce radical changes when they discover the limits to, and effects of, quango abolition. Indeed, the *Herald*'s description (in Cairney, January 2007: 20) of Scottish Labour's attitude to quangos could apply to most governments — it 'promised to consign quangos to a bonfire when in opposition but, since it gained experience of government, it found them both useful for delivering its objectives and hard to cut back when it tried'.

The first attempt in Scotland took place in 2001 (McGarvey, May 2001: 41; Winetrobe, May 2001: 10; August 2001: 47–8). The number of quangos fell, and their reported overall cost as a proportion of total managed expenditure fell from 12% to 10% in two years, but this was not on the same scale as reform in Wales (Winetrobe, February 2003: 8; Winetrobe, June 2003: 5). The modesty of the reforms partly reflected unanticipated problems. For example, many quangos had legal responsibility for their own staffing levels and major reform would require extensive legislation. The Scottish Executive also realised that quangos (or NDPBs) had widely different remits and responsibilities, suggesting that a blanket policy was difficult if not impossible (Winetrobe, August 2003: 6). There were some instances in which the bonfire agenda was fuelled by other events. Widespread criticism of the conduct of Scottish Enterprise prompted calls for Scotland to follow Wales and transfer enterprise to a government department, or at least move some of its functions to separate bodies or local authorities (Christie, September 2006: 58–9; Cairney, September 2007: 12). Further, conflict over the management of Scottish Water prompted calls for its reorganisation (or indeed its privatisation or mutualisation — Cairney, May 2006: 16; Cairney, May 2008: 13). The Crofters Commission has also been subject to continuous criticism despite regular legislative action (Cairney, September 2007: 13). Yet, the prospect of large-scale reforms had receded by the end of the Labour-Liberal Democrat era.[20]

---

[20] See also Winetrobe, November 2004: 7 and Cairney, January 2007: 20 on the suspicion that too many Scottish Executive appointments to quangos (70%) 'had links to Labour'. See Winetrobe, February 2002: 9-10; Winetrobe, May 2002: 8; Winetrobe, August 2002: 5-6 on claims of 'cronyism' and public appointments, addressed by the Public Appointments and Public Bodies (Scotland) Bill which established a Commissioner for Public Appointments in Scotland.

The SNP Government made a similar commitment to reduce the quango state, although perhaps with the added focus on the detriment to the private sector of an excessively large public sector (Cairney, January 2007: 20). It was helped by a Scottish Executive commissioned (Howat) report that recommended immediate review of the 'crowded landscape' of public bodies 'to determine whether fewer organisational entities could be more effective at delivering outcomes and could do so at a reduced cost' (see Cairney, January 2008: 12). It also became caught up in the quangos numbers game, in which as much attention is focused on the *number* of bodies as their cost and, more importantly, their efficiency when delivering public services (Cairney, May 2008: 12–3). This was highlighted by Andy Kerr MSP, a sort of poacher-turned-gamekeeper who, as a former minister, knew the tricks to keep quangos numbers low. In particular, Kerr highlighted the Scottish Government practice of funding 'task forces' or 'short term groups', instead of an official non-departmental public body, to deliver a public service (Cairney, May 2008: 13).

Perhaps surprisingly, given its strong image of governing competence, the SNP became involved in too many high profile instances of controversy over fairly peripheral policy issues just because quangos were involved. The first example involved the cost and controversy regarding the reform of SportScotland. The SNP refused, unsuccessfully, to relocate it to Glasgow and was obliged by the Scottish Parliament not to abolish it in the wake of Glasgow's successful Commonwealth Games 2014 bid (Cairney, January 2008: 12). Instead, it would be merged with the Institute of Sport and both bodies' chairs would lose their jobs, prompting much critical attention about the politics rather than efficiency of the move (which came into doubt later—Cairney, September 2008: 9). The second involved Creative Scotland, a proposed (originally by the Scottish Executive—Cairney, May 2006: 16) new body merging the functions of the Scottish Arts Council (which funds individuals and arts bodies) and Scottish Screen (which funds film making) at a cost of £3.3m (Scott, May 2009: 82). This plan was first disrupted by farcical scenes in the Scottish Parliament when opposition MSPs did not seem to realise that they could not reject the financial memorandum of the Creative Scotland Bill without causing it to fall (the principles of the bill had clear support in plenary and committee—Cairney, September 2008: 19). The fallout also contributed to the declining status of Linda Fabiani before she was replaced as Minister for Europe, External Affairs and Culture by Mike Russell in February 2009 (Russell replaced Hyslop as Education Secretary in December 2009). However, it did not reverse the SNP's 'agenda on abolishing or merging quangos' (Scott, January 2009: 67; Scott, May 2009: 83; Cairney, September, 2009: 52).

The example of Scottish Parliament-commissioned bodies (Scottish Public Services Ombudsman; Scottish Information Commissioner; Co-mmissioner for Children and Young People in Scotland; Commissioner for Public Appointments in Scotland; Scottish Commission for Human Rights; and the Scottish Parliamentary Standards Commissioner) perhaps typifies the problem with bonfires. The Scottish Parliament wanted these bodies to provide more scrutiny of government activity, but they have had to let them get on with it and pay handsomely for the privilege. The Finance committee looked into its £6m spending on such bodies in 2006, but found itself in a familiar quandary: 'ensuring the financial accountability of these bodies while also allowing them the independence to fulfil their duties' (Cairney, January 2007: 25). A special committee re-examined the issue in 2009 (Cairney, September 2009: 39), but it recommended little more than a continuous scrutiny of their activities (and to consider removing overlaps in their responsibilities) (Review of SPCB Supported Bodies Committee, 2009).

Central Local Relations: the Effect on Pressure Participants

Chapter 4 outlines a potential irony to the Scottish Policy Style – groups are encouraged to believe that they are influencing policy at the stage of policy formulation, only to see that influence diminish as policy is implemented. The more that governments make policy commitments that lack detailed restrictions, and leave the final outcome to the organisations that deliver policy, the less groups see their initial influence continued during implementation.

Although the devolution monitors often outline greater central-local tensions from 1999–2007, the devolution of power to local authorities *has* been a key feature of Scottish policymaking since 1999 – at least when we compare implementation styles in Scotland and England. For example, Scotland introduced very high standards for housing quality and very ambitious legislation to tackle homelessness but, in both cases, did not take a strong line on implementation (Cairney, 2009d: 366). Similarly, it introduced ambitious legislation to deliver free personal care in Scotland but did not ring fence the money, leaving local authorities to consider the provision as part of their overall funding strategy (McGarvey and Cairney, 2008: 215).

The election of an SNP Government marked a further shift in that central-local relationship, producing the potential to exacerbate tensions between interest groups and government when policy implementation is so devolved (the 'bottom-up' not 'top-down' approach to policy implementation). An interesting feature of this strategy is that it has the potential to produce new policymaking relationships, with groups perhaps obliged to lobby 32 local authorities rather than one Scottish Government. Just as devolution produced 'territorial policy communities' (Keating, Cairney and Hepburn, 2009), the Scottish and local government relationship has the potential to produce further devolved networks of policymakers and groups.

These new relationships may also be complicated by the new economic climate in which governments and local authorities are seeking ways to make efficiency gains and spending reductions. Both factors prompt us to reflect on the first decade of group-government relations: does it reflect a particularly Scottish culture of cooperation and the pursuit of consensus, or does it reflect the once favourable, but now undermined, conditions that were conducive to a particular style at a particular time? Can we identify the same types of close relationships between groups and local authorities or does the further devolution of power, combined with the new economic climate, produce new tensions and challenges for groups with limited lobbying resources?

Case Study: Compulsory Education

The case study of education suggests that many groups distinguish between their influence at the point of Scottish Government choice and the eventual policy outcome when it is implemented by local authorities. The perception of vague national policy prescriptions, combined with considerable local authority discretion, is a particular feature in education and a more pronounced feature since the combination of an SNP government from 2007 and the new economic environment. These issues are best demonstrated with two key examples: teacher pay & conditions and the Curriculum For Excellence.

Devolution initially contributed to one of the quietest periods of industrial relations in Scottish education. A number of things happened at the same time: regular and often informal contact between unions and the Scottish Government became much more frequent; they found that they agreed on many (if not most) aspects of education policy; and the pay and conditions of service agreement between the teaching profession, local authorities and Scottish Government, following the McCrone report, provided the 'lubricant' for smooth group-government relations for many years (see also chapter 8). The style of the McCrone consultation in education appeared to be markedly different in tone to previous reviews. The previous 'Millenium Review' of pay and conditions, conducted before devolution, was rejected by the main unions, with the EIS reporting a 98% rejection and its general secretary Ronnie Smith criticising the 'proposals and the government's handling of them' (BBC News, 1999; see also Buie, 1999a and 1999b on the tensions created within the EIS during the process). One particular sticking point, that dogged negotiations for years, related to the balance between the national and local negotiating roles; teaching unions have generally rejected calls by some local authorities to further devolve pay and conditions bargaining to the local authority level (based on fears that some local authorities wanted to merge teacher pay deals with other local authority employee deals—Munro, 1998—and fears that local negotiations would mirror the shift to local, and strained, negotiations regarding further education colleges).

The McCrone review was commissioned by the new Scottish Executive in September 1999 to examine teacher pay, promotion and conditions of service and the wider context, including: (a) how pay and conditions should be negotiated (following the Executive's decision to disband the Scottish Joint Negotiation Committee); and, (b) how they contribute to the promotion and retention of teachers and 'improving standards of school education for all children in Scotland' (Scottish Executive, 1999). The review, chaired by Gavin McCrone, was praised by the EIS for its, 'refreshing style in which the teacher is actually placed at the centre of the educational process. The report itself is devoid of much of the managerialist rhetoric which so characterised the Millennium proposals and, in many ways, is a genuine attempt to address some of the real concerns of a demotivated and demoralised profession' (McIver, 2000). This reception reflected a particular review style designed to 'avoid the mistakes of the millennium committee' (interview, member of McCrone group, 2006). The review team visited schools, talked to teachers and was careful to phrase the report in a more sympathetic way; in 'more teacher-friendly language than the millennium committee'. It contributed to an agreement which: simplified teacher career structures; introduced the new Chartered Teacher Status (to allow salary increases based on further University qualifications); guaranteed newly qualified teachers a one-year contract; set a maximum 35 hour week for teachers (including a maximum class contact time of 22.5); set annual CPD levels to 35 hours per year; made a pay award of 23% from 2001–4; signalled an increased investment in support staff; and introduced the tripartite Scottish Negotiating Committee for Teachers (SNCT) to replace the Scottish Joint Negotiating Committee (Scottish Executive, 2001; SPICe, 2007). The agreement also paved the way for the devolution of negotiations on issues (such as local authority inspections of schools, teacher numbers or the deployment of staff) to local NCTs. The headline action was the significant pay rise, but the style of the consultation, the language of the report and the commitment to national negotiations was also important since it set in place the machinery to produce relatively consensual pay agreements between unions, government and local authorities for ten years.

Yet, by 2011, we saw the potential to return to a period of industrial disputes under the same policymaking arrangements. From the perspective of some teaching unions, the SNCT no longer operates in a tripartite way. Instead, we have witnessed a two stage process. First, many local authorities have been considering proposals, to change teacher terms and conditions, within their own committees rather than taking them directly to the SNCT. They include plans by Glasgow to increase teacher contact hours from 22.5 to 25, and by Renfrewshire and Aberdeen to bring in other staff to teach the extra 2.5 hours. Second, COSLA and the Scottish Government have engaged in bilateral negotiations, building on their new relationship and their agreements set out in the Concordat, to produce plans to take to the SNCT – a process that unions may feel undermines the spirit of tripartite agreement. Perhaps more significant is the tone of wider debates, with some suggestion that teachers did disproportionately well from the earlier McCrone agreements and that they should therefore shoulder a disproportionate share of the new economic burden (based on the rule of thumb that education is 80% of a local authority budget and wages represent 80% of education spending). Certainly, the agenda of the SNCT now regards how much money to cut. The original Scottish Government/COSLA proposal to reduce the national wage bill by £60m was rejected by unions, followed by more agreement on £45m, tied financially to the condition that the Scottish teaching force is no less than 51,131 FTE and that previous COSLA proposals to reduce sick pay are rejected (EIS, 2011).

These more recent developments prompt us to reconsider the nature of the agreements: did they reflect the policy style we now associate with devolution or were they only made possible by the favourable economic conditions that allowed significant morale-boosting pay rises to the profession? Are they under threat by the new bilateral relationships between central and local government? Much will depend on the Scottish Government's reaction to the McCormac review of the McCrone agreement (it did not recommend increasing teaching hours, but did recommend more flexibility in the use of non-contact hours – see Scottish Government, 2011c). McCormac had a shorter timescale than McCrone and has significantly different terms of reference, focused partly on the 'cost and size of the teacher workforce in the context of the current financial climate' (Scottish Government 2011; BBC News, 2011) in the context of a 2007 HMIe report stating that McCrone delivered industrial harmony but not an increase in attainment.[21] So, not only are there new tensions associated with an economic climate not yet faced since devolution, but also signs that the 'Scottish policy style' itself may also suffer.

Yet, the latter conclusion may be to underestimate the scale of the current economic crisis. An agreement to reduce teacher pay by such a significant amount seems unprecedented in the modern era — suggesting that if the SNCT delivers an agreement in this year and after the McCormac review, it will represent the success of a body that has operated well for over ten years. Indeed, it may be a better marker of success than a body that delivered a substantial pay rise during a period of financial stability. It will signify the ability of the Scottish Government to dissuade local authorities from going their own way on key issues and to persuade teachers to accept a significant pay reduction instead of industrial action. This task would have been much more difficult if conducted by the UK Government or old Scottish Office, or by a Scottish Government without a good track record on pay and conditions on which to draw.

The issue of pay and conditions is often linked closely to a consideration of the school curriculum — particularly since the McCrone review sought to reintroduce flexibility into the way that teachers operated in the classroom. The assumption was that teachers taught to the Scottish educational equivalent of the bible — the 'yellow book' — because it was a protective device; without it, teachers feared that local authorities would place additional demands on their time. The aim of the review team was partly to trade more favourable pay, and a wider recognition of the important job that teachers were doing, for more flexibility in teaching hours and the way that they taught the curriculum. While McCrone's recommendations on teaching hour flexibility was not taken on board in the Scottish Executive report (prompting McCrone later to bemoan a 'clock-watching' profession — Rice, 2002), the agenda on curriculum reform did gather pace.

Devolution initially contributed to the production of a curriculum review that attracted the support of all major political parties and produced only limited dissent from education groups. Indeed, it is surprising that an issue that seemed so innocuous during research interviews conducted in 2006 should prove so significant by 2011. It

---

[21] 'A key test of the success of the Teachers' Agreement must be its beneficial impact on young people and their learning. As yet the evidence of that impact is very limited' (HMIe, 2007).

began with the 'National Debate' in 2002 (itself a sign of the new possibilities of devolution) which prompted the Scottish Executive to highlight a commitment to 'simplified assessment' and a review of the curriculum (as well as make a commitment to 'smaller classes at crucial stages', 'improved information for parents' and 'more control over budgets for headteachers'—Scottish Executive, 2003). The Scottish Executive then established the Curriculum Review Group in 2003 which produced the broad policy, *A Curriculum for Excellence,* in 2004. This agenda was taken forward by Learning and Teaching Scotland (fire-resistant until 2011, when it merged with the HMIe to become Education Scotland), which commissioned research in 2005, specified the curriculum's key features in 2006, produced the 'draft experiences and outcomes' from 2007 and published the new curriculum guidelines in 2009 (for the detailed timeline see LTS, 2011a).

The process was fairly low key throughout, in large part because this was a classic valence issue and the aims were unobjectionable — with many interviewees referring to the 'motherhood and apple pie' aspect of curriculum reform. This has two related aspects. First, we can highlight the high presence of *consensus* around broad themes such as 'successful learners', 'confident individuals', 'responsible citizens' and 'effective contributors' (who wouldn't want these things?), professional consensus on the key aims for curriculum reform — such as to close the 'achievement gap' for people in poorer backgrounds and improve, for some, the transition to work through vocational courses — and Scottish professional consensus on the aim of maintaining an equitable comprehensive system furthering a broad education (see LTS, 2011b). Second, low key can also mean *low attention*, with few actors, outside a small professional world of active and interested practitioners, aware of the details of the policy.

This image of curriculum reform changed markedly during the implementation process, with local authorities, schools and teachers displaying highly variable levels of preparation and support for the new arrangements. A shift of attention from the broad aims during policy formulation to the details during implementation produced considerable disquiet, with many individuals (including parents and teachers), unions and local authorities expressing uncertainty about the meaning, and the practical implications, of curriculum reform. The issue appears to reinforce the perception of minimal national policy prescriptions, combined with considerable local authority discretion, since the idea behind the 3–18 curriculum is that local authorities and schools can design their own ways to help students learn (with help from the LTS if requested), with the confidence that the education inspectorate, HMIe, will not tell them they are doing it wrongly and that the Scottish Qualifications Authority (SQA) will provide examinations that reflect the curriculum and how it is taught (not vice versa).

However, there are some differences when compared to the issue of pay and conditions. First, there is less concern about the need to lobby 32 local authorities; curriculum development is largely a professional issue with minimal local authority 'corporate' involvement (unless it relates to the resources to aid implementation). Second, the new economic environment has not produced hard choices in the same way. Instead, participants are concerned about the lack of resources to implement a new policy. Third, there is perhaps less to unify the profession. Curriculum reform is often portrayed as a clash of cultures between primary and secondary teachers. The former may be better able to apply a curriculum based on interdisciplinarity and a further move away from testing. The latter may be more concerned about the future of their specific disciplines and the uncertainty regarding the future of external assessments (and perhaps the workload involved in internal assessment), given the move away from the 8 Standard grade in S4 and 5 Highers in S5 model (still a key indicator for many universities) towards a more flexible structure. Overall, there is a greater sense of business-as-usual in this case, with the new central-local relationship having no great effect on curriculum reform.

Conclusion

The monitors describe frequent and significant tensions in the Scottish central-local relationship, although we need to qualify this statement in several respects. First, there will always be tensions between governments that share responsibilities so closely. Unlike in chapter 5, we are not talking about governments that enjoy a much clearer division of responsibilities. Instead, the relationship involves shared responsibilities, with central government setting the policy direction and providing most of the funding, and local governments not only implementing policy but also setting some of their own priorities according to local circumstances and a local electoral mandate. Second, the central-local relationship is generally less fraught than its UK government counterpart. The 'Scottish Policy Style' is more likely to involve developing personal relationships and relying less on impersonal regulations and punitive targets — largely because Scotland is smaller and this approach is possible. Third, these relationships changed over time. The early years of devolution were marked by relative uncertainty and perhaps a measure of ambivalence. On the one hand, many local authorities and local authority groups were key supporters of devolution, in part because they were the most affected by UK Conservative government policies in the 1980s and 1990s. Policies such as compulsory competitive tendering, the enforced sale of council housing, the poll tax, and local government reorganisation (and the proposed sale of Scottish Water) contributed to a feeling among local authorities that devolution in 1979 could have protected them somewhat. Further, in many ways, this support for devolution paid off. In particular, Scottish local authorities now operate in a profoundly different context in which they are in regular contact with government and generally enjoy good working relationships. On the other hand, the formation of a Scottish Parliament and Executive had the potential to challenge local authorities by introducing another body that could legislate and use funding to influence local service delivery. Consequently, in the early years we witnessed a combination of optimism and joint working on the new relationship, with a sense that local authorities may be subject to top-down control.

Fourth, however, we should not exaggerate the top-down role. It is tempting to contrast a tension-filled top-down first era, from 1999–2007, with a bottom-up period marked by mutual central-local respect from 2007. Yet, the Scottish Executive era was also frequently marked by a bottom-up approach to implementation, in which it would make policies and set priorities but then devolve important details to local authorities. Examples such as average class sizes show us the difference between headline-hitting top-down policies and the more day-to-day process of negotiating with local authorities during implementation (although STV was introduced despite opposition from Labour-led councils and COSLA). In this context, the SNP approach *accelerated* a shift further away from 'top down diktats'. The shift of ring fenced budgets from 22% to 10% perhaps sums this up—as a shift from a low number to an even lower number (the SNP Government has also generally taken a very similar approach to quangos).

At the same time, we should not ignore the power of perception, and further devolution in this vein has prompted many pressure participants to bemoan the reduction of central control and accountability of the Scottish Government and Parliament as well as, more importantly, the reduction in their ability to influence policy at the formulation and implementation stages. Indeed, in the absence of a powerful Parliament, it may be 'civic Scotland' that acts as the biggest obstacle to the Scottish Government's approach. This is demonstrated somewhat by the significant role played by education unions in maintaining a central government interest in schools and teachers, but the issue requires further research.

Chapter 7

Changes in Public Attitudes

A key finding from social attitudes studies in Scotland before devolution was that Scotland had unusually high levels of national identity when compared to Wales, Northern Ireland and England. When asked to choose between a Scottish and a British identity, a comfortable majority chose Scottish. When asked to identify themselves on a national identity continuum, the majority responded that they were at least more Scottish than British. When given a free choice, far more chose Scottish although, crucially, a smaller majority also responded that they were British. This is key context for the run up to devolution. Although it is problematic to read-off attitudes to constitutional change simply from feelings of national identity (and that policy change of the magnitude of devolution requires much more than a degree of public demand), we can say that this expression of national identity translated into support for devolution within the Union rather than independence from it.

The most popular post-devolution questions regard the effect that devolution has had on national identity and constitutional preferences.[22] Or, in the language of the pre-devolution days, did it mark a stepping stone to independence or kill it stone dead? There are a number of potential sources of change to attitudes in this respect. For example, devolution as an event had the potential to provide some sort of closure for supporters of devolution. Or, the performance of devolved institutions, and the effects of particular policy decisions made in Scotland, may influence public perceptions of the success of devolution. In turn, people may reconsider if devolution should be maintained or extended. More recently, the elections of SNP

---

[22] There is also a wealth of information in the monitors on voting intentions in various elections and by-elections.

governments in 2007 and 2011 have raised questions about the prospect of independence and whether or not more people now support it.

In most cases, events from 1999 have had a minimal effect on feelings of national identity and constitutional preferences. Most notably, the election of the SNP did not coincide with rising support for independence. Its successful term of office, from 2007–11, resulted in a remarkable election landslide but an unremarkable shift in attitudes to independence. Further, while people have been generally disappointed with devolution, the performance of devolved institutions, and many policy decisions, this has not diminished support for devolution itself. In short, devolution has *not* made a difference. Indeed, the recent economic crisis in the UK may have a greater effect on the devolution debate.

To demonstrate these arguments, the chapter is set out as follows. First, it charts pre- and post-devolution trends in Scottish national identity. Second, it explores attitudes in Scotland towards constitutional change. Third, it presents the evidence on public perceptions regarding the effect of devolution and the performance of devolved institutions. Fourth, it outlines post-devolution attitudes in England and Scotland regarding the fairness of the devolution settlement. Finally, it reviews the extent to which policy decisions made in Scotland reflect Scottish public opinion.

Levels of National Identity

There are three main ways to measure Scottish national identity in surveys: the forced or best choice question in which the respondent must choose between Scottish and British (or other); the free choice question which allows the respondent to choose up to 3 identity responses within the UK (Scottish, British, English, etc.) and the 'Moreno' question which gauges Scottish identity along a continuum, from 'Scottish not British' to 'British not Scottish' (see Curtice, May 2001: 23–5 for an unusual combination of Moreno and best choice).

Tables 7.1–7.3 outline the long term analyses of the best choice, Moreno and free choice questions. Table 7.1 is the most striking. It shows that, when people are forced to choose, the vast majority choose Scottish over British. The 'Scottish' figure is relatively low in 1979 (but still a majority at 56%), reflecting the partial success of the 'no' to devolution campaign (McGarvey and Cairney, 2008: 30–1). However, it has been between 72–80% since 1992. Notably, levels of Britishness have not fallen further since devolution. Most of that erosion occurred during the Conservative Government years, 1979–97 (Curtice, September 2006: 30). The Moreno question (table 7.2) produces a less extreme picture, since people can express their Scottish identity without rejecting their Britishness (in 2005, 57% agreed and 34% disagreed with the statement 'I feel British as well as Scottish and do not want to stop being British'—Curtice, 2006: 56). The results from different surveys in 1992 perhaps show the potential for a degree of inconsistency when different surveys are conducted. However, in general, the long term results are clear. The proportion of people who describe themselves as 'Scottish not British' generally ranges from one-quarter to one-third of the Scottish population (with a low of 19% in the SES 1992 survey, and a high of 40% in 1991). Further, the proportion of people who respond 'Scottish not British' or 'More Scottish than British' has a range (with one exception) of 55–69%.

Again, devolution has had little impact on these figures. Further, levels of Scottishness appeared to *dip* in the lead up to the SNP's Scottish Parliament election victory in 2007 (Curtice, January 2008: 48). As Curtice (September 2009: 25) notes: 'It seems that the existence of devolution continues not to have any long-term impact on national identity in a country in which Scottish identity was already far stronger than British identity before the Scottish Parliament was established'. The free choice question provides similar figures (albeit only up to 2003). It suggests that, while levels of Scottishness remain consistently high, the proportion of Scottish residents who also consider themselves to be British rose after devolution, from a low of 47% in 1999 to a high of 58% in 2003 (table 7.3). In other words, a key source of support for the Union 'has not so far been significantly weakened further by the advent of devolution' (Curtice, May 2004: 23).

Table 7.1 Forced/Best Choice National Identity Preferences 1974–2007

%	1974	1979	1992	1997	1999	2000	2001	2002	2003	2004	2005	2006	2007
Scottish	65	56	72	72	77	80	77	75	72	75	77	78	72
British	31	38	25	20	17	13	16	18	20	19	14	14	19

Sources: Curtice (May 2008: 44); Rosie and Bond (2003: 118); McGarvey and Cairney (2008: 77)

Table 7.2 Moreno Question 1986–2009

%	86	Sep-91	Apr-92	SES 1992	Row 1992	Apr-97	Sep-97	1998	1999	2000	2001	2003	2005	2006	2007	2009
Scottish not British	39	40	32	19	37	37	29	26	25	32	36	31	32	26	24	26
More Scottish than British	30	29	29	40	27	26	30	33	32	28	30	34	32	29	26	31
Equally Scottish and British	19	21	29	33	25	22	28	26	26	27	24	22	22	29	24	29
More British than Scottish	4	3	3	3	4	3	2	3	3	3	3	4	4	4	5	4
British not Scottish	6	4	6	3	6	7	8	7	11	9	3	1	5	10	10	9

Sources: Curtice (September 2009: 24; September 2006: 31); Brown et al (1997); Denver et al (2000: 156); Rosie and Bond (2003: 118). SES (Scottish Election Study), Row (Rowntree-commissioned survey).

Table 7.3 Free Choice National Identity 1997–2003

%	1997	1999	2000	2001	2002	2003
Scottish	82	84	87	86	83	84
British	52	47	52	50	56	58
Both	38	35	43	41	43	47

Source: Curtice (May 2004: 22)

Other, often more detailed, measures of identity are available (for example, see Curtice, August 2004: 19 on the proportion of Ethnic Pakistanis who see themselves as more Scottish than British). Rosie and Bond (2003: 120) and Denver et al (2000: 29) describe the important finding that Scottish respondents feel significantly closer to a 'Scottish person of opposite class' than an 'English person of same class' (they are also much more proud of the Saltire than the Union Jack – Curtice, May 2002: 27). This finding is notable because it marks the relative importance of territorial over social background (the last survey to identify class over territory in this sense was conducted in 1979) and almost any other source of identity (only being a parent ranks higher – Curtice, May 2002: 26). It also highlights the possibility of an anti-English sentiment underpinning Scottish national identity. Indeed, a key theme of the monitors regards the extent to which high levels of Scottish national identity are linked to civic nationalism (in which you are generally considered to be Scottish, or some equivalent, if you live in Scotland) or ethnic nationalism (in which you are Scottish by birthright or other means). The main link between the two issues is that the largest non-Scottish population in Scotland is English-born (and many Scots live in England).

The monitors discuss, periodically, Scottish attitudes to who can claim to be Scottish. For example, in 2001, 75% respond that people who immigrate into Scotland cannot be considered Scottish, compared to 15% saying that they can (Curtice, May 2001: 24–5). There is some movement by 2005, but the majority (54% plays 33%) still require more than Scottish residence. In 1999 only a small majority believed that 'people who live in Scotland but were not born in Scotland should be entitled to a passport in an independent Scotland' (Curtice, May 2001: 24–5). This rises only to 62% by 2004 (33% against) among 'majority Scots' (born in Scotland, not English, not Muslim, and without a partner born outside Scotland – Curtice, May 2004: 23; Miller, 2008: 4).

Further answers (from all respondents) suggest that English residents in Scotland should fake a Scottish accent and keep their birthplace secret if they seek acceptance. While 44% 'would regard someone who was born in England but now lives permanently in Scotland as "definitely" or "probably" Scottish ... 70% said that they would regard a non-white person with a Scottish accent as "definitely" or "probably" Scottish' (Curtice, May 2004: 23). The latter rose to 90% by 2005, and the colour of the Scottish-accented person's skin makes no difference (Curtice, September 2006: 30). However, the response differs if the respondent knows that the person in question was born in England; only 44% think that someone born in England with a Scottish accent is Scottish (42% if that person is not white, 15% if they have an English accent, and 11% if they are also not white – Curtice, September 2006: 32). Overall, as Curtice (September, 2006: 31) notes: 'It would seem that the children of immigrants to Scotland who are born and brought up in the country are readily accepted as Scottish, irrespective of race or colour, but that their parents will to some degree be regarded as "outsiders"' (see also Curtice, May 2002: 29–30 on mixed Scottish attitudes to immigration; Curtice, November 2003: 22–4 and January 2008: 51–2 on perceived and expressed levels of prejudice). However, perhaps some comfort can be taken from Scottish attitudes to English people. Curtice (August 2000: 7; August 2002: 18–19; May 2006: 37) notes the generally high proportion of Scots who like the English and would support England in the (football) World Cup or European Championships (as long as they don't 'lord' it over the Scots – Curtice, January 2006: 56) There is also no evidence presented to suggest, in surveys of social capital, that people are less likely to ask an English neighbour if they can borrow a sink plunger or £5 for milk (Curtice, January 2006: 62–3).

Constitutional Preferences

These expressions of national identity are, to a large extent, reflected in attitudes to constitutional change. As far as most people are concerned, devolution is (or at least should be) here to stay. Indeed, while our current attention is focused on the prospect of independence, it is worth noting that we paid serious attention to the opposite view only ten years ago. Now, support for a return to the days without a Scottish Parliament is relatively low and has been below 10% since 2006, compared to a high of 24% in May 2003 (although the questions asked in tables 7.4 and 7.5 are different). Some early monitors expressed concern about the effect of particular crises on the 'perceived legitimacy' of the Scottish Parliament, but support for devolution has remained high throughout (Curtice, May 2002: 23–5).

A regular finding in the monitors is that there is generally more support in Scotland for devolution (and some kind of extension to it) rather than independence. However, this finding is not always clear and much depends on the question asked (Curtice, April 2007: 31–4; January 2008: 41; February 2000: 9; see also Mitchell, April 2005: 16 – polls 'are biased in favour of the status quo' or 'have a pro-independence bias' – and Curtice, May 2006: 36 – the format used for table 7.5 'evinces higher support for independence than does asking people to choose between independence, devolution and no parliament'). There is also some variation when we compare responses from people with different backgrounds or affiliations (see, for example, Curtice, April 2007: 31 on party affiliation and Curtice, May 2002: 24 on age).

When asked to choose simply between independence, devolution and no Parliament, devolution tends to come out on top and often secures a majority of responses (as from 1999–2003 in table 7.4). The additional distinction between devolution with or without tax powers for the Scottish Parliament (table 7.5) often makes a small difference and, in some cases, it raises the combined support for devolution to 60% (as in 2001 and 2007; it fell below 50% in 2004 and 2005 – Curtice, January 2006: 44). Support for independence fluctuates from just below one-quarter (in January 2000 and 2007) to just above one-third of responses (in September 1997 and 2005). It reached a high of 37% in September 1997, following the successful 'yes to devolution' campaign. However, it reached a low of 24% in 2007 and rose only to 28% by 2009.

These figures suggest two main things. First, the rise in vote for the SNP from 2007 was not caused by a rise in support for independence (Curtice, January 2008: 39). Rather, the most convincing explanations for its victory come from a discussion of valence politics and the idea that Scottish Labour was viewed negatively as a government, while the SNP, its leader and its vision were viewed positively (Johns et al, 2009; Curtice, 2009). The SNP was also able to exploit differential voting patterns, in which it always does relatively well in Scottish Parliament elections (chapter 2). Yet, attitudes to constitutional change, linked strongly to levels of national identity, do play an important part.

Table 7.4 Constitutional preferences in Scotland 1998–2005

%	Sep 97	Feb 98	May 98	Jan 99	Feb 99	Jan 00	Feb 00	Sep 00	Feb 01	May 01	May 03	May 05
Independence	28	28	33	26	24	23	27	24	27	25	22	29
Devolution	38	48	48	53	54	54	46	55	53	56	52	45
No Parliament	30	21	17	18	18	19	22	18	16	17	24	18

Source: Curtice (February 2000: 7; May 2001: 21; August 2003: 16; January 2006: 55). The question asked was: 'Thinking about the running of Scotland as a whole, which one of the following would you like to see? Scotland being independent of England and Wales, but part of the EU? Scotland remaining part of the UK but with its own devolved Parliament with some taxation and spending powers? Scotland remaining part of the UK but with no devolved Parliament?'

Table 7.5 Constitutional preferences in Scotland 1997–2009

(%) Scotland should ...	May 97*	Sep 97	99	00	01	02	03	04	05	06	07	09
be independent, separate from UK and EU or separate from UK but part of EU	26	37	28	30	27	30	26	32	35	30	24	28
remain part of UK with its own elected Parliament which has some taxation powers	42	32	50	47	54	44	48	40	38	47	54	49
remain part of the UK with its own elected Parliament which has no taxation powers	9	9	8	8	6	8	7	5	6	7	8	7
remain part of the UK without an elected parliament	17	17	10	12	9	12	13	17	14	9	9	8

Sources: 1997–2007 Curtice (May 2008: 35); 2009 Ormston and Curtice (2011: 164). *Note: May 1997 figures extracted (in 2011) by John Curtice from the original dataset. The May 1997 poll was taken during the General Election campaign and the September poll during the devolution referendum campaign. The two independence options (in or out of EU) were combined to give the totals above. A differently worded question in 2007 produced 31% for independence, 49% devolution and 12% fewer/no powers (Curtice, April 2007: 32). In 2009, one produced 21%, 67% (41% it should have more powers/26% it has the right level) and 8%, and another 27% independence, 47% devolution with tax powers, 22% devolution no tax powers (Curtice, May 2009: 17; September 2009: 18).

For example, the SNP was able to mobilise more effectively those voters with a natural affinity to independence (it attracted three-quarters of independence supporters in 2007, compared to half in 2003), largely at the expense of Labour which may have successfully reduced support for independence at the cost of alienating those that remained in favour (Curtice, January 2008: 39–40). It also has considerable support among voters that hold a strong sense of Scottish national identity without necessarily favouring further constitutional change; the proportion of the SNP's vote from this larger source increased in 2007 (Curtice, January 2008: 41). As Curtice (2009: 65) notes, 'the SNP ... was able to persuade in particular those who already favoured independence that the party was capable of providing Scotland with good government'.

Second, the SNP was only partly successful in its governing strategy. Its aim was to inspire people to choose independence by demonstrating to the public that it could govern competently using its powers under devolution (along the lines of 'if you think this is good, think what we could do with more powers'). There is minimal evidence to suggest that the SNP shifted overall attitudes to independence during its first period in office (Curtice, January 2009: 18). One poll conducted in 2008 suggests that the SNP's achievements made the population only slightly more likely to vote for independence than before (32% more likely, 27% less likely, 35% no difference—Curtice, May 2008: 38). Another suggests that far more people (58%) view a successful SNP Government as evidence that it can have 'the best of both worlds by remaining part of the UK' than those (29%) who think it should become independent (Curtice, May 2008: 39). This outcome reflects more longstanding perceptions that further devolution would allow people to 'enjoy the advantages of "independence" without the pain or risk of "separation"' (the idea that independence is 'disruptive' and expensive attracts 57% agreement (32% disagree) and 'extremely risky' secures 63% (24%)—Curtice, January 2006: 51–3).

These findings were reinforced by a poll suggesting that the SNP could only benefit so much from 'standing up for Scotland's interests'; that the Scottish Government was as much to blame as the UK Government for problems in intergovernmental relations (Curtice, May 2008: 39; chapter 5). The SNP merely contributed to a partial recovery of previous levels of support for independence following the dip in 2007 (see Curtice, May 2008: 37–8, who discusses the lack of media appreciation of this point). However, the SNP did demonstrate its governing competence (Cairney, May 2008: 83–4)—a factor that helps explain its landslide election victory in 2011 (the primary aim of most political parties) and gives it a further chance to pursue independence with a referendum in 2–3 years (note that most respondents favoured a referendum in principle—Curtice, May 2006: 37—and before 2011— Curtice, June 2003: 22–3; May 2008: 43; September, 2009: 19—but not during an economic crisis—Curtice, May 2009: 20).

Tables 7.4 and 7.5 suggest that independence would not be successful if voters were presented with a multi-option referendum. However, things change markedly when we restrict the focus to independence. If we remove the multi-option survey and give people a choice between independence or not, then independence sometimes achieves a majority of responses. Table 7.6 gives a flavour of the high degree of fluctuation, suggesting that support for independence changes not only over time (often markedly in just a few months) but also according to the way that the question is asked (although note Curtice's September 2009: 19 point that 'the precise wording of the question on the ballot paper may make less difference once the subject has been thoroughly aired in a referendum campaign'). The main problem for the SNP is that most of the over-50% scores for independence came in 1998. While support rose briefly to 51% in 2006, it has since fallen to well below 50%. Indeed, it fell from 46% in February 2007 to 33% in April 2007 (almost all of those responses became undecided—Curtice, September 2009: 16).

Table 7.6 Support for Scottish Independence 1998–2009

%	1998	1999	2000	2001	2006	2007	2009
For	48-56	38-49	47	45	51	33-46	38-42
Against	35-44	42-50	43	49	39	44-46	50-54

Source: adapted from Curtice (September 2009: 16–17).

Note: the hyphens denote a range of scores from multiple polls taken in that year. In most cases the question asked is: 'In a referendum on independence for Scotland, how would you vote? I agree that Scotland should become an independent country; I do not agree that Scotland should become an independent country'. The level of indecision/refusal varied from 9–18%. An SNP-commissioned poll in 2006 found 46% for and 39% against (Curtice, May 2006: 36).

As table 7.7 suggests, even less support comes from surveys which ask people to choose 'to retain the Scottish Parliament and Executive in more or less their current form, or to establish Scotland as a completely separate state outside the United Kingdom but inside the European Union' (Curtice, April 2007: 31).

Table 7.7 Support for a Separate Scottish State, 2003–7

%	Apr-03	Apr-05	Nov-06	Mar-07
In favour of retaining present Scottish Parliament	55	46	50	51
In favour of completely separate state outside the UK	29	35	31	28

Source: Curtice (April 2007: 31).

Note the scary term 'separate state' in these surveys and what happens when the wording varies (see Curtice, September 2008: 43):

- In 2003, an SNP-commissioned poll produced 44%/44% when people were asked to choose between 'yes, for Scotland to become an independent country in Europe, or no, against Scotland becoming an independent country in Europe' (Curtice, February 2003: 17).

- A Daily Mail-commissioned poll found 38% support for a 'fully independent Scotland' and 49% for a 'devolved Scotland' (Curtice, June 2003: 22).

- In the same survey used for table 7.7 in April 2005, 44% 'would be happy' if 'Scotland one day became a fully independent country' and only 32% would be unhappy, with 24% unsure or not bothered; 44% agreed (and 41% disagreed) with 'It's simple: the Scottish people are a separate nation and they should have their own independent country to reflect that fact'.

- In 2005, a BBC-commissioned poll finds 63% support for 'Keeping Scotland within the United Kingdom as it is now' and 33% for 'Allowing Scotland to leave the United Kingdom and become an independent country'. 46% agreed (30% disagreed) that 'An independent Scotland on its own would be able to win greater advantages from the European Union than Scotland as only part of the UK' (Curtice, January 2006: 53–4).

Marginally more support for independence can be found in recent surveys (post-2007 election) that: (a) use the wording of the SNP's referendum question (table 7.8); or (b) use it to structure the question before asking respondents to choose between 'I would vote YES (i.e. for Scottish independence)' or 'I would vote NO (i.e. against Scottish independence)' (Curtice, September 2008: 42; May 2009: 15–17; September 2009: 14).

Table 7.8 Support for a Negotiated Independence Settlement, 2007–11

%	Aug-07	Nov-07	Mar-08	Jun-08	Oct-08	Jan-09	May-09	Aug-11
Agree	35	40	41	39	35	38	36	39
Disagree	50	44	40	41	43	40	39	38

Source: 2007–9 Curtice (September 2009: 14); 2011 Dinwoodie (2011). The referendum question is: 'I agree [I do not agree] that the Scottish Government should negotiate a settlement with the government of the United Kingdom so that Scotland becomes an independent state'

The former wording attracts more support, in part because it does not ask respondents to commit themselves to independence as much (we are invited to agree to negotiations). A win for independence negotiations (41% plays 40%) is reached twice, once in March/April 2008, following a significant recovery from its position after the 2007 election (Curtice, January 2008: 42), followed by six slender defeats in polls conducted from June 2008–May 2009, before a slim win in 2011. These results suggest that there is little to separate the yes/no votes using this question. However, the latter wording generally produces a more comfortable majority for the 'no' vote, from 48%/36% in July 2008 to 57%/28% in August 2009 (Curtice, September 2009: 15).

Similar results can generally be found in January 2007 even if we really mess about with the question wording:

- there is 51% approval and 36% disapproval to the question 'Do you approve or disapprove of Scotland becoming an independent country?'; but,

- 56% would 'like the Union to continue as it is/has done', compared to 32% that would 'prefer the Union to end' [meaning that Scotland would become an independent country]; and,

- 53% believe that 'The Union is worth maintaining' compared to 33% that think the opposite (Curtice, April 2007: 32–3).

Attitudes were also reinforced in 2008 by the economic crisis. A highly biased question, identifying the UK Government's £37 billion investment in Scottish banks, finds that 28% are less likely, and 16% more likely, to support independence as a result (although the experience generally reinforced the existing beliefs of yes/no voters — Curtice, January 2009: 18). However, the less biased 'Does the current financial crisis make you more or less likely to support independence for Scotland?' still produces a wide gap, with 42% less and 24% more likely (Curtice, January 2009: 18). The SNP-commissioned question 'I agree that the Scottish Government should negotiate a new partnership so that Scotland becomes an independent country' secures only 37% of responses, compared to 52% who do not agree (Curtice, May 2009: 16), and a BBC commissioned poll with a similar wording produces 42% for and 50% against (Curtice, September 2009: 17).

The Conservative (and Liberal Democrat) win in the 2010 UK General election, coupled with a democratic deficit in Scotland, is likely to reinforce existing attitudes to, and only produce marginally higher support for, independence. Consequently, it 'might make Mr Salmond's task of winning a referendum easier, but seems unlikely to guarantee him success' (Curtice, January 2009: 20). This view is supported, albeit indirectly, by survey respondents. While, in 1997, 59% thought it was likely that Scotland would become independent within 20 years (and 39% thought it unlikely), this fell to 28% (69%) by 2003 (we can see a similar drop in the perceived likelihood that devolution will 'make it more likely that Scotland eventually leaves the United Kingdom', from 37% in 1999 to 25% in 2003 — Curtice, May 2004: 16). The SNP Government has given those expectations a boost, but still only 38% (58%) of respondents in 2009 think Scotland will be independent by 2029 (Curtice, September 2009: 24). Note that the figures are lower if you ask about 10 years time (25% predicted independence in 2000 — Curtice, February 2000: 8) and much higher if you say 'sometime in the future' which secured 51% in 2001, compared to 22% never, 6% next 20 years and 11% next 10 (Curtice, May 2001: 23; in 2005, 28% thought it would happen by 2035 — Curtice, January 2006: 54).

A more positive finding for the SNP is that support for independence was at its highest during a period in which people were thinking seriously about constitutional change in the run up to devolution. In this sense, subsequent findings may only represent background noise until people come to reconsider their preferences seriously when they find that they actually have to make a choice after a campaign. Or, many SNP supporters may settle for further devolution (Curtice, April 2007: 34), particularly since the dividing lines between independence and 'devolution max' are rather blurry (chapter 10). For example, in an independent Scotland in the EU, most people want to keep the pound and perhaps the Queen, retain UK armed forces and keep the BBC (Curtice, May 2008: 41–2; September 2008: 43–4; see Curtice, May 2001: 25–6; February 2002: 21–2; August 2002: 21 on Scottish opposition to the Euro; compare with Curtice, May 2001: 22 which shows that only 38% wanted devolved railways and 21% devolved responsibility for abortion).

There is considerable evidence that people would vote for more powers to be given to the Scottish Parliament: 66% agreed in 2007, and 'agree' has always enjoyed a majority since 1999 (Curtice, January 2008: 43; see also Curtice, May 2001: 22; May 2004: 19; January 2006: 55). In particular, most devolution supporters favour tax-raising powers for the Scottish Parliament (table 7.2), while several surveys suggest that most people favour the idea of the Scottish Parliament being more responsible for taxation overall. A small majority agreed from 2001–3 (52%, 57%, 51%) and 2007 and 2009 (57%) that the 'Scottish Parliament rather than Westminster should be responsible for raising taxes to cover public spending' or 'Now that Scotland has its own parliament, it should pay for its services out of taxes collected in Scotland' (Curtice, November 2002: 14; January 2008: 43; Ormston and Curtice, 2011: 169). When the question wording was made particularly clear in 2001, a much larger majority (63% plays 27%) thought that the Scottish Executive should be 'responsible for setting and collecting taxes in Scotland' (Curtice, May 2001: 22; compare with vaguer questions in Curtice, May 2008: 40 and September 2008: 44).

There is also majority support for the devolution of welfare benefits and pensions, even though a small majority does *not* want greater autonomy to lead to differences in public service standards and levels of benefits (Curtice, May 2004: 19). Only defence and foreign affairs are seen by respondents as a UK responsibility, although most wanted the Scottish Executive to have a say in the UK response to 9/11 (also note that attitudes to the Iraq war had minimal effect on the 2003 Scottish Parliament election, although ethnic Pakistanis 'deserted Labour in droves' – Curtice, January 2008: 42–3; September 2009: 17; November 2001: 26; June 2003: 34–5; August 2004: 23). Foreign affairs may relate more to sharing diplomatic space than engaging with the EU, with one SNP-commissioned poll showing a small margin (42% plays 40%) in favour of the Scottish, not UK, Government representing Scotland in the EU (although it is not clear how this could be achieved in the absence of independence – Curtice, May 2009: 18–19).

The SNP is also in a far stronger position now than it was in 2007, in relation to parties in the Scottish Parliament and the UK Government (which generally seems reticent about challenging the SNP's right to hold a referendum on its terms). While it may struggle to achieve a referendum along the lines of the likely popular 'Scotland getting "full powers to run its own affairs"' (Curtice, April 2007: 34), and there is a residual issue about the competence of the Scottish Parliament to legislate on the constitution (which might affect the question wording), it will now have more control over the question asked of Scottish voters.

Evaluations of Devolution and the Performance of the Scottish Parliament

The evidence on public perceptions of who runs, and should run, Scotland (table 7.9) is difficult to link to attitudes on constitutional change, partly because the results are not entirely clear (for example, there is either a lack of public awareness of the importance of the EU or an inability to express that knowledge in surveys; and, a sudden rise in belief that local authorities are most powerful, in 2004, perhaps comes three years too soon). If we focus on the 'Scottish Parliament/Executive' row, we find that support for its influence is high, but it fell consistently until 2006, perhaps as people became increasingly aware of its influence (in the context of an understandable tendency to view UK institutions as the most powerful – Curtice, 2004: 221). In other words, people may have been using the question to express a desire for the Scottish Executive to have *more* influence – an expression that diminishes as they come to believe that it has influence. If so, the 2007 figure may be encouraging for the SNP Government, since an increasing proportion of people believe that it has, and should have, the most influence (see also Curtice, May 2004: 19 – people who think devolved institutions are doing well often want them to have more powers).

These results also relate, to some extent, to evaluations of the *performance* of Scottish institutions – but other questions can be found for that purpose. Good examples relate to surveys which ask how well Scottish institutions provide a 'voice' for Scotland or stand up for, or act in the best interests, of Scotland. Such questions also feed into discussions of valence politics in Scottish Parliament elections (chapter 2; Johns et al, 2009).

Table 7.9 Who ought to have (who has) the most influence over the way Scotland is run?

%	2000	2001	2003	2004	2005	2006	2007
Scottish Parliament/ Executive	72 (13)	74 (15)	66 (17)	67 (19)	67 (23)	64 (24)	71 (28)
UK Government	13 (66)	14 (66)	20 (64)	12 (48)	13 (47)	11 (38)	14 (47)
Local councils	10 (10)	8 (9)	9 (7)	17 (19)	15 (15)	19 (18)	9 (8)
European Union	1 (4)	1 (7)	1 (5)	1 (6)	1 (8)	1 (11)	1 (9)

Source: Curtice (January 2008: 45–6; September, 2008: 47–8). 'Ought to have' is the main figure and 'has' is in brackets. Early surveys contained 'Scottish Parliament' and this was changed in 2004 to Scottish Executive' with no real effect on the results (Curtice, January 2006: 48). The figures for the Scottish Executive (ought) are higher in devolved areas such as health and education (Curtice, January 2008: 46; September, 2009: 17). Compare with Curtice (May 2006: 36), which shows a much smaller gap in perceptions of the influence of the four levels of government. See also Curtice (May 2001: 22): 51% thought that 'London Labour' had too much influence over the Scottish Parliament (35% 'about right', 6% 'too little', 8% don't know). See Curtice (2004: 220) on comparable perceptions in Wales.

The decline in the belief that the Scottish Parliament has made Scotland's voice stronger does not match Scottish Labour's decline *perfectly*, but we do get a broad sense of disenchantment following early optimism, perhaps punctuated by Labour's defence of the Union in the run up to the 2003 and 2007 elections. The rise in 2007 is more likely to relate to the election of the SNP, which does relatively well on this question (see Curtice, January 2008: 56) and seems more willing 'to air its disagreements with the UK government in public' (Curtice, September 2008: 44). 2007 is also the first year that more people (47%) felt the 'Scottish Parliament is giving ordinary people more say in how Scotland is governed' than felt it was 'making no difference' (45%), although this could relate, in the minds of some, to issues of power *within* Scotland (a majority responded 'no difference' from 2000–6 — Curtice, September 2008: 46; 79% in 1997 and 64% in 1999 thought that it *would* give ordinary people more say — Curtice, February 2002: 20). As Ormston and Curtice (2011: 167) note, the irony for the SNP is that this rising confidence in Scotland's voice may *reduce* support for independence, as more people believe that devolution is starting to work and they can have the 'best of both worlds' (see above).

Table 7.10 'Perceived Impact of Scottish Parliament on Scotland's Voice in the Union'

	2000	2001	2002	2003	2004	2005	2006	2007	2009
Made Voice Stronger	52	52	39	49	35	41	43	61	52
No Difference	40	40	52	41	55	50	49	32	40
Made Voice Weaker	6	6	7	7	7	6	6	4	5

Source: Curtice (January 2008: 47; September 2009: 22). Note from Curtice (February 2002: 20; 2004: 223) that 70% thought the Scottish Parliament *would* give Scotland a stronger voice in the UK (in surveys in 1997 and 1999).

Other questions on the performance of devolved and UK institutions may also feed into attitudes towards constitutional change—for example, low levels of belief in the ability of the UK government to work in Scotland's interests may be linked to high levels of belief in the need for further devolution or independence. However, as Curtice (January 2008: 47) notes, we should not get too excited about predictably higher levels of trust in the Scottish Executive compared to the UK Government (outlined in table 7.11). Further, the more important *trends* in these figures show an overall decline in trust in the Scottish Executive until 2006 (although note that the 1999 peak, when people didn't have any experience on which to draw, and the 2000 near-trough, when the Scottish Parliament had no time to do much, are misleading). While its decline is initially proportionately lower than the UK Government's, 'the devolved institutions are not immune from the mood of scepticism towards politics and political institutions that has been widely detected in previous research' (Curtice, January 2008: 48). Again, the 2007 figures seem to show a notable SNP-related rise in trust in the Scottish Government, although note that the UK Government's rise in trust is proportionately higher ('it seems that people are also inclined to feel that the UK Government has been persuaded to be more sensitive to Scotland's needs too' — Curtice, September 2008: 45).

Table 7.11 Trust in Scottish and UK Governments to work in Scotland's interests 1999–2007

%		1999	2000	2001	2002	2003	2004	2005	2006	2007
Just about always/Most of the time	Scottish Executive	81	54	65	52	62	52	56	51	71
	UK Government	32	17	22	19	21	22	23	21	35
Only some of the time/ Almost never	Scottish Executive	16	43	34	45	35	47	40	45	26
	UK Government	66	80	77	77	78	76	74	76	62

Source: Adapted from Curtice (January 2008: 47; September, 2008: 45–6) which separate the four main categories. The questions asked: 'How much do you trust the UK government to work in Scotland's best long term interest?'; 'How much do you trust the Scottish Executive to work in Scotland's best interests?' (before 2004 it was Scottish Parliament, not Scottish Executive). A related survey, examining their relative abilities to 'make fair decisions', shows a much smaller gap (Curtice, January 2008: 48), while far more (52%) thought that the Scottish Government 'cares more about the needs and interests of you and your family' than the UK Government (16%). In 2006, 48% agreed (31% disagreed) that the Scottish Parliament 'Can be trusted to make decisions in the best interests of Scotland' (Curtice, May 2006: 35).

The most specific questions probe views on the achievements of the Scottish Parliament, which refers to devolution as a whole, and the performance of the Scottish Executive/Government specifically (although sometimes the distinction is not clear—Curtice, June 2003: 21). The SNP effect is difficult to judge because we have no consistent figures on the Scottish Parliament's achievements from 2001–7. Rather, what we can say is that satisfaction with the Scottish Parliament improved from a sluggish start then reached a plateau quite quickly (table 7.12).

Figures on the more direct question suggest that the SNP Government's initial approval rating (52% approve, 27% disapprove) is much better than its predecessor's, which ranged from 30–35% in four similar polls conducted from 2003–7 (Curtice, May 2008: 54; June 2003: 21; January 2006: 83; April 2007: 62). Yet, much depends on the timing and wording of questions. For example, First Minister Donald Dewar personally received approval ratings from 46–63% ('good job') in 1999 and 2000 when the Scottish Executive only attracted 24% willing to say it was 'very or fairly successful' (Curtice, February 2000: 9; August 2000: 8; November, 2000: 26). In 2003, 49% thought that the Scottish Executive coalition had worked well, compared to 42% not very/at all well (Curtice, June 2003: 22). In 2007 this rose to 52% versus 34% (Curtice, April 2007: 63; see also Curtice, May 2004: 25–8 on attitudes to the voting systems that might produce coalitions). However, the Scottish Executive does relatively badly if people are asked about particular policy issues (see Curtice, June 2003: 37; see also Winetrobe, August 2004: 3 who suggest that the Scottish Executive and Scottish Parliament were well aware of the dim public view of their performance). Most clearly, we can see a decline in Labour approval, from Dewar's 47% in 2000 (Curtice, May 2000: 7), to McLeish's 43% in 2001, and McConnell's 29% in 2003 and 30% in 2007 (note that few other ministers or opposition leaders are recognised very well by the public — Curtice, May 2000: 8; August 2000: 7–8; May 2001: 28–30; May 2004: 21; April 2007: 59). We can also see remarkable levels of Alex Salmond popularity (Curtice, June 2003: 38–41; January 2006: 79; May 2006: 46; April 2007: 59–61; January 2008: 57–8; May 2008: 52–4; September 2008: 60–1; January 2009: 27–9; May 2009: 27–8; September, 2009: 37–9; see also Bort September 2007 and May 2008: 25–6 Salmond's popularity in the media).

If we remind ourselves that devolution is only 12 years old, we see that the more important figures relate to the early years of devolution when the Scottish Parliament was not as established and there was considerable doubt about its likely success in the eyes of the public. In this light, the figures seem worrying at times because few people felt that devolution was delivering much benefit (tables 7.12 and 7.13), an outcome that Curtice (May 2000: 8) links initially to intense media criticism (see chapter 1).

Table 7.12 The Scottish Parliament has achieved:

	Feb-00	Sep-00	2001	2009
A lot	5	11	25	20
A little	64	56	56	53
Nothing at all	27	29	14	15

Source: Curtice (May 2001: 21; September 2009: 20–1). In 2009 the question was 'Since the Scottish Parliament was [introduced] in 1999, do you think it has achieved a lot, a little, or nothing at all?'. In 2000 and 2001 it was 'From what you have seen or heard, do you think the Scottish Parliament has achieved a lot, a little, or nothing at all?' A separate survey asks people to approve/disapprove of the 'record to date of the Scottish Parliament as a whole'. In 2003 it secured 37% approval/49% disapproval, 42%/39% in 2006 and 39%/39% in March 2007 (Curtice, April 2007: 62).

Table 7.13 The effect of the Scottish Parliament on the way that Britain is governed, 2000–3

%	2000	2001	2002	2003
Improved it a lot	5	3	5	2
Improved it a little	30	32	26	28
Made no difference	44	54	48	56
Made it a little worse	5	5	8	6
Made it a lot worse	4	3	7	3
It is too early to tell	9	2	3	1

Source: Curtice (May 2004: 16–17). Compare with Curtice (2004: 228).

These perceptions are confirmed by surveys which ask related questions:

- One question in 2000, on the Scottish Parliament's performance, produced 27% for good, 31% for poor and 34% ambivalence (Curtice, May 2000: 8).

- Another produced 27% satisfied with 'the performance of the parliament in first year', with 57% dissatisfied and 33% ambivalent (Curtice, August 2000: 7–8).

- In 2001, 45% were satisfied with the way the Scottish Parliament was 'being run', compared to 39% dissatisfied (Curtice, May 2001: 23).

- In 2003, 24% thought the Scottish Parliament had made 'a real positive difference to life in Scotland and has been a success so far', compared to 48% 'little positive difference ... disappointment so far', 12% 'no positive difference .. failure so far' and 13% 'negative impact ... should be scrapped' (Curtice, February 2003: 17).

- 29% thought that the 'Scottish Parliament has improved the way Scotland is governed' a lot or a little, compared to 11% made it a little/a lot worse, and 57% 'no difference' (Curtice, August 2003: 16).

- 30% were satisfied with 'what the Scottish Parliament has done for Scotland since it was established in 1999', compared to 38% dissatisfied (Curtice, June 2003: 22).

- In 2006, 33% felt that the Scottish Parliament worked well but 61% thought it could be improved a lot, 57% agreed that it spent 'too much time debating issues over which it has no power' (15% disagreed), and more people *dis*agreed that devolution has increased Scotland's influence on the UK (37%/31%) and EU (38%/28%) (Curtice, May 2006: 35–6; slightly more people were satisfied with their local council, and satisfaction seems to go down as the institutions become more remote).

- Devolution is worst off when people are probed about particular policy areas. While most people had high hopes about the effect of the Scottish Parliament on education, the NHS and the economy, far fewer thought that it made things better. Rather, better/no difference are fairly evenly matched, with the exception of education following the SQA debacle and most questions on the building of the Scottish Parliament (Curtice, February 2002: 20–1; May 2004: 15; see chapter 4 and Curtice, November 2000: 20–1 on the SQA; evaluations of the Scottish Executive when building the Scottish Parliament are 10% positive, 85% negative—Curtice, June 2003: 21; compare with Curtice, August 2003: 17).

- In 2009, 41% felt that devolution has been a 'good thing', while 46% replied 'no difference' and 9% replied 'bad thing' (Curtice, September 2009: 21).

- While 33% and 29% felt that devolution has produced a better health service and standards in schools, 52% and 41% noted 'no difference' and 9% and 12% replied 'worse' (Curtice, September 2009: 21).

Yet, such attitudes did not necessarily have a negative impact on attitudes to the *principle* of devolution, particularly since they often improved markedly by 2001 (when devolved institutions had been given the 'opportunity to achieve something' — Curtice, May 2001: 24) and perhaps because the Scottish Parliament is viewed more favourably in wider terms, such as a body 'more open and accessible to the public' (49% agree, 28% disagree—Curtice, May 2006: 35). As Curtice (May 2002: 23; February 2003: 17) notes, although people may be disappointed about the effect of devolution or the performance of the Scottish Parliament, this has 'not undermined the perceived legitimacy of the institution' and 'support for the principle of a Scottish Parliament remains strong':

- When asked if 'having its own parliament has been good/bad for Scotland', 43% said 'good' in 2000 (45% in 1999), 21% bad (15%) and 36% (40%) did not know or care (Curtice, February 2000: 8).

- When probed further, 48% thought that the devolved institutions were 'good for Scotland in principle', while 37% thought they were good 'in practice' (compared to 13% bad and 35% no difference in principle, 16% and 41% in practice) (Curtice, May 2000: 7).

- Support for the maintenance of a Scottish Parliament remained high at 69% in 2002 (20% no and 11% unsure; a Scottish Parliament with tax varying powers secures 64% yes, 24% no, 12% unsure—Curtice, May 2002: 24 and 62% in 2003 (27%, 11%)—Curtice, June 2003: 21).

The problem for most people is not that devolution has made things worse (better usually attracts more support than worse). Rather, devolution 'has not made any difference' (Curtice, April 2007: 43; Curtice, 2004: 225). In this context, the solution for most people is to give the Scottish Parliament more powers to be more effective (Curtice, May 2000: 7–9; May 2006: 35), particularly since most people still blame UK institutions for perceived failings in issues such as Scottish healthcare, education, and its economy (Curtice, January 2006: 80–4). For example, a plurality often responds that the NHS has gotten worse in the last year, but more people blame UK, not Scottish, institutions (Curtice, April 2007: 44–5; January 2006: 79; and many feel it is better than the NHS in England—Curtice, January 2006: 84; compare with Curtice, September 2006: 32–5).

Or, people simply do not care about or pay attention to, devolution; their knowledge of how devolved institutions work 'remains astonishingly low' (Curtice, April 2007: 47). This is confirmed in various ways: by Scottish Parliament-commissioned qualitative and quantitative research in 2001 and 2003 (Curtice, November 2001: 28; May 2004: 20); questions on 'knowledge of Government activity' (Curtice, January 2006: 49; May 2006: 34) and 'knowledge of politicians' (Curtice, January 2006: 55); and, Curtice (August 2003: 17) on public interest in politics. Further, only 25% felt that the Scottish Parliament had made an impact on their lives (Curtice, May 2001: 23) and there was significant disinterest in the outcomes of Scottish Parliament elections (Curtice, August 2003: 17; Curtice, 2004: 222).

Fair Shares and the Future of Devolution

This general lack of public attention is useful background for an examination of perceptions of fairness. The financial settlement in Scotland has 'all the characteristics of an issue likely to explode on to the political agenda at some stage' (Mitchell et al, 2001: 66). Much of its explosive potential comes down to the issue of fairness, with the August (2000: 10) monitor presenting the widespread prediction that 'if services in Scotland are seen to be getting a less generous deal than their counterparts south of the border (or, indeed, vice versa) it will surely fuel arguments about the character of the devolutionary settlement'. As Ormston and Curtice (2011: 157; see also Bort, January 2008: 31–2) note, elite and political commentator concerns now generally regard an *English* backlash as most likely, based on the higher per capita levels of spending in the devolved territories. Yet, few serious discussions of finance have taken place since devolution, even during heightened attention to the economic crisis from 2008.

As chapter 9 discusses, this outcome is caused partly by strategies pursued by actors within the UK and Scottish executives to make the funding settlement semi-automatic and removed from tension-filled departmental or territorial bargaining. This strategy is helped by the fact that very few people know much about the details of policymaking or devolved policy processes. In particular, Condor (2010: 30) found, in over 1000 qualitative interviews, that the lack of an English backlash reflects 'little evidence that people knew much about the fiscal relationship between Scotland and England'. On the other hand, relative ignorance is not a guarantee of *eternal* low attention. Indeed, a sudden lurch in public interest is often more likely if the intensity of people's views is subject to change as they begin to pay attention. Instead, we have a case that should interest students of punctuated equilibrium theory (Baumgartner and Jones, 2009), since it may not take much for stability to be replaced by instability.

In this context, it is interesting to know what people think of Scotland's financial settlement even if we are not convinced that their attitudes are based on much knowledge. It seems that the majority of respondents in England only express resentment about Scotland's share of public expenditure when they are told by commercial polling organisations that it is high (Ormston and Curtice, 2011: 159)! When merely asked about their perception of Scotland's position, the plurality responds that Scotland receives 'Pretty much its fair share', although we can now detect two key phases. In the first, from 2000–7, the proportion that thinks Scotland gets *at most* a fair share is always higher than a combination of 'much more' and a 'little more than its fair share': from 63% and 21% in 2000 to 45% and 32% in 2007 (2011: 159). In the second, the reverse is true—36%/41% in 2008 and 34%/40% in 2009 (2011: 159). This does not translate into a visible English 'backlash', since English respondents often calculate their interests in relation to the past (or other social groups) rather than other territories such as Scotland (Condor, 2010: 530), but attitudes are changing to some extent. There is no greater sense in England that Scotland should become independent to reduce economic unfairness (2011: 159), but there is growing support for the idea of an English Parliament (as distinct from regional assemblies). In 1999, the status quo was supported by 62% and an English Parliament 18%; in 2009 the status quo secured 49% compared to 29% for an English Parliament (support for regional assemblies was 15% in 1999, reaching 26% in 2003 before falling to 15% in 2009) (2011: 161–13).

Conversely, 'Scotland has appeared somewhat more content with its place in the Union than it was previously', partly because respondents are now less likely to feel that Scotland loses out economically (2011: 165). In 2000, 37% felt that Scotland received 'its fair share' or more of government spending, while 59% thought it received less.[23] In 2005, 42% were content and 49% dissatisfied and, by 2009, 53% were content and only 37% dissatisfied (2011: 165). We can see the same trends when people in Scotland are asked 'whose economy benefits more from having Scotland in the UK?'. In 2000, England received 42%, Scotland 16% and 'both equally' 36%; in 2005, it was 36% England, 21% Scotland and 35% 'both equally'; and, by 2009, it was 28% England, 24%

[23] Even then, independence was not viewed as a better option—in a separate survey in 2000, 20% thought that people in Scotland would be better off in an independent Scotland, with 39% replying 'worse off' and 37% 'no difference' (Curtice, February 2000: 8); even though 30% thought that petrol would be cheaper in an independent Scotland (15% more expensive, 40% 'about the same'—Curtice, November 2000: 20). 'Better off' fell to 13% in 2003 (Curtice, June 2003: 22)

Scotland and 40% 'both equally' (2011: 166; in 1997 it was 50% England, 11% Scotland, 31% 'both equally' — Curtice, May 2002: 22-3). These figures compare with those of a differently worded question in Curtice, (January 2006: 52): 32% of respondents in Scotland believed that the UK spent a disproportionate amount per capita in Scotland, while 38% did not and 30% didn't know; and, 42% supported that subsidy, while 34% did not and 23% had no firm view.

The solution seems to be that Scotland should pay for Scottish services using taxes collected in Scotland. This option has, since devolution, commanded a large majority in England (82% in 2009) and a small majority in Scotland (57% in 2009), even though most people in Scotland feel that taxes would rise in Scotland (Ormston and Curtice, 2011: 169-71). However, as chapter 10 suggests, the reforms produced by the Calman Commission may only make it *look* like Scotland is taking responsibility for its own finances. Given the low levels of knowledge of devolution in the UK, this may be enough to satisfy most of the public (compare with Ormston and Curtice, 2011: 173-4).

Attitudes Towards Public Policies

The monitors devote considerable attention to attitudes in Scotland towards particular policy issues (see chapter 8 on public policy). These attitudes are important, but they also show us the often-indirect link between social attitudes and policy decisions when, for example, ministers 'get ahead' of public opinion (as many policymakers did when they introduced smoking bans — Cairney, Studlar and Mamudu, 2012) or when different decisions are made in Scotland despite similar social attitudes in Scotland and England (Jeffery, 2006). For example, Curtice (February 2001: 26) notes that Scotland respondents are 'slightly keener' on government-funded care for older people, while Curtice (September 2006: 36) finds no less demand in Scotland for 'choice' in the NHS. We should also note the tendency for public attention to be limited, generally to controversial issues that represent a tiny proportion of government activity. For example, although higher education was described by the monitor as 'important political battleground' and the 'first real issue to occupy the politicians minds this year', one of its flagship policies (tuition fees) received muted media coverage because it was crowded out by attention to 'section 28' (see below) during the passage of the Ethics and Standards in Public Life bill (of which section 28 is a small part — February 2000: 25-6; August 2000; 18; see chapter 7; Winetrobe, June 2003: 64 also notes that tuition fees and free personal care barely registered during the 2003 election campaign). Similarly, while few people beyond the mental health profession would notice a reform of mental incapacity legislation, its potential to introduce 'euthanasia "by the back door"' guaranteed it attention (May, 2000: 24).

In broader terms, policymakers may often try to gauge the 'national' or 'public mood' when making decisions, but they do not have the ability to capture that mood accurately, and have to rely on imperfect information. Or, they use information selectively to reinforce their own attitudes towards policy decisions — a strategy that often poses low risks since 'the public' can only pay attention to a very small proportion of policy decisions (for a classic discussion, see Schattschneider, 1960). Indeed, in some cases, ministers may take decisions even if they think they will be unpopular, as in the case of the SNP Government's decision to release the Lockerbie bomber (although this was opposed by a 'far from overwhelming' majority, partly because only a small majority believe that Mr al-Megrahi was guilty — Curtice, September 2009: 28; see also Winetrobe, August 2002: 47 on Nelson Mandela's intervention).

The issue of 'section 28' has become a classic example of the gap between social attitudes and public policy (other possible examples include the issue of Catholic schools, cannabis use, alcohol licensing, the structure of NHS services, immigration, homelessness and universal free school meals).[24] The Scottish Executive and Parliament came together to pursue what many MSPs thought would be a quick win for devolution, by passing legislation removing a controversial prohibition, introduced by the UK Conservative Government in 1988, on the 'promotion' of homosexuality. Yet, the move appeared to be opposed by a majority of respondents. Levels of support/oppose

---

[24] See Curtice (May 2002: 27-9; February 2003: 18-19; June, 2003: 33-4) on separate Catholic schools but note that while most people (including non-church-attending Catholics) may no longer support separate schools, there is little active support for, and likely active opposition to, a major change (and Jack McConnell briefly considered merging some Catholic/secular school campuses). Public policy may effectively be converging with attitudes on cannabis, since custodial sentences for cannabis use are increasingly unlikely (although the majority-supported prescription of cannabis is not yet policy in the UK — Curtice, May 2002: 27-9). Curtice (November 2003: 21) finds public concern with the Scottish Executive's moves to liberalise licensing laws. The NHS issue is less clear, but most people prefer the idea of local hospitals to the idea of specialist services (Curtice, May 2004: 23). Yet, the latter was partly recommended by the Kerr report (Cairney, January 2006: 118) and often pursued by the Scottish Executive before 2007 (see chapter 8). Curtice (January 2006: 64-6; see also September 2009: 29-30) remarks on the difference between the Scottish Executive's 'Fresh Talent' policy and majority disagreement with the statement that 'Scotland needs to attract more immigrants'. Flagship Scottish Executive policy on homelessness removes the idea of priority need still supported by the more judgemental public (Curtice, January 2008: 52-3). More (57%) want means tested school meals than non-means tested (35%) (Curtice, May 2008: 45).

ranged from 30%/50% to 34%/66% in January 2000, depending on the wording used by different newspapers. 87% of respondents to a privately funded postal referendum opposed the policy, although turnout was quite low (34.5%, much lower than the famous referendum on water privatisation in 1994), partly because many supporters of the policy boycotted the poll (Curtice, August 2000: 8–9). Still, as Curtice (February 2000: 12) notes, 'a body which had been created in order to ensure that public policy was more attuned to the needs and wishes of Scots had in fact embarked on a change to which the clear majority of the Scottish public was opposed'. Curtice (August 2000: 8) highlights the potential for a smaller opinion-policy link: the critical campaign pushed for a commitment by the Scottish Executive to include, in their new guidance, 'references to the merits of marriage'. Yet, this provision was *not* included in Scottish legislation (SPICe, 2000a: 38). In fact, this omission marks it out from equivalent legislation for England and Wales (Keating et al, 2003: 120–1).

The section 28 experience perhaps provides evidence of a much closer link between government policy and the preferences of a relatively small group of pressure participants such as local authorities, teaching unions and voluntary organisations (chapter 4). However, of course, pressure participants are more successful when they share the same attitudes as the Scottish Executive (see SPICe, 2000: 32). Further, there are instances in which policies receive majority public, but very mixed pressure participant, support—such as the focus on young people when addressing anti-social behaviour (90% support the Scottish Executive line—Curtice, November 2003: 21; see also Curtice, August 2004: 21–2 on arts funding).

The Section 28 experience may also have provided a cautionary tale for politicians seeking a quieter life. Certainly, Winetrobe (May 2002: 65) highlights the experience of Scottish Executive policy on smacking children in these terms (it initially sought to ban the hitting of any child under three, then changed its decision) (Winetrobe, November 2002: 34 also links it to the 'power of parliamentary committees'). Curtice (November 2003: 24) suggests that the Scottish Executive may have avoided the issue of gay marriage and civil partnerships because it was concerned about a 'possible public backlash' (although 41% supported gay marriage, 30% opposed and 24% were ambivalent; see also Winetrobe, February 2004: 42; note that this is a live issue again—see BBC News 8.8.11). Further, its reforms of family law have generally not gone too far ahead of public opinion (with the exception of gay adoption—Curtice, January 2006: 57–62; Cairney, January 2006: 124) and may indeed contribute to changes in opinion (Curtice, January

2008: 52). Then there are issues which have both majority pressure participant and public support. 'Free' personal care for older people seems to fall into this camp, although Curtice (September 2006: 37) notes that its public support is perhaps 'rather less than would be anticipated given its status as a celebrated example of the advantages to Scotland of devolution': 57% support it unconditionally, while 41% favour the means test; 66% do not agree that people should be responsible to pay for their own care when older (it is 32% for pensions).

The Scottish Executive initially trod carefully on one of its few 'flagship' policies – the ban on smoking in public places. Early surveys suggested that 52% were in favour of a ban, with 36% against, but with many differences according to the age and social backgrounds of respondents (Curtice, August 2004: 21). Things also change when we ask about complete versus partial bans, allowing ASH Scotland to argue that 80% wanted a smoking ban, and the Tobacco Manufacturers' Association to argue that 77% did not want a comprehensive ban (Cairney, 2009e: 478–80). Similarly, Curtice (January 2006: 57) argues that the Scottish Executive introduced a comprehensive smoking ban 'in the face of public opposition' because only 25% wanted a complete ban in pubs and bars, while 58% wanted restrictions to certain areas and 15% no restrictions. Its strategy was to 'change the attitudes and behaviour of people in Scotland' (January 2006: 57), and this has proved successful in many countries including Scotland and Ireland (Cairney, 2009: 480). The Scottish Government appears to be taking a similar approach with alcohol policy and minimum pricing in particular (which 55% oppose and 40% support – Curtice, May 2009: 20–1), hoping that the normalisation of the policy, and support form key medical and public health groups, will change public attitudes over time (Cairney, September 2008: 100–1).

In other cases, survey results show that policymakers often have a degree of leeway when making choices. For example, in 2000, the majority of respondents believed that 'some' students should contribute to the cost of their higher education tuition fees, either 'while studying' (19%) or 'once earning' (40%), compared to 37% who believed that 'none should pay' (Curtice, February 2000: 10–2). These attitudes proved conducive to the Scottish Executive policy of subsidising then deferring tuition fees (the 'graduate endowment') although, notably, they are vague enough to be consistent with the UK Government's introduction of top-up fees payable as soon as people reach a certain wage level (which most Scots oppose – Curtice, June 2003: 33–4).

Scottish attitudes to other issues such as nuclear power are also not absolute. While there is a clear preference to develop renewable energy, and considerable concern about nuclear power, a small majority (54%) would support nuclear power stations 'if they helped to avoid us being dependent on energy imported from overseas' (Curtice, May 2006: 39). This may be a crucial distinction in the context of increasing reliance on increasingly-expensive gas imports (a live issue in the summer of 2011). In other words, the SNP's pro-renewable stance is popular, but it (or a successor party) has some room to breathe on nuclear power if it ever needs it (also note that the imports angle was lower, than uncertainty regarding how to dispose of nuclear waste, in the minds of Labour and the Liberal Democrats in the Scottish Executive when they agreed to postpone a decision until after the 2007 election—Cairney, September 2006: 77; January 2007: 86). Similarly, more people may favour renewable energy, but that support dips when people are asked about the issue of ugly pylons. As Curtice (May 2009: 21-2) argues, public attitudes are not as fixed or extreme as they are often portrayed: 'It seems that while people are sympathetic towards renewable energy, they only want it if is neither unsightly nor costly, and if needs be they accept that nuclear power may also have to be part of Scotland's energy mix' (see also Winetrobe, November 2004; 44; Cairney, January 2006: 127; and Cairney, April 2007: 94; September 2009: 60 on the controversial 'Beauly to Denny line').

In other words, public opinion is often a weak guide for established governments—but how important is it during elections? In 2007, it is not difficult to link the SNP's increasing electoral success to its policies which generally chime well with the public (while noting that the parties can also influence those priorities when campaigning), including priorities such: as 'refusing to site in Scotland any new nuclear weapons', setting targets on climate change, minimising the role of the private sector in building schools and hospitals, increasing the visible police force and opposing the closure of local hospitals (Curtice, April 2007: 49-52). Yet, we should be careful with such measures, because many score well in terms of salience but there may be a small margin between public support and opposition (examples include free prescriptions, building nuclear power stations and renewing Trident (although opposition to siting Trident in Scotland is clearer)—Curtice, January 2008: 49; May 2008: 46-7; September 2009: 30). Further, as local tax reform may show, policies can seem popular in advance—see Curtice, April 2007: 50; January 2008: 50; May 2008: 46; January 2009: 20—but unpopular when they produce quiet winners and vocal losers. In addition, the public can only pay attention to a very small proportion of policy decisions—which may lead them to use rules of thumb, such as an assessment of how 'effective' they think each party may be in government. This is something that the SNP in particular benefited from (Curtice, January 2008: 58–60; May 2008: 54; see also chapter 2 on valence politics). Overall, public opinion on policy is important, but in the context of limited attention and the uncertain opinion-policy link described above, it is understandable that we generally focus so much on one major policy issue (constitutional change).

Conclusion

Social attitudes studies in Scotland have long shown that Scotland exhibits unusually strong levels of national identity, and support for devolution, within the UK. Since 1999, the central focus of research has been to gauge devolution's effect on national identity, voting patterns, and attitudes to constitutional change. A perhaps-surprising finding is that devolution has had a clear effect on voting patterns (chapter 2) but a minimal effect on national identity and attitudes to constitutional change in Scotland. The majority of Scots still feel remarkably Scottish, but the majority also expresses a further British identity if they are not forced to choose between the two. Devolution is still the most popular choice in Scotland. The success of the SNP from 2007 has not taken place because of rising levels of Scottishness or because support for independence has risen.

Perceptions of institutional effectiveness are almost as notable. There is a wealth of information on effectiveness and perceptions about who should run or fund particular services, but they do not have a major effect on attitudes to the principle of devolution. Instead, they show that people had unrealistic expectations of devolution which were never met; they were bound to be disappointed (chapter 1). However, unlike early media attitudes to devolution, that disappointment does not produce a negative change in attitudes to devolution itself. Rather, they support greater devolution as a means to make devolved institutions more effective. Or, people generally express ambivalence or minimal interest in devolution, linked to the generally-high belief that devolution has not made much of a difference to their lives.

The election of the SNP from 2007 has had an effect on these attitudes, but not in the way it had hoped. Instead, more people are starting to think that devolution is making a positive difference—something that may lessen their demand for what is often perceived to be a risky and potentially expensive voyage to independence. If anything, the economic crisis and the current agenda about public sector retrenchment may have as much of an effect on the future of constitutional change. In other words, there is growing support in England for change, if not in the form of devolution then at least in the greater representation of England and, perhaps more importantly, a greater devolution of fiscal responsibility to Scotland.

Much less has been written about public perceptions regarding specific policy issues in Scotland, but the monitors give enough information to suggest that the opinion-policy link is just as weak as in other political systems. Devolution has brought policymaking closer to the Scottish public, but that public can only pay so much attention to policy decisions. Devolution has helped produced a small number of important policy differences in Scotland, but surprisingly few can be linked to distinctively Scottish policy preferences. Public preferences may help parties win elections, but they do not give a consistent steer to those parties after they have won. In this sense, Scotland's attitudes are distinctive but its political system is not.

Chapter 8

Changes in Public Policy

We can look back on two contrasting visions for public policy in Scotland after devolution. First, we might have expected a lot of activity and policy divergence. The famous phrase 'Scottish solutions for Scottish problems'[25] sums up the idea that Scotland has distinct policy problems that require distinctive solutions, and perhaps that these solutions can only be produced in a devolved Scotland with dedicated policymaking institutions. It also highlights (although we are asking a lot from a five-word phrase) the likelihood of an avalanche of new and exciting policies after devolution, if only because there would be a backlog of legislation for which Westminster had no time. Second, we might have expected a net *reduction* in activity, as a relatively conservative Scotland breaks free from UK government policy processes often characterised as excessively innovative. A vote for devolution may have been 'a vote to change institutions in order to stay the same' (Mitchell, 2005: 26-7), in the context of the idea that devolution in 1979 could have prevented the worst excesses of the Thatcherite policies that were relatively unpopular in Scotland (McCrone and Lewis, 1999: 17; McGarvey and Cairney: 32-9; Cairney, May 2006: 70).

These contrasting visions are important reference points when we come to assess the difference that devolution has made to public policy. As with all public policy evaluation, this is not an objective process. Rather, we try to gauge the success and failure of policy by questioning the extent to which it lives up to our expectations. In the Scottish case, we either expect a great deal of change or very little; our expectations are likely to be unfulfilled if we expect a lot (as in the discussion of new politics in chapter 1) or we might be pleasantly surprised if we expect very little (surely the key to a contented life). The tendency in the Scottish policy literature is to identify unrealistic expectations, largely to point out that they were not fulfilled (for example, Keating et al,

---

[25] See Parry, 1993: 44 for an example of its use by the Scottish Office in 1993.

2003; McGarvey and Cairney, 2008: 199). It also reflects the wider finding in the policy literature that change tends to be incremental in most political systems. While contemporary theories of public policy seek to explain major policy change, they do so on the understanding that it is rare; that incremental change is the norm. This point is particularly strong if we consider the importance of policy implementation, which may take years or decades to arise (Cairney, 2012).

Of course, 'policy divergence' is not the same as 'policy change'. The former suggests that the policies of two political systems are moving (or moving *further*) apart, while the latter suggests that policy in one system is moving away from the policy of its past. Therefore, we may have significant policy change in Scotland without it marking divergence (as when both governments pursued legislation on anti-social behaviour), while moderate change in Scotland may help produce divergence if policy changes radically in England (as when the UK Government introduced student tuition fees of up to £9000 shortly after the Scottish Government abolished the graduate endowment). Further, that divergence may only be temporary – a process that we can link to the phrase 'laboratory of democracy' (used initially to describe policy diffusion across US states). Policy may diverge in the short term, only to converge in the long term as governments learn lessons from each other and emulate their decisions (Hazell, 2001: 292; Keating et al, 2012). Or, in many cases, UK government policies have a direct or indirect effect on Scottish policies which often limits divergence (particularly when both governments are led by the same party).

To explore these issues, the chapter is set out as follows. First, it summarises the literature on policy change in Scotland and relates this evidence to equivalent discussions in the monitors. Second, it delves into the details of the monitor coverage to explore how policy developed in key areas such as health, education, justice, transport, housing and the media. Local government policy is covered in chapter 6 and economic policy in chapter 9. The most 'Europeanised' policy areas, such as agricultural and environmental policy, are discussed more in chapter 5, since most policy discussions relate largely to Scotland's constrained position rather than substantive policy issues (particularly when we discuss fishing) (Cairney, January 2006: 124; Bell, May 2001: 44). There is no dedicated section comparing policy from 1999–2007 and from 2007 onwards, largely because the election of an SNP Government did not mark a major change in policy direction (for its 'First 100 days' achievements' and first legislative programme, see Cairney September 2007: 76–80). The SNP Government's more notable effects can be found in local government (chapter 6) and, to a lesser extent, in finance (chapter 9) and IGR (chapter 5).

Evolution, Not Revolution

The early monitors covered policy through the lens of the newly created Scottish Executive coalition, exploring the likely tensions in their views on issues such as education (November 1999: 28). They do not refer as much to policy divergence as we might expect. Indeed, the tone of the first report (November 1999: 28-30) often suggests the opposite: there is evidence of learning in health, when Scottish Health minister Susan Deacon's shift of 'policy emphasis away from waiting lists to waiting times' was '"copied" by UK Health Secretary Alan Milburn'; there is a key focus on initiatives to remove old Scottish practices (on feudal tenure—a 'classic case of a Scots law reform measure which had never made it to the top of the list of priorities for parliamentary time at Westminster'—May 2000: 23), follow an established approach in England and Wales (introducing national parks); address issues of power *within* Scotland (land reform, which introduced a community 'right to buy' and public 'right to roam'—*also* 'one of the best examples of a public policy area expected to be given greater priority under devolution'—Winetrobe, May 2001: 52; August 2001: 50; February 2002: 50; May 2002: 64; February 2003: 44; November 2003: 52); while Scottish policy on education largely involves valence issues (i.e. we all agree with the policy aims) such as spending more money and legislating to try to increase standards in schools (August 2000: 18-19). Overall, we have policy change, and we have a sense in which a backlog of (often rather technical) legislation has been passed, but no real sense of a big bang marking a new and divergent Scottish policy agenda.

A notable exception is Winetrobe's (August 2001: 45) discussion, which notes that issues, such as tourism and culture, now arise higher on the Scottish agenda. More importantly, he notes a small number of issues, including mobile phone masts, that have received more scrutiny and attention, with 'this enhanced policy process' leading to 'substantially different outcomes from what may have emerged through the old Scottish Office and UK Parliament arrangements' (August 2001: 45-6). We might also point to initiatives such as the 'national debate on education' (Winetrobe, February 2002: 48; May 2002: 63; August 2002: 48; McGarvey, May 2002: 50; Winetrobe, February 2003: 44) and the greater attention given to the idea of a third party right of appeal to planning application (opposed strongly by business groups—Winetrobe, August 2004: 49; Cairney, September

2006: 78) to highlight events that may not have happened or received as much attention without devolution.

Less positively, Winetrobe (August, 2003: 37) notes that, by 2003, there was still a sense of legislative diarrhoea in the Scottish Parliament which did not dissipate after four years (i.e. the initial period 'loaded with legislation that were building up from the pre-devolution era'). Further, the monitors note a general impression of limited policy success in the first three years (or a Scottish Executive inability to demonstrate 'actual and visible policy delivery' — Winetrobe, August 2001: 12), an outcome accentuated by new leader Jack McConnell's initial promise to 'do less, better' (in part to demonstrate Scottish Executive stability following the death of Dewar and resignation of McLeish — Winetrobe, February 2002: 46) and his instruction to ministers 'not to come up with a raft of new initiatives, but to focus on delivering what is already there'(see also Woods, 2002: 6; although note his attempted initiation of a more 'exciting' second Scottish Executive term — Winetrobe, February 2003: 4).

In other words, there was a lot going on, but often with little to show for it. Indeed, we may get the sense that legislation was used less to pursue policy innovation, and more to establish a dominant relationship over the Scottish Parliament (chapter 3). Or, legislation was used to maintain Scotland's image in relation to the UK. There is a consistent sense in the monitors that Scottish policy is made with one eye on England, based on the idea presented by the UK Government that the devolved territories are not keeping up. In particular, there is constant reference in UK Labour-led policy debates to 'modernising' (Winetrobe, February 2003: 43), and a 'growing perception, however justified, that the more radical, Blairite policies are finally bearing fruit in England, whereas the Executive's approach of piling in ever-greater amounts of money, but apparently without the same degree of radical reform, is not' (Winetrobe, April 2005: 41; similar claims were made in 2007 — Cairney, January 2008: 109–10).

However, the pressure to keep up is more or less strong in different policy areas, depending largely on the agenda-setting ability of the UK Government, the direct comparability of services (NHS waiting times are often the most-used for comparison), and the often-problematic availability of information required to compare services reliably: 'the indicators of service performance are either non-existent, not sophisticated or subject to competition in the selection of evaluation tools' (Cairney, January 2006: 114; compare Andrews and Martin, 2006 with Cairney, 2009d and Keating et al, 2012 on this point). In broader terms, it is not always easy to say what policy is and therefore how successful it is (Cairney, January 2008: 103). Consequently, Scotland is often embarrassed by UK Government commentary, but it is also able to use its preferred measures, such as its 'self-assessed report card' that rated its policy delivery highly (Winetrobe, February 2003: 5; Winetrobe, June 2003: 4), its strategy updates which rate its enterprise and lifelong learning policies highly (Cairney, January 2007: 85) or its data on waiting lists showing that 'outcomes in Scotland are, in many cases, as good as or better than in England' (Permanent Secretary John Elvidge in Cairney, January 2006: 118). A similar approach was taken by the SNP Government (Cairney, January 2008: 110; September 2008: 98). These debates went into overdrive during the coverage of devolution ten-years-on, with English-based think tanks particularly keen to challenge the idea of devolved success (Cairney, May 2009: 49–50).

This early monitor coverage is a good indication of the overall direction of Scottish policy and the constraints involved. The policy literature on Scotland (e.g. Keating, 2005; 2010; McGarvey and Cairney, 2008; Keating and Cairney, 2009; Keating, Stevenson, Cairney and Taylor, 2003) suggests that devolution did not produce radical policy divergence. Rather, we witnessed evolution rather than devolution. As chapter 4 suggests, the phrase 'Scottish solutions to Scottish problems' often refers more to the 'Scottish policy style', or the way in which the Scottish Government *processes* policy in cooperation with pressure participants, than policy divergence (Cairney, 2008; 2009a).

However, there is plenty of evidence of policy *change*, with issues often displaying low divergence but high significance for other reasons. For example, although Scottish and UK legislation on anti-social behaviour was similar (Winetrobe, May 2004: 3; Winetrobe, August 2004: 49; McGarvey, August 2004: 38), Scottish policy was marked by the almost negligible use of anti-social behaviour orders by local authorities (see below). Although both governments passed legislation to further housing stock transfer (in part because Treasury rules effectively precluded alternative strategies—chapter 9; Cairney, January 2006: 116; Cairney, May 2006: 17; McGarvey and Cairney, 2008: 192), the policy was more significant in Scotland because there was more stock to transfer (2008: 213; Stirling and Smith, 2003: 147; McGarvey, June 2003: 54) and the policy would have been harder to introduce in the absence of a Scottish Parliament (see Mitchell in McGarvey and Cairney, 2008: 200). There is also a small number of unexpected issues which may affect Scotland disproportionately, such as ECHR rulings on distinctly Scottish practices, including 'slopping out' in prisons (Winetrobe, May 2004: 53; April 2005: 36–7; Cairney,

September 2006: 76; May 2009: 65; September 2009: 50). Consequently, we need to consider both the formulation and implementation of policy to get a full picture of change in Scotland since devolution.

Devolution Monitors and Policy Areas

Transport, Rural and Environmental Policy

While transport policy receives relatively little attention in the monitors (compared to health and education), it is also one of the first areas to produce divergence based on different Scottish problems and demands. In particular, UK-wide initiatives to introduce congestion charging and workplace parking licensing schemes were initially on the Scottish agenda, only to be rejected following public and business leader opposition, weak MSP support and local authority reluctance to implement the measures (MacMillan, November 2000: 58; Saren and Brown, February 2001: 61; see also February 2000: 24 – 'This is the only part of the [Transport] Bill which really demonstrates any substance'). The only congestion-charging scheme to be proposed was not popular, prompting Edinburgh City Council to hold a referendum, rejected in 2005 (Winetrobe, November 2002: 35; April 2005: 43; see also Cairney, September 2007: 80 on the abolition of bridge tolls). This divergence in policy (congestion charging is used increasingly in England, and London in particular), combined with other issues such as the future of ferry provision in Scottish islands, a dedicated Highlands and Islands transport authority, and the rail link from the Borders to the central belt, provides one of the best examples of 'Scottish problems', since access to rural areas tends to be higher on the agenda than measures to reduce congestion in Scotland, compared to England which has more dense urban areas (May 2000: 27–8; August 2000: 21–4; August 2003: 38–9; Keating et al, 2003: 123).

Scotland may also have distinctive problems when it comes to rural policy, a vague term 'reflecting a desire within the European Commission to broaden agricultural policy, with a new focus on the "economic, social and environmental needs of people living in rural areas"' (McGarvey and Cairney, 2008: 211; Keating, 2005: 204; Jordan and Halpin, 2006). As a relatively rural country, with a low population density outside of a small number of major cities, it has different demands related to health, education and transport. These issues arise periodically in the monitors, including the examples of doctor cover in rural areas (below) and Scottish Government attempts to prevent the closure of rural schools (Cairney, September 2008: 99; 107; May 2009 66–7). There is also some evidence of distinctive implementation of the

EU Common Agricultural Policy, related to Scotland's higher proportion of small farms and its much greater reliance on meat rather than crops as a source of income (and its administration of single farm payments — Cairney, January 2007: 85; January 2009: 58; see also Cairney, May 2009: 70 on its 'days-at-sea' policy to implement the EU Common Fisheries Policy). Yet, there is little to report in the monitors, perhaps largely because the big decisions on agriculture are made elsewhere (chapter 5) and because 'rural' policy is a term used to describe things going on elsewhere in health, education, transport and agricultural policy (McGarvey and Cairney, 2008: 212). The monitors generally highlight small sums of money dedicated to ad hoc funds on initiatives such as 'rural stewardship' (Cairney, September 2006: 76).

The same can be said about environmental policy, since this has become of the EU's key responsibilities and the Scottish Government is generally responsible for implementation (which produces occasional differences, such as the Scottish Executive reluctance to incinerate waste — Cairney, April 2007: 93; May 2008: 91). There are three main exceptions. First, Scotland has the potential to produce a disproportionate amount of renewable energy. While such projects were announced regularly before devolution (see for example Cairney, September 2006: 76-7; January 2007: 86; April 2007: 94), they were championed in particular by Alex Salmond from 2007 in tandem with the SNP's opposition to new nuclear power stations (chapter 5; Cairney, January 2008: 108; January 2009: 56; although see September 2009: 60 on the problematic implementation of renewable incentives). Second, Scotland can set its own climate change targets (it set a more ambitious target than the UK in 2009), even if the measures may be symbolic or very difficult to track until well after the current government has left office (Cairney, September 2008: 95; January 2009: 56-7; May 2009: 69; September 2009: 60). Again, this rapid acceleration of existing policy was a feature of the SNP's first term (Cairney, April 2007: 94). Third, the balance of power between agricultural and environmental lobbies may be tipped towards the former in Scotland (but the latter in England) because agricultural spending is much higher than environmental spending and industries such as meat (and timber and fish) play a more important part in the Scottish economy (which might affect the implementation of EU policy — see for example Cairney, January 2007: 85 on transporting live animals). The same may be said about the balance between transport and the environment, with the M74 alone costing £445m and the Forth bridge over £1bn (Cairney, May 2008: 91; September 2008: 107; the Edinburgh tram project may cost over £700m, but this issue tells us more about party politics than public policy—chapter 3; Cairney, April 2007: 95; May 2009: 69).

Health

The transport experience highlights a key tenet in policy analysis: 'different kinds of policy have different characteristics and are associated with different styles of politics' (Cairney, 2012: 22–3; John, 1998: 7–8). In other words, Scottish policy making may be distinctive, but Scottish transport policymaking also differs from Scottish health policymaking. As in all areas, there are several sources of health policy distinctiveness. First, there are distinctive *problems* related to Scotland's poor health record and its '"sick man of Europe" tag', despite higher spending on health, primarily because it has large deprived areas (particularly in Glasgow) (MacMillan, November 2000: 55; Leicester, 2000b: 34–43). Second, there may be distinctly Scottish consultation *practices* in terms of the 'Scottish policy style' (see chapter 4 and note in health the alleged tendency to consult closely with the medical profession, often at the expense of patient representatives—August 2000: 25–6; MacMillan November, 2000: 58; compare with MacMillan, November 2000: 55 and Saren and Brown, February 2001: 56 which highlight 'consultation with hundreds of patients' on the Scottish NHS plan). Third, there are often distinctly Scottish *solutions*, including moves to focus increasingly on public health policy and health inequalities in Scotland (Leicester, 2000b: 38–9; Jervis and Plowden, 2001: 30; although not always to the extent noted in Wales—Hazel, 2001: 257).

However, there are also strong forces for similarities and convergence. First, the overall policy context is the same across the UK. The NHS is generally a tax-funded service, open to all, and free at the point of use. In these terms, the NHS model is similar across the UK even if it addresses different problems and administers policy in very different ways (Jervis and Plowden, 2000: 8). Second, medical profession influence is evident across the UK and it often produces policies that would not be chosen by electorally-obsessed politicians. For example, the Kerr report on the NHS in Scotland called for the greater centralisation of some acute services, to produce the critical mass of patients required to train doctors in specialist procedures, often at the expense of popular local hospital services (Cairney, January 2006: 118; some notable closures were halted by the SNP against Kerr's wishes—Cairney, September 2007: 84—but supported by other experts—Cairney, January 2008: 107). This move was reinforced by the EU Working Time Directive which limited the amount of time that junior doctors could work and be on call (although few people really know how many hours that doctors work), and it may even have been influenced by the use of public-private-partnerships to fund hospital building (Cairney, September 2006: 73; see chapter 9 on PPP). The medical profession is also described by Woods (2001b: 4–5) as a key influence on the implementation of health policy ('workforce issues have the potential to blow the Executive's plans off-course').

Third, there are strong pressures to keep up with 'modernisation' reforms in England; to minimise waiting times in the NHS and demonstrate healthcare efficiency and/or effectiveness in a department that accounts for one-third of the Scottish Government's (DEL) budget (May 2000: 30–3; August 2000: 24–7; MacMillan, November 2000: 55; Saren and Brown, February 2001: 55; note that attention to journey times arises periodically in transport policy—August 2000: 21; Cairney, January 2007: 87—as do the education equivalents, pupil testing and exam results—Cairney, January 2009: 55—and class sizes, below). Indeed, the language of waiting times and lists, how they compare in Scotland and England, and how honest ministers are about the figures (or at least how they are calculated and presented), has always dominated Scottish debates—hence their almost ever-present discussion in the monitors (Winetrobe, February 2002: 47; May 2002: 63; August 2002: 47; November 2002: 34; February 2003: 43; June 2003: 67; February 2004: 42; August 2004: 50; November 2004: 42; April 2005: 42; see Cairney, January 2006: 115; 117–18 and May 2006: 72 on 'hidden waiting lists'; Cairney, September 2006: 74; see also Woods, 2001a: 27–8; Woods, 2002: 7; 15).

Cairney (April 2007: 91) reports a brief move by the Scottish Executive away from a waiting time fixation but, by the next report, the new SNP Government had introduced its plan to abolish the Scottish Executive's 'hidden' waiting lists and to introduce the idea of a patient's right to a waiting time guarantee enshrined in legislation (Cairney, September 2007: 77). Combined with a bill to introduce local health board elections (or at least pilots in some parts of Scotland—Cairney, January 2008: 107), the SNP's policy was geared towards the localisation of health decision-making and accountability (Cairney, September 2007: 80; Scott, January 2009: 66; May 2009: 81). The SNP government also introduced new targets related to the first GP referral rather than the first hospital visit. Although its patient rights bill was amended in Parliament (before it passed in 2011), to make clear that the patient's charter involves limited legal redress, the waiting time and list game has now been firmly institutionalised. The Scottish Government has contributed to the sort of unintended consequences and gaming by health authorities that have become so associated with targets in England (Cairney, May 2008: 84; September 2008: 98; January 2009: 49; May 2009: 57–8; compare with the move in the UK from targets to 'guarantees' – Cairney, September 2009).

These dual pressures – distinctive problems and processes but common agendas – may explain first Health Secretary Susan Deacon's dual commitments to 'develop distinctive solutions for Scottish needs' and the 'shared commitment of the UK Government and the Scottish Executive to deliver a 21st century patient-centred NHS' (August, 2000: 27). It may also explain why so much attention was paid in 2000 to the amount of time that elapsed between the publication of the NHS National Plan for England and Wales and the 'equivalent Scottish Health Plan' and why, 'The challenge for the Scottish Health Minister is whether she can match the English and Welsh plans' (MacMillan, November 2000: 54). In other words, in areas such as health we can see the strongest pressure to converge and even to coordinate policy within the Labour party. Consequently, 'For the most part, the Scottish strategy is fairly similar to the English Plan' (Saren and Brown, February 2001: 57).

In this context, it is notable that one of the first Scottish Executive initiatives was to reorganise the NHS in a way that marked significant divergence from England and began to reinforce its distinctiveness on administration, targetry and the private sector. While the UK Government extended the idea of an internal market, in which organisations such as 'foundation' hospitals competed for the 'business' of local commissioning bodies, the Scottish Government sought to remove it (Saren and Brown, February 2001: 54–5; Woods, 2001b: 3; Greer, 2004; Hazell, 2001: 256–7). Rather than giving hospital trusts more autonomy to compete (as in England), it placed them more firmly in the hands of health boards, 'reminiscent of the days when hospitals were "directly managed units" of health authorities and boards' (Jervis and Plowden, 2001: 11; see also Greer, 2001: 29). It then introduced legislation in 2003 to finish the job (Winetrobe, August 2003: 36).

The first Scottish NHS plan also places less emphasis on the use of targets or, if it sets targets, they are couched in a rather qualified way, without the precise and punitive language we see in the NHS in England (Saren and Brown, February 2001: 55). This is a general feature of UK-Scottish Government comparisons; the caricature of top-down UK Government targetry is often contrasted with a more flexible Scottish system (Cairney, May 2006: 72; September 2006: 74; January 2007: 74; September 2009: 54), even though the Scottish Executive was not averse to *occasional* bouts of top-down policymaking (see Cairney, May 2006: 71–2 for the examples of Lewis MacDonald and the appearance of top-down dental policy reform, and Tom McCabe changing the retirement age of local government workers, driven by EU rules; Cairney, May 2008: 85 discusses the Scottish Government's surprisingly top-down approach to the new GP contract).

The Scottish Executive bought and effectively renationalised a private hospital to aid its reduction of waiting times – the opposite of moves in England to encourage the use of the private sector to deliver NHS services (Winetrobe, August 2002: 47; February 2004: 42; Jervis and Plowden, 2001: 12). Health Minister Malcolm Chisholm was also reported to be 'refusing to regard patients as "consumers"' – in contrast to the rhetoric pursued by the UK Government (Winetrobe, November 2003: 53). This policy tone was extended by the SNP Government, with Health Secretary Nicola Sturgeon keen to keep the private sector out of NHS delivery and describing a '"battle of ideas" between an ethos of public service and mutuality and one driven by the private market' (Cairney, September 2008: 98; May 2009: 56; although this was complicated 'by her decision to remove the ban on patients, in exceptional cases, "topping up" their medical provision' and receiving private treatment at reduced cost – Cairney, January 2009: 48; May 2009: 57).

There is also notable divergence in one of the Scottish Executive's flagship policies – personal care for older people (see Simeon, 2003; Woods, 2001b: 5–7; Woods, 2002: 8; Bell, November 2001: 48–50; Saren and Brown, February 2001: 9–13). The key source of divergence came from the Scottish Executive's decision to fund personal care provision universally (for those who were assessed and met the criteria), both for people living at home (who would pay no fee) and in care homes (who would only pay 'hotel costs'). The UK Government's preferred approach was means-tested personal care. The policy can potentially feature in several chapters of this book:

- as an example of unusual parliamentary pressure (McGarvey and Cairney, 2008: 101; Simeon, 2003);

- as a source of tension within the Scottish Executive coalition (the Liberal Democrats were more in favour of the policy – see Winetrobe, November 2004: 42 for former minister Sam Galbraith's description, 'a right-wing Liberal policy forced on Labour');

- as a source of tension within the UK Labour party and between Scottish and UK governments (the UK Government favoured means tested personal care arrangements and Labour ministers wanted Scottish ministers to agree; McLeish made the announcement '*before* an approach was made to the Treasury' — Mitchell, 2004: 22-3; see also Saren and Brown, February 2001: 50 — 'Scottish Labour MPs were known to be furious about the decision to implement the Sutherland report in full');

- as an example of policy learning that did not lead to transfer between the Scottish and UK executives, despite UK pressure participants pointing to Scotland and 'arguing that a separate policy was discriminatory' (Winetrobe, August 2002: 47; Cairney, May 2006: 74-5; January 2008: 109-10);

- as an example of the idea that Scotland is a well resourced 'land of milk and honey' (chapter 9; Bell, February 2001: 48-9). Other examples include plans announced in 2004 to deliver a 'national free bus fare' scheme for over-60s (Winetrobe, November 2004: 43; April 2005: 43), free eye tests (Cairney, May 2006: 75-6), the funding of certain expensive medicines for cancer patients (Cairney, January 2007: 81), the McCrone review of teacher pay (below), the abolition of student tuition fees (below), the introduction of free prescriptions and the freezing of council tax (Cairney September 2007: 77; January 2008: 107; May 2008: 85; January 2009: 49; Bort, January 2008 — but note that almost 90% of prescriptions in England are free — Keating et al, 2012).

However, its place in *this* chapter is secured because the policy is an excellent example of the difference between policy choices and their implementation — a point flagged early and consistently by Winetrobe (May 2002: 63; February 2003: 45; June 2003: 67; May 2004: 60; April 2005: 42; Bell, February 2004: 31-2; compare with social work policy and the successful smoking ban implementation in Cairney, September 2006: 69; note that there may be greater problems of implementing care policy in England — Bell, May 2002: 51). Winetrobe notes particular concern regarding the dispute between care homes, local and central governments. Indeed, this tension proved to be the main obstacle to the successful implementation of the policy in care homes: local authorities argued that the Scottish Executive provided insufficient funds for the policy; care homes argued that local authorities provided insufficient funds for personal care and hotel costs; and, care homes used high hotel costs for some patients to subsidise the perceived shortfall in funding (Cairney, September 2006: 69–70; May 2008: 88; McGarvey and Cairney, 2008: 215). In other words, the Scottish Executive provided £145 per person per week for the policy, but many people did not receive the full financial benefit (they also lost their entitlement to UK benefits previously used to part-fund personal care) (2008: 215). Pressures related to implementation, and the perception that care costs would be unsustainable in the long term, prompted a review of the policy in 2005, but little was resolved. While, by 2007, the policy seemed less problematic (Cairney, January 2006: 119; April 2007: 90), it soon hit the headlines again in 2008, with the Scottish Government facing evidence of patchy coverage (with some local authorities more likely to maintain long waiting lists or charge for some care) but also mindful of its commitment not to interfere in local authority policymaking (Cairney, May 2008: 88–9; September 2008: 99).

These examples of major divergence in policy *choices* are limited. However, there are also examples of *practices* that develop differently, partly because problems are addressed by separate bodies often dealing with different problems or operating in a different environment (see Cairney, January 2008: 109–10). A good example is NICE (National Institute for health and Clinical Excellence), a UK body which assesses the effectiveness of health technologies, including medicines, and makes recommendations to health authorities on whether or not they should be funded by the NHS (note that it does not have the capacity or time consider all technologies). Scotland has separate bodies to perform this function. The Health Technology Board for Scotland was established in 2000 (see May 2000: 32; GPC Scotland, April 2000; GPC Scotland, June, 2000: 7; GPC Scotland, September: 4; Woods, 2001b: 11; Woods, 2002: 14; it was later subsumed within NHS Quality Improvement Scotland, then Healthcare Improvement Scotland) and it performed a similar function, assessing multiple technologies in a similar way (often for services as a whole). Further, the idea was that it would adopt NICE recommendations 'in the Scottish context' and perform its own technology appraisals which 'relate specifically to health priorities that have been identified in Scotland' (Saren and Brown, February 2001: 60–1). Then, the Scottish Medicines Consortium was established in 2001 (and strengthened in 2003). It makes recommendations to the Area Drug and Therapeutics committees of Scottish health boards on single medicines (almost all recommendations are accepted). A process has developed in which NICE and the SMC perform different functions and co-exist without necessarily having to cooperate. The SMC is generally quicker to assess medicines (and it considers most available medicines) and English (and international) health authorities often make decisions based on its recommendations; NICE assesses multiple technologies, produces more evidence over a longer period, and its recommendations are often adopted in Scotland (in these cases, their recommendations supersede those of the SMC) (interview, SMC, 2006; see Healthcare Improvement Scotland, 2011). Consequently, we have evidence of divergence in operation but regular convergence in health policy — with the exception of a small number of cases where Scottish health boards approve funding for a medicine but English health authorities do not (note the *occasional* examples of people crossing the Scotland-England border to 'benefit from better health care' — Cairney, January 2007: 81–2; this hardly represents the English public 'backlash' discussed in chapter 7 and Jervis and Plowden, 2001: 19).

Another example is the consultant (doctor) contract issue, which arose when doctors in Scotland voted to accept the terms of a new contract in 2002 while doctors in England voted against (Winetrobe, November 2002: 34; although the talks in Scotland broke down too — an event which Winetrobe, August 2003: 38 links to 'UK government interference' — before contracts were signed in Scotland and England — Winetrobe, November 2003: 53). One part of the difference is the difference in the ability of doctors in England to command fees for private practice (for which there is generally a greater demand or provision in England). Yet, there are also key similarities, including the high stakes related to NHS waiting times which give doctors power during negotiations. Indeed, the Scottish Executive came under heavy criticism in 2005 for 'spending NHS funds on "crisis management" rather than long term capacity' when the details of overtime payments to doctors to 'clear the backlog' were revealed (Cairney, January 2006: 117; May 2006: 75). The contract talks were also driven by the need to 'meet the European Working Time Directive' which limited the number of hours a doctor could work per week, a stipulation that affected most doctors on call in rural areas (Cairney, May 2006: 75; McGarvey and Cairney, 2008: 161; see also Cairney, April 2007: 91–2; September 2007: 83–4 on different arrangements for nurses' pay).

Mental Health

Mental health links well to several of the reasons given for the need for political devolution: administrative devolution had already allowed policy to develop separately, producing new problems and solutions; devolution allowed parliamentary space for legislative reform; and, there is evidence of policy learning, with the UK Government drawing on Scotland's experience on mental incapacity policy (Cairney, January 2007: 77–80). Further, the strongest single example of a divergence of policy styles comes in mental health (Cairney, May 2006: 71; Cairney, January 2007: 77). The Millan review of mental health legislation is first discussed by Saren and Brown (February, 2001: 59; see also Woods, 2001b: 9; Woods, 2002: 11–12) listing recommendations which include potentially-divisive 'Measures to allow for some patients to be compulsorily treated in the community rather than hospital' (previously, the restricted number of beds effectively restricted the number of compulsory detentions) (Saren and Brown, February, 2001: 59). This may be why Winetrobe (November 2002: 34; June 2003: 67) twice describes the bill as 'controversial' (it may also be because the bill took two days to process in Parliament, with Presiding Officer David Steel concerned that the Scottish Parliament was being 'bounced' with too many amendments — Cairney, 2006b: 189–92).

As such, it takes careful consultation to ensure the passage of a bill built on the support (or, in some cases, reduced opposition) and expertise of pressure participants. This was in evidence in Scotland, and the bill passed smoothly, because the Scottish Executive placed considerable emphasis on patient rights and state responsibilities. In contrast, the UK Government suffered constant problems and eventually withdrew its bill (which included provisions on preventative detention) in favour of a limited bill addressing little more than its ECHR commitments, largely because almost all pressure participants objected to its emphasis on public safety and the preventative detention of mentally ill people (Cairney, January 2007: 77; Cairney, 2009a). The implementation of mental health policy is more difficult to track, because some outcomes (such as an increase in prescribing medication for depression, or a reduction in psychiatric hospital beds) may be a sign of success to some but failure to others, and the issue of resources and the level of realistic success is ever-present (see for example Cairney, January 2007: 78–80; April 2007: 90–1; January 2008: 107; May 2008: 88; January 2009: 51; and Buckland 2011; see Cairney, May 2008: 99 on a 'manically depressed and suicidal man … apparently advised [by NHS24] to "drink a glass of warm milk"'). We also get a different impression of convergence and divergence in mental health if we go beyond this kind of legislation. The UK Government was much more likely to learn from the Scottish experience on mental incapacity. Further, both governments tended to learn from each other on issues such as depression, 'recovery' and wellbeing (although the UK Government delivers such policies in markedly different ways – Cairney, May 2008: 87; May 2009: 58).

Public Health

Public health provides one of the highest profile examples of policy innovation and occasional divergence (before policy transfer and learning within the UK). The Scottish Executive had made an early commitment to enhance anti-smoking measures (May 2000: 30), but the first signs of innovation came from the attempts by Nicola Sturgeon (then opposition MSP) to introduce legislation to ban tobacco advertising, largely because the UK Government was taking too long (the eventual outcome was UK legislation applied to Scotland) (Winetrobe, November 2001: 63–4). We can see a similar process with the comprehensive ban on smoking in public places. Initially, a quite-limited member's bill was introduced by SNP MSP Stewart Maxwell to 'regulate smoking in food premises' (Winetrobe, August 2003: 38) and this rose up the political agenda quite quickly, especially when it received health committee support (Winetrobe, August 2004: 50). The Scottish Executive then made a deal with Maxwell, to trade (a) Maxwell's support for a comprehensive bill for (b) the Scottish Executive's praise for Maxwell's efforts (and legislation he could easily get behind) (Cairney, 2007a). This was followed by a huge Scottish Executive consultation on the smoking ban and, more amusingly, a trip by Jack McConnell to Ireland, organised largely to symbolise his road-to-Damascus change of mind and his shift of support to a measure that became his best chance to 'show the current administration to be capable of ambitious policy-making' (Winetrobe, November 2004: 42).

The smoking ban is one of the very few examples of the IK Government following Scotland in a high profile area (for lower profile examples, on healthy eating campaigns, missing persons schemes and DNA storage, see Cairney, September 2008: 107; May 2009: 64; Keating et al, 2012). Indeed, it is notable that the cause of the comprehensive (rather than partial, exempting pubs and clubs) ban in England came from a free vote of MSPs, not the UK Government (Cairney, 2007b). In any event, this one measure of tobacco policy is misleading because tobacco policy as a whole is generally similar across the UK (Cairney, January 2006: 116) and policy still continues in tandem, such as when both raised the smoking age to 18 (Cairney, 2007: 83; September 2008: 101; May 2009: 59; September 2009: 57).

As chapter 7 suggests, the Scottish Executive was careful to make sure that the smoking ban would not be electorally expensive. While it expected some unpopularity, it also knew that it had SNP and Liberal Democrat support and that social attitudes to smoking bans shift after the legislation passes. The Scottish Government appears to be taking a similar approach with alcohol policy, although it has been undermined (until 2011) by cross-party opposition to measures such as minimum pricing. The treatment of alcohol policy from 2007–11 was unfortunate given that the Scottish Executive seemed to be heading in broadly the same direction until 2007 (Cairney, April 2007: 92). It began with agenda-setting plans to tax the sellers of alcohol for NHS treatment, followed by proposed legislative measures to raise the legal age to 21, introduce minimum pricing for alcohol, reduce the drink-drive limit and limit drinks promotions (Cairney, May 2008: 86; January 2009: 50; May 2009: 59–61) as well as to use licensing laws to further prohibit alcohol promotion (Cairney, September 2009: 57). As in the case of tobacco, alcohol policy has some appeal to governments with limited budgets because it is primarily a 'regulatory' policy that costs much less than 'distributive' policies such as personal care (Mitchell, 2004: 27).

Drugs policy enjoys an unusual position, having a high profile in a small number of cases (usually drug-related deaths) but often one of the lowest profile policies of its kind. This is largely because the Scottish Executive does not want to advertise its tendency towards 'harm reduction' policy, keeping drug users alive long enough to reform their behaviour, rather than the more populist low tolerance and abstention (a policy rejected quietly in the UK in the 1980s after it was blamed for the rise in drug-related HIV infection). This policy was effectively reaffirmed from 2005, with most measures designed to help reduce drug related deaths through better care and training, 'improvements to joined-up government' and health education (Cairney, January 2006: 117; May 2006: 74–5; September 2006: 75). It appeared to come under threat following a high profile case of the death of a two year old who drank his parents' methadone. However, the £1.7m announced for an abstinence drug treatment represents a small proportion of NHS spend and is better seen as a pilot and another option for people who choose to go 'cold turkey' (Cairney, January 2007: 83). This approach continued from 2007 (Cairney, September 2007: 83). The Conservatives pushed successfully for more abstinence-based treatments as part of their cooperation deal with the SNP Government, but these programmes took place within the context of an overall harm-reduction focused service (Cairney, May 2008: 86; September 2008: 102; January 2009: 51; September 2009: 56).

Higher Education

The first major source of potential Scottish Executive coalition conflict, policy change *and* divergence came from the reform of tuition fees. It abolished up-front fees in favour of a 'graduate endowment' of about £2000, payable after graduation. It had commissioned the Cubie review which proposed quite ambitious reforms — reintroducing some student grants, abolishing up-front fees for all Scottish students, and asking students to make a contribution when earning over £25000 (SPICe, 2000b: 2). The reforms were diluted to some extent, partly because Scotland was tied closely to the UK system of student loan and fee repayment (Cairney, September 2006: 71; Cairney, 2006: 434). However, they still caused significant policy change and divergence, and represented to the Liberal Democrats 'as much as they were going to get', given the reluctance of the Labour Party to entertain a different policy in Scotland (February 2000: 25; MacMillan, November 2000: 52–3).

The reforms were described negatively by Tony Blair when Prime Minister (Winetrobe, November, 2002: 35), but there is less evidence of direct interference when compared to free personal care. Instead, the UK Government produced its own policy in 2003, to introduce top-up fees, that had a major knock-on effect in Scotland. It is interesting to note the unusual degree of concern in Scotland about the knock-on effect, and most notably the 'fear that the UK Government's policy will produce both an increase in students and a relative decline in resources leading to loss of staff to English Universities', which produced regular calls from Universities to fill the funding gap or, occasionally, for Scotland to follow the UK Government lead (Winetrobe, February 2003: 44; August 2003: 39; November 2003: 54; May 2004: 59–60; August 2004: 47; Cairney, April 2007: 93; January 2008: 106; May 2008: 90; January 2009: 55–6; May 2009: 67; September 2009: 59). We can also detect a prolonged period of uncertainty about the Scottish Executive's response, with a detectable strain within the Scottish Executive coalition and Jack McConnell feeling the need to state that 'there will be no top-up tuition fees for Scottish higher education students as long as I am First Minister' (Winetrobe, February 2004: 40). This announcement was followed by a provision in Scottish legislation to allow ministers to vary fees for UK students not living in Scotland — introduced following 'the concern that more English students will study medicine in Scotland (crowding out Scottish students who are more likely to work in the Scottish NHS after graduation)' (Cairney, January 2006: 119).

While the rise of fees for medical courses from £1200 to £2700 in 2005 was seen by some as the 'slippery slope' to top-up fees in

Scotland, the election of the SNP in 2007 ensured movement in the opposite direction. The SNP abolished the graduate endowment in 2008 – probably its highest profile and most important piece of legislation from 2007-11, even if it did not fulfil its additional pledge to help pay off loans taken out by former students to pay for their graduate endowments (Cairney, January 2008: 106; September 2008: 106; January 2009: 55; May 2009: 67). This has become a live issue again, following the decision of the UK Government to allow Universities to charge £9000 fees, prompting the Scottish Government to allow Scottish Universities to charge the same to UK students not living in Scotland. Consequently, there is added potential for a legal case (based on an appeal to the ECtHR) on the issue of charging students in the rest of the UK as a form of discrimination (McGlauchlin, 2001).

Compulsory Education

Winetrobe (November 2002: 35; see also Cairney, May 2006: 74) describes education as a 'key front in the "devolution diversity" debate on the future direction of the public services', following early signs that Tony Blair was critical of Scotland's reliance on comprehensive schools. Yet, compulsory education became increasingly removed from that debate because Scotland has had its own education system for centuries and it is difficult to compare its operation and outputs (such as exam results) in the same way that we can with health. There have been various attempts to provide Scottish-style league tables, but they are generally designed to take into account the social composition of pupils (Cairney, January 2006: 121). Similarly, while ministers occasionally make pronouncements on dealing with 'failing schools' (Winetrobe, February 2004: 40; McGarvey, August 2004; 36), there is nothing like the English media culture of naming and shaming head teachers (see also Cairney, May 2009: 65; September 2009: 59 on the 'blame culture' in social services). Further, while Jack McConnell toyed with the idea of 'selection', 'specialist schools' (Winetrobe, November 2004: 42), 'schools of ambition' ('with the First Minister letting it be known that old "progressive" policies have failed' – Winetrobe, April 2005: 42; Cairney, January 2006: 121; September 2006: 75), and 'skills academies' (Cairney, January 2007: 84) little policy innovation was in evidence.

Education was more likely to enter the divergence debate as part of the idea that Scotland is well funded compared to England (see chapters 7 and 9 and above; compare with Winetrobe, August 2004: 47 on funding constraints prompting the Scottish Executive to 'fall more in line with UK policy'). In effect, this is a UK-Government inspired focus on funding and efficiency through the back door. As chapter 6 notes, the McCrone review of teacher pay was notable for its style as much as its substance (see MacMillan, November 2000: 54 on its positive effect on the EIS, Scotland's largest teaching union). Yet, it is difficult to ignore the size of the pay deal, with a rise of 21.5% over three years offered by the Scottish Executive (Saren and Brown, February 2001: 62; accounting for one-quarter of Scotland's increased budget — Bell February 2001: 46–7; followed by a 4-year 10% deal in 2004 — Winetrobe, August 2004: 47). Its importance at the time was perhaps overshadowed by higher attention to the SQA fiasco and its aftermath (see Saren and Brown, February 2001: 62–4 and chapter 4), but it soon returned amid claims that teachers were not fulfilling the terms of the deal, that the costs of the settlement were 'getting out of hand' and that the Scottish Executive was not delivering 'improved efficiency' (Winetrobe, May 2002: 63; August 2002: 48; February 2003: 44; June 2003: 66; May 2004: 60).

The deal became a key source of party-political tension following concerns by the Scottish Parliament Audit Committee that it had not led to better educational attainment or 'value-for-money', and by the education inspectorate HMIe that it had 'limited impact.' Jack McConnell's reply was that the absence of strikes helped secure educational attainment, while the Scottish Executive pointed to 'unprecedented stability' in schools and presented the deal as the solution to low morale and recruitment (it was close to its 53000-teachers target by 2007 which, combined with falling school rolls, reduced the pupil-teacher ratio markedly), and the HMIe lauded the post-agreement local negotiating processes (Cairney, September 2006: 72; January 2007: 75; April 2007: 93). In other words, the Scottish Executive defended the first and subsequent deals (as did the Scottish Government in 2007 — Cairney, January 2008: 104–5). It was not until 2011 that teachers were offered a much-reduced offer in the light of new economic constraints (chapter 6).

One of the highest profile policy issues regarded the pursuit of reduced class sizes (an aim that has similar resonance in England). It is education's equivalent of waiting times and receives disproportionate public and media attention (Winetrobe, June 2003: 66; August 2003: 39; April 2005: 42; Cairney, May 2006: 74; September 2006: 75). The election of the SNP ensured that more attention would be paid to class sizes, largely because it set targets and allocated money for local authorities to achieve it, but it did not enforce targets with legislation or ring fence the money (chapter 6; Cairney, January 2008: 104; May 2008: 90; January 2009: 53; September 2009: 58–9; May 2009: 65–6; see Cairney September 2008: 104–5 on the link between PPP and class sizes). This presents us with two measures of policy success (top-down and bottom-up), discussed further in chapter 11.

Justice

The Scottish legal system was one area protected under the Union of 1707 and Scots law remains distinct within the UK. Scotland has its own court system and often its own behaviour, based, for example, on the greater ability of High Court judges to use their discretion when passing sentence (judges in England and Wales receive more guidance from the UK Government) and the separate nature of legal education, qualification and socialisation. Yet, justice is also an area which requires considerable intergovernmental cooperation to avoid legal loopholes (when, for example, someone could come to Scotland to avoid punishment in England) and it accounted for a large proportion of Sewel motions (chapter 5). Further, it is an area in which we have seen considerable policy convergence across Europe, driven by legislation to allow the Scottish and other legal systems to become consistent with the laws associated with the European Convention on Human Rights. The Scotland Act 1988 incorporated the ECHR into Scots law (February 2000: 19), meaning that all Scottish Parliament legislation must be compliant. In 2000, the Scottish Executive introduced a bill to amend various aspects of the law to make it ECHR complaint (on issues such as tribunals for mandatory life prisoners — MacMillan, November 2000: 8) and in 2006 it introduced a bill to establish a Scottish Commissioner on Human Rights (Cairney, April 2007: 19). Further, since 1999, there have been many court cases with public policy consequences in justice and other areas (see, for example, chapter 4 on the independence of temporary sheriffs, this and chapter 5 on 'slopping out' and chapter 10 on the recent Cadder and Fraser cases; see MacMillan, November 2000: 40 on planning appeals; Winetrobe, August 2001: 38; November 2001: 51-2 on mental health law; Winetrobe, February 2002: 39 on self governing schools; Winetrobe, May 2002: 55; August 2002: 39-40; August 2003: 34; August 2004: 39 on fox hunting; Winetrobe, April 2005: 36-7 on prisoner segregation; Trench, April 2007: 74 on 'the disclosure of an accused's sexual history in trials for sexual offences'; and, Trench, January 2008: 90-1 on the relationship between court delays and the right to a fair trial).

Keating et al (2003: 130) argue that coalition government made an early difference to justice policy, with 'less emphasis on hard-line law and order policies' associated with Jim Wallace's tenure as Justice Secretary. Further, Wallace made decisions often in the face of Labour ministers who sought a more punitive approach, before Labour secured the justice portfolio from 2003–7 (2003: 130). Winetrobe (August 2002: 45) identifies tensions in May 2002 when Jack McConnell created a justice policy group that excluded Wallace, a move 'interpreted not just as an attempt by Labour to make law and order a "Labour" issue, but … also linked to the abortive attempts to reshuffle Wallace out of the Justice portfolio'. Justice was a 'central election issue' and, by June, the Scottish Executive had begun to consult on measures to address anti-social behaviour, including the 'electronic tagging of children' (Winetrobe, August 2003: 38), a Labour-led measure that put strain on its relationship with the Liberal Democrats (November 2003: 54).

The Anti-social Behaviour bill proved troublesome during its passage (February 2004: 42), particularly since it arose during a period of embarrassing pressure on the Scottish Executive (regarding, for example, the escape from prison of a convicted murderer) and faced criticism from a wide range of bodies, including the Commissioner for Children and Young People, senior police officers and clergy (Winetrobe, May 2004: 57; August 2004: 49). Yet, it passed because 'the Lib Dems have generally fallen in line with Labour despite obvious misgivings' (Winetrobe, August 2004: 49). After the legislation passed, the Scottish Executive hired a truck to go on a roadshow to advertise the new measures (Cairney, September 2006: 76). However, ASBOs never took off in Scotland. They doubled in two years after a slow start, but were effectively abolished by the Scottish Government (Scott, September 2006: 53; Cairney, May 2006: 70; Cairney, January 2007: 86; September 2008: 103–4; May 2009: 63; compare with the number of women in prison, which has doubled since devolution – Cairney, September 2006: 76 – perhaps contributing to a shift from prison sentences to community orders for those who fail to pay fines below £500 (a key cause of female imprisonment) – Cairney, January 2007: 87).

Justice remained high on the Scottish Executive's legislative agenda throughout its 2003–7 term, with bills passed from 2005 on sexual offences, the management of offenders, criminal injuries compensation, the tagging of offenders on parole, sentencing reform, football banning orders, drug testing, penalties for knife crime, and sectarian marching (Cairney, January 2006: 123–4; compare *The Herald* 2011 and Scottish Government 2011a on the *use* of football banning orders). Labour's last legislative and policy programme before 2007 included measures on prisoner release, prostitution, knives, hate crime, kerb crawling (seeking sex from prostitutes) and measures to reduce reconviction rates (Cairney, September 2006: 76; January 2007: 86; April 2007: 94–5).

The SNP agenda on justice was distinctive to some extent with, for example, Justice Secretary Kenny MacAskill linked strongly to its agenda on sentencing reform and the eventual abolition of prison sentences below six months in favour of community service (Cairney, May 2008: 89; September 2008: 103; January 2009: 52; May 2009: 62). At the same time, much of the SNP's response was in reaction to external pressures (prison overcrowding) and the move to home detention and community sentences was an acceleration of previous Scottish Executive policy (Cairney, May 2008: 89; September 2009: 58; see Winetrobe, November 2004: 44 on the Scottish Executive's 'early release' prison scheme). MacAskill was also subject to intense pressure on the issue of knife crime, but this tells us more about party politics under minority government than about Scottish Government policy (Cairney, May 2009: 62-3; September 2009: 58). Indeed, all major parties had fairly punitive agendas, while most attention focused on what seemed to be small beer given the Scottish Government's range of responsibilities—the SNP's commitment to increase police numbers by 1000 (Cairney, September 2007: 78; May 2008: 89; May 2009: 64; September 2009: 58).

Housing and Homelessness

Housing policy displays a combination of policy divergence and innovation but also implementation problems and reserved policy constraints. For example, the Scottish Executive introduced innovative legislation on homelessness in 2002. It was based on an almost-complete acceptance of 59 recommendations of a task force populated by housing and homelessness groups such as Shelter, which described it as 'providing the country with the most progressive homelessness policy in the UK and arguably Western Europe' (McGarvey, November 2002: 28; see also Woods, 2002: 8 on the NHS homelessness plan). However, the same groups became disenchanted a few years later when there was no ministerial weight behind implementation and no new money to help local authorities implement (McGarvey and Cairney, 2008: 215-6; Cairney, 2009d: 366). It was also undermined by legislation on anti-social behaviour (which removed social housing entitlement to those subject to an ASBO) and the 'right to buy' social housing (Cairney, January 2006: 115). The consequence of a wider definition, and problematic implementation, produced a significant rise in homelessness and the low likelihood of the Scottish Government meeting its target of eradication by 2012 (Cairney, January 2006: 115; May 2006: 77; September 2006: 78).

Chapter 9 suggests that the large scale voluntary transfer (LSVT) of council homes to housing associations was a Scottish Executive policy made out of necessity and a lack of room to manoeuvre on Treasury rules (but see also reports of stock transfer representing a 'resounding success' in Cairney, May 2006: 77). It also supported people's 'right to buy' their council and housing association homes. However, from 2005, this policy came under increasing pressure as the availability of social rented homes reduced (Winetrobe, April 2005: 43). The Scottish Executive reduced, incrementally, public entitlement to the right-to-buy (following the sale of 500000 homes from 1980–2007, contributing to 67% owner occupation in Scotland—Scott, January 2007: 56). South Ayrshire was the first to seek Scottish Executive permission stop its tenants buying their homes (to maintain its social housing stock) in 2004, followed by many others (McGarvey, August 2004: 38; Cairney, September 2006: 78; April 2007: 90; see Cairney, January 2007: 76 on a report finding mixed results of the right-to-buy). The Scottish Executive also met a commitment to provide '18000 affordable homes by 2006' (Cairney, September 2006: 78). The Scottish Government continued these policies, restricting further the right to buy and funding new council housing (Cairney, May 2008: 92; September 2009: 111; January 2009: 58; May 2009: 71; September 2009: 61).

Media Policy

The monitors devote the bulk of their attention to the role and behaviour of the media (as discussed in chapter 1) rather than government policy on the media, at least beyond the general discussion of the decision by the Scottish Parliament not to regulate the media despite their tense relationship. Although the Scottish Parliament has faced significant criticism from the media, it decided not to curb media access. Instead, the Consultative Steering Group's Expert Panel on Media Issues recommended 'minimal rules' for broadcast proceedings, widespread accreditation not only for national media but also local and specialist journalists and 'considerable access to MSPs by accredited journalists' (November 1999: 7). This emphasis on accreditation—and therefore exclusion of 'single-issue journalists operating as lobbyists' (November 1999: 7–9) stood it in good stead following 'lobbygate' which centred on claims made to undercover journalists by John Reid's son Kevin (who worked for Beattie Media) that he could guarantee privileged access to ministers (November 1999: 10; Shephard, August 2001: 15; Mitchell, November 2001: 6). The issue also established early on that parliamentary attempts to conduct investigations of such matters in private (which eventually exonerated all ministers concerned, as did Donald Dewar's own investigation) would not go down well with a media sold on the idea of new politics as open and accessible (November 1999: 7–9). Thus, the Scottish Parliament's overall approach to the media reflected to a large extent its wider rhetoric on transparency and accountability.

One of the biggest topics in media policy concerns the prospect of dedicated Scottish BBC news broadcasting (a question for the BBC rather than the UK Government directly). In particular, a long debate surrounded the establishment of the 'Scottish Six' or Six O'clock News run by BBC Scotland and reporting on Scottish, UK and international news. While a greater focus on Scottish political and social issues may make sense following devolution, there are also questions regarding finance, practicability (does it have enough journalists and resources to replicate programmes originally organised in London?) and the signal that dedicated Scottish coverage sends to the voters. In particular, its critics highlighted the ability of separate broadcast news to further the devolution divide and encourage the 'SNP's independence agenda' (February 2000: 5–6). Initially, the compromise offered by the BBC was to reject the 'Scottish Six' but offer a 20-minute Newsnight Scotland programme at 11 o'clock on BBC2. The issue rumbled on, but very quietly (Curtice, August 2004: 22; September 2008: 54 suggests that the Scottish Six is low on agenda of the public and attitudes are fluid) until Scottish Television introduced its own Scottish Six (Cairney, September 2009: 62). The issue of broadcasting in general became higher profile following the election of the SNP Government in 2007, but much revolved around a demand for greater representation within the BBC, more resources for Scottish media and Scottish Government support for a Scottish digital network (Cairney, May 2009: 72). The SNP also published its plans for the media in an independent Scotland as part of its National Conversation (Cairney, September 2009: 61)

Conclusion

With the benefit of hindsight, we have good reasons to hold very limited expectations about policy divergence in Scotland: few of us *really* believed that there would be a rush to major policy change; governments in all political systems face constraints on their ability to change policy; change in Scotland may not cause policy divergence; and, even if it does, that divergence may be replaced by convergence in the longer term. Further, most discussions of policy divergence tend to be predicated on the idea of different policy *choices*. Yet, it may take years if not decades for those choices to be implemented and to have an appreciable effect. Or, incomplete implementation may produce limited divergence.

Chapter 8 identifies a small number of 'flagship' policies — including personal care, tuition fees, mental health, smoking, NHS reform — many of which also mark divergence from UK Government policy. We have also found in several chapters that a key difference may be the 'Scottish policy style'; the way that policy is processed in Scotland. Our focus moves from policy choices to the way that policy is made. Yet, our discussion of top-down policymaking and targetry in the UK highlights a blurry boundary between policy and policy style. As Greer and Jarman (2008) note, the key divergence in approach may relate to their use of 'policy tools'. While the Scottish Governments set broad goals and accept a degree of partnership or varied implementation, the UK Government is often associated with an approach in which it introduces targets and also a series of punitive measures if the targets are not met. While this comparison was perhaps most interesting when Labour was in government in both Scotland and the UK, the 'Scottish way' clearly continued after 2007 (as predicted in Cairney, April 2007: 89). In this light, the idea of policy style takes on a greater importance, since the administration or implementation of policy is often as important as the policy choices themselves (see Cairney, 2011c).

How should we assess devolution given this evidence on public policy and policymaking in Scotland? Hazell (2001: 255) argues that a key purpose of devolution was to allow the devolved nations to 'get away from "one size fits all" policies imposed by Westminster and Whitehall, and to develop their own policies better suited to local needs. If devolution does not lead to differentiation of policy then it will prove a serious disappointment to those who voted for it'. This perhaps suggests that people will be disappointed by a lack of policy innovation and divergence. Yet, the devolved territories can also produce divergence merely by stepping off the train; by allowing the UK Government to be innovate but without taking part. We should also be careful about the idea of locally produced policies. Health policy sums this up best, because most of us would think that most of the UK population supports a tax funded NHS open to all UK residents and generally free at the point of contact. Chapter 7 also suggests that Scots like some of the ideas behind the choice agenda in England. In that context, it is difficult to know what the Scottish Government could do differently to avoid disappointing the Scottish public. Perhaps policy innovation may also refer to the way that policy is processed and implemented rather than a complete shift in policy substance. We might also suggest that the public pays little attention to policy and that its knowledge of government may be restricted to a small number of flagship or controversial policies (such as 'free' personal care). Again, this suggests that the Scottish Government does not have to do much to keep its supporters happy.

Overall, we have notable policy change, but we also have fewer and fewer reasons to treat Scotland as an arena for unusual policymaking or policy outputs. The phrase 'Scottish solutions for Scottish problems' may be best used to describe what happens when devolved institutions become responsible for their own policy processes. 'Problems' in this sense can refer to the wider policy literature definition—issues that require policymaker attention—while 'solutions' are the ideas considered or adopted by policymakers (Cairney, 2012b). In this sense, Scotland becomes a useful case study of an area with some unusual characteristics, but also a source of information on public policy that is not so different from most other studies. There is a limited number of 'flagship' policies because policymakers only have the attention and resources to devote to a small number of policy initiatives. Those policy choices also take a considerable time to implement, while many may not be implemented fully or at all. Consequently, policy can only change and/or diverge so much in such a short space of time. Note that some of the major projects analyse policy over several decades (e.g. Baumgartner and Jones, 2009). Consequently, we may only have enough information on policy divergence after a generation shift. Perhaps by this time we will be less interested in comparing Scottish and English policies and more interested in the broader question of why policy changes.

Chapter 9

Finance

There are two key points to note about public finance in Scotland. First, public expenditure is one of the most important factors in devolved and Scottish politics, but also an area that has changed very little since devolution. This is largely because Scottish finance receives only sporadic attention, and few actions are taken before that attention passes. Second, the issue of finance sums up the difficulties of reporting on devolution without the benefit of hindsight. The economic landscape was changing dramatically just as the monitors ended in 2009. One of the most important factors in a discussion of finance, in the first ten years of devolution, relates to the high levels of public expenditure in Scotland. High levels of expenditure in England, at the same time, helped reduce attention to relatively high per capita spending in Scotland (Heald and McLeod, 2005: 496). They combined with the maintenance of the Barnett formula, used largely to alter the budgets of the devolved governments at the margins, to keep UK public attention to devolved expenditure remarkably low. Further, while elite attention to Scottish finance rose before and after the publication of the Calman Report in 2009 (chapter 10), there are still no concrete plans for fundamental financial reforms.

In this light, the main focus of the devolution reports has been the Barnett formula and its effect. For example, much has been written about the ability of the formula to reduce Scotland's financial advantage. We can also identify the links between finance and intergovernmental relations, exploring the role of the UK Treasury in determining Scotland's budget and the ability, desire and willingness of the Scottish Executive to spend it in a distinctive way (although note that few governments take a non-incremental approach to budgeting). The latter topic raises a wider issue about the role of the Scottish Executive in economic affairs. The main economic levers, to determine interest rates and the mix between the major taxes, and to borrow money to finance capital projects, were not devolved. Rather, the Scottish Executive's economic role is restricted largely to the distribution of public money and, to some extent, the promotion of economic regeneration. It is therefore difficult to identify a 'Scottish Treasury' in any meaningful sense, particularly since the UK Treasury still has a greater role than the Scottish Government in this area. This is the context in which we can view new SNP initiatives. The Scottish Government's approach may be distinctive, but it takes place within a context of limited room for manoeuvre. Indeed, this room is shrinking, following an economic crisis which has reduced the Scottish budget for many years to come.

This chapter explores these issues as follows. First, it outlines the background of, and attention to, the Barnett formula. Second, it explores the idea of, and evidence for, a 'Barnett squeeze'. Third, it considers the Scottish Government's discretion to spend its budget. Fourth, it examines the economic levers available to the Scottish Government, and the evidence of a Scottish Treasury. Fifth, it considers the limited role of the Scottish Government in areas such as large scale capital projects and housing stock transfer. Finally, it examines the role of the SNP within this context, as well as the new era of economic constraint.

Scottish Public Expenditure and the Barnett Formula

One of the most important aspects of Scottish politics — how devolved governments are funded — often received very low attention in the monitors. For the most part this is because, in contrast to the changing political landscape, Scotland's fiscal relationship with the UK Government has 'remained largely unaltered' (Keating, 2005; 2010: 168). Further, the changes to its overall budget have been largely automatic and marginal, spending changes have tended to be incremental, with no real evidence of a fundamental review of the way that the Scottish Executive or Government spends its budget, and the Scottish Parliament's ability to alter Scottish income tax by three pence in the pound (the 'Tartan Tax') was never used.[26] Consequently, there is very little to report if nothing much is changing. It is often important to report on the absence of important change, since the funding settlement raises important issues about the fairness of the territorial distribution of funding and how it relates to the UK's economic strategy. However, we can only remark on the same thing, the now-cliché dog that didn't bark, so many times!

---

[26] In fact, the Scottish Government decided not to pay the fee to maintain its ability to vary the tax (BBC News 2010). See also Woods (2002: 6) on the Scottish Executive's rejection of its use.

In the absence of these major changes, the monitors have generally focused on the effects of the current arrangements. In particular, they explore the effect of the Barnett formula on the Scottish Executive's budget. The Barnett formula was introduced in the 1970s and later named (by Professor David Heald) after Joel Barnett MP, Chief Secretary to the Treasury from 1974–79. It now covers most of the Scottish Government's budget and approximately 60% of public expenditure in Scotland (the rest is spent by Whitehall departments). The system is based on an initial funding settlement supplemented by changes determined by the Barnett formula, which adjusts the Scottish settlement in line with changes to the English budget. The initial funding settlement cemented Scotland's higher per capita spending, because it was determined almost entirely with reference to Scotland's budget at that time. The Barnett formula alters this settlement at the margins. It is based on Scotland's share of the UK population rather than its initial share of the UK budget. We calculate the change to the budget for England, and then award 'Barnett consequentials' to the devolved territories, based on an estimate of their population sizes and the extent to which the policy area is devolved (for example, the more clearly devolved health and education produce more consequentials than transport — Keating, 2010: 170).

Much debate revolves around what the Barnett formula was designed to do (see McGarvey and Cairney, 2008: 180–8; Keating, 2005: 122–123; 2010: 172–3; Heald and McLeod, 2002: 151; Heald and McLeod, 2005: 497), and it is useful to separate analytically the practical, agenda setting and financial aims. One suggestion is that the formula represented a practical, interim measure devised in the run up to political devolution in 1979. The Treasury's plan was to negotiate a new system with the new Scottish Assembly, based on a Treasury-commissioned needs assessment study. When devolution did not materialise, this plan was dropped and Barnett remained (although note that Scotland's settlement is often defended in terms of need — Keating, 2010: 173). While the Treasury could have acted unilaterally, it would have gained very little (the effect of a 3–5% reduction in Scotland's budget would represent much less than 1% of the Treasury's budget) and would have provoked a negative response in Scotland at a time of constitutional unrest. Barnett also represented, to the Treasury, a way to avoid spending a disproportionate amount of time on protracted annual budget negotiations for sums that were small when compared to its overall commitments (Heald and McLeod, 2002: 150). A key tenet of the 'policy communities' literature is that policy issues are often portrayed as dull affairs to limit public interest and participation.

If an issue can be successfully presented as a 'technical' subject for experts, related to a problem which has largely been solved, power can be exercised behind the scenes by a small number of participants (Baumgartner and Jones, 1993; 2009; Jordan and Maloney, 1997; McGarvey and Cairney, 2008: 181).

In this sense, the Barnett formula represents a successful attempt by decision-makers in Scotland and the UK to keep the big and potentially most contentious questions of funding off the political agenda. Barnett initially 'solved' the problem of Scottish advantage without provoking the type of reaction that would fuel calls for constitutional change (this was certainly a requirement in the run-up to the 1979 referendum). The annual budget rounds then became almost automatic, with the only scope for negotiation around the 'technical' issue of Barnett consequentials (there is some room for negotiation on the level of devolution, and hence the level of comparability, in some areas such as transport, trade and industry) and ad hoc issues (such as the funding of swine flu vaccines — Cairney, September 2009: 56).

A further suggestion is that the formula was devised to satisfy two camps — the initial maintenance of Scotland's higher budget would satisfy the Scottish Office, while the Barnett formula would satisfy calls to reduce Scotland's advantage in the long run. There is considerable disagreement on the latter point. While a strict and accurate application of the formula suggests that it would eventually reduce per capita spending levels in Scotland to a level similar to England (Bell, 2001), Midwinter (2004a; 2004b) argues that this was never the stated aim and that it did not happen (even during the Conservative years of government — Keating, 2010: 172-3). Perhaps a more likely aim was to prevent any further advantage to Scotland and then bring Scotland's per capita spending closer to the figure identified in the Treasury's needs assessment. Any such equalising effect is called the 'Barnett squeeze' (rather misleadingly, because it only occurs when public spending increases).

Each side has avoided reforms since a very clear sense of winning and losing would result from any deviation from the status quo (and in Scotland there is a large public sector to lose — Cairney, September 2006: 72-3; May 2009: 53; September 2009: 55). This strategy was helped considerably during the 1999–2007 period by significant rises in UK and Scottish public expenditure. The types of disagreements on the adequacy of the funding settlement that we are now witnessing between the UK and Scottish Governments (beginning in 2007 — Cairney, January 2008: 105) did not arise. These factors help explain why fundamental issues of territorial finance only tended to arise when linked – in the eyes of actors who are not normally involved – to other events such as the election in 2007 of a nationalist party just before the rise of a Scottish Prime Minister in the UK (also note Hazell's 2001: 261 suggestion that UK Government attention to Barnett reform was low when so many Scots were in the Cabinet). They were also considered, to some extent, during the production of the Calman Report (chapter 10).

Public Expenditure and the Devolution Monitors

The 'Barnett Squeeze'

The tone of the early reports reflects the fact that Barnett remained off the agenda for a long time, despite having 'all the characteristics of an issue likely to explode on to the political agenda at some stage' (Mitchell et al, 2001: 66). Its first mention merely states that the historically-secretive Treasury has finally begun to publish statistical details of the programmes covered by Barnett (February 2000: 16). The August (2000: 10) monitor presents the widespread prediction that 'if services in Scotland are seen to be getting a less generous deal than their counterparts south of the border (or, indeed, vice versa) it will surely fuel arguments about the character of the devolutionary settlement'. Yet no serious discussion of Barnett took place until 2001, when Bell (May 2001: 43) and Mitchell et al (2001: 66; see also Hazell, 2001: 260; Jervis and Plowden, 2001: 19; Woods, 2001c: 4–5) reported rumours that the UK Government would review it, as part of a wider review of local and regional funding in England. In fact, it was only particular ministers such as John Prescott and Peter Mandelson that favoured a review, with Tony Blair and the Treasury keen to play the issue down. Similar rumours came to nothing in 2007 (Trench, January 2008: 79). Indeed, Graham Stringer MP has claimed that UK Government officials have tried their best to persuade MPs not to raise the issue of Barnett (Trench, January 2008: 88; Trench, May 2008: 73–4).

An early review was unlikely because, according to the earliest reports, the Barnett squeeze was apparent and the formula was perhaps working as intended (although note the difficulties of finding reliable figures – Heald and McLeod, 2002: 159; Heald and McLeod, 2002: 512). The November (2000: 38) report states that the Barnett squeeze 'is now quite discernible', predicting that the effect of the comprehensive spending review and the squeeze would account for £1bn less money by 2003–4 for Scotland than if its spending rose at the same rate as England. This argument is repeated in Bell and Christie (2001: 145; see also Mitchell et al, 2001: 67 but compare with Heald and

McLeod, 2005: 514). Bell (February 2001: 44–7) identifies in particular the large rises in education and health spending in Whitehall departments which cannot be matched in Scotland, arguing that 'if the Barnett formula is not replaced, levels of per capita expenditure in Scotland and England will converge' (see also Jervis and Plowden, 2001: 8–9; Woods, 2001c: 4–5). Further, Scotland's growing list of spending increases in Scotland — including on public sector salaries, tuition fees and free personal care — limit further policy innovation in the short term and are unsustainable in the longer term. Bell (August 2002: 37) also identifies a further squeeze based on the comprehensive spending review figures from financial years 2003–4 to 2005–6 (see also Trench, May 2009: 88). Yet, the existence of any overall squeeze is disputed by Schmueker and Adams (2005) and Keating (2010: 175) suggests that Scotland's losses were partially reversed from 2005.

To a great extent we can explain this difference of interpretation in three main ways. First, we can look beyond Barnett to Scotland's overall share of public expenditure. From 1997/8 to 2001/2 it remained constant at 10.3% of the UK total despite a fall in its population. Scotland's spending per capita rose from 17% to 20% above the UK average (Bell, November 2003: 41). This rise, despite a relative fall in Scotland's Departmental Expenditure Limit (i.e. the part of the budget covered by Barnett), took place because of a rise in spending outside the DEL. For example, in this period social security payments rose from 4.8% to 8.4% above the UK average, suggesting that 'it is the social security system, rather than the Barnett Formula' which provides an automatic stabilising effect (Bell, November 2003: 42). Scotland's share of UK public expenditure was also boosted by its disproportionate share of, and a significant rise in, agricultural spending. Further, although housing policy is covered by Barnett, the £1.4bn of Treasury money to help Scottish local authorities write off council housing debts (provided they transferred their housing stocks to housing associations) was not. It is spending in these areas that accounts for the maintenance of Scotland's 'advantage', demonstrating that 'the squeeze has not come about because the formula does not work as the textbook definition suggests' (Christie, January 2006: 106).

Second, we can examine further the idea of a Barnett squeeze in some areas. Bell (November 2003: 43; see also Cairney, January 2007: 84 on education) suggests that, in the largest spending areas under devolved control (most notably health, education and transport), spending patterns reflect what 'one would expect had a Barnett squeeze been in place'. Keating (2005: 145) also suggests that the formula has 'begun to bite' in some policy areas. While spending per head in these areas is still higher in Scotland, it may be less so than before devolution. This suggests that we can identify a quasi-squeeze within an overall pattern of funding continuity, particularly in health where spending per capita is roughly the same as in the North East of England (HM Treasury, 2009). The complication with this interpretation is that any 'squeeze' in particular areas involves a choice by the Scottish Executive to fund some areas but not others. In other words, the gap in health is reduced partly because the Scottish Executive made a decision to spend the money elsewhere.

Third, as Bell (November 2004: 31) suggests, the confusion caused by comparing overall expenditure per capita, and expenditure covered by Barnett, may be further exacerbated by policy developments (such as top-up fees in England) and non-comparable policy conditions (such as the higher levels of private schooling in England).

In any event, the term 'squeeze' is misleading because it only occurs when funding increases. For example, in 2002 it could be used to describe annual rises in the DEL element of public expenditure of just below 5% in Scotland, compared to rises in England of just above 5%. Thus, consistent rises in Scottish public expenditure gave successive Scottish governments 'a strong resource base on which to promote the growth of public services', while real rises in absolute spending may reduce the issue of a squeeze to 'second-order importance to most voters' (McGarvey, November 2002: 28; see also Bell, November 2004: 32-6 on the details of spending changes). In other words, the squeeze took place in the context of significant growth in UK budgets; when 'resources are plentiful and the problem is one of unprecedented underspending' (Heald and McLeod, 2002: 165). Consequently, Bell's (August 2001: 37) prediction that the Scottish Executive's 'end year flexibility' (EYF) reserves for unforeseen events 'will be increasingly difficult to maintain as the "Barnett-squeeze" takes effect' proved pessimistic, with those reserves reaching about £900 million by 2008 (see also Bell's August 2003: 32 criticism of Executive underspends as a contributory factor in Scotland's low growth). Indeed, only since 2008 have these reserves seemed under threat, following relatively low increases in the Scottish budget from 2008-9 (Trench, May 2009: 88) and then the decision by the UK Coalition Government to phase out EYF from 2010 (Sandford, 2011: 9).

The Freedom to Conform?

A key related topic regards a dilemma posed by the permissive nature of devolved spending: devolved governments do not need to spend their budgets in the same areas as the UK Government; and, Barnett consequentials derived from changes in spending in England do not have to be spent on the same policy area (Heald and McLeod, 2002: 151). At the same time, the UK, Scottish and Welsh governments were all led by Labour and we would expect a degree of policy uniformity, based on: their attachment to similar ideals; the UK Government's ability to set the agenda; and, its desire to avoid the embarrassment of devolved governments going their own way. In this context, a key question arose: should they spend consequentials on the same policy areas and risk appearing to be merely emulating the English lead, or deviate from popular spending increases and be seen to lag behind on issues such as health (even though Scotland already spends more on it) (May 2000: 11–12)? This discussion of power and discretion continued, with Bell (May 2002; 52–3) highlighting the lack of UK Government recognition that the devolved territories could go their own way, and Mitchell (2004: 23) arguing that the 'Executive's spending priorities and plans have followed those of Whitehall remarkably' (compare with the Wales devolution monitor coverage of First Minister Rhodri Morgan's 'clear red water' speech—Osmand and Mugaseth, February 2003: 3).

This theme of emulation continues throughout the monitors, and it seems that either way is problematic. For example, Bell (May 2002: 52–3) and McGarvey (November, 2002: 29–30) point to the practical problems associated with the decision to follow the UK Government lead on health spending increases, including reduced money for other services and a questionable ability to increase effectiveness when health spending is already so high. However, there may also be political problems when the Scottish Executive goes its own way. For example, its economic strategy *Closing the Opportunity Gap* appeared to focus more on the equitable distribution of funds when compared to the UK Government's use of public spending to boost economic growth. This may further the view of Scotland as a subsidised nation, with measures focused on 'improving the living standards of the Scottish people' (McGarvey, November 2002: 29). Further, its economy appeared to be doing no better than before, and it was close to recession in 2001 and 2002 despite the UK's steady growth (McGarvey, November 2002: 29). The Scottish Executive made a firmer commitment to focus more on economic growth than social justice from 2003 (Christie, January 2007: 59), although we can link this as much to Scottish business group pressure as the UK-Scotland link (McGarvey and Cairney, 2008: 239).

The Scottish Executive also felt pressure to emulate the UK's use of Public Service Agreements (PSAs), by moving from an input-based budgeting system based on how much services cost, towards an outcomes system in which service deliverers must use their budget to meet targets (Bell, February 2003: 37; even though the process is problematic — Bell, May 2004: 50–1; Bell, November 2004: 32; Christie, January 2006: 104–5). There were also more recent signs that the Scottish Executive would follow, or even attempt to go beyond, the Treasury's 'efficiency' agenda (Christie, January 2006: 105–6; Christie, May 2006: 59; Winetrobe, November 2004: 7) which includes public sector job cuts, particularly in the civil service (Winetrobe, August 2004: 6; even though the Scottish Executive may prefer to boost its policy capacity with more civil servants — Cairney, January 2006: 15).

However, in most of these cases the waters are muddied by the fact that Scotland does not control all of the levers necessary to deliver policy, while developments in the UK may affect Scottish-based targets, often indirectly. Indeed, in some cases, such as higher education, indirect UK effects may push and pull Scottish targets: demand for employees in the south-east of England may affect a Scottish target to increase graduates as a proportion of the Scottish workforce; while the introduction of tuition fees in England may affect Scottish Universities and the mobility of Scottish students (Bell, February 2003: 37; Bell, February 2004: 32). In other cases, such as efficiency targets, the Scottish Executive may be driven primarily by an attempt to jump before being pushed — although in both the UK and Scotland the efficiency drive may be more about *looking like* departments are saving money while providing the same service. As Audit Scotland suggests, when evaluating the Efficient Government Initiative, the Scottish Executive struggles to demonstrate efficiency savings (rather than just reduced spending in some areas) because it has not produced reliable measures of efficiency (Cairney, January 2007: 21; see also Christie, May 2006: 60–1).

Further, the statement that its economic growth tends to be lower than the UK as a whole is misleading: (a) because the UK average is maintained by London and the South-East, with Scotland often enjoying the fourth highest Gross Value Added (GVA) per capita (Christie, September 2006: 56); and (b) because new methods to determine Scotland's Gross Domestic Product (GDP) (using regularly updated, not historical, weights) suggest that it has 'been growing at broadly the same rate as the rest of the UK' (Bell, February 2004: 31). This point may not be publicised too much in Scotland for fear that it shows that Scotland has less need than other regions (Christie, September 2006: 56).

What is the Economic Role of the Scottish Executive
Is there a Scottish Treasury?

The main economic levers, to determine interest rates and the major taxes (such as income, corporation and value added) and to borrow money to finance capital projects, were not devolved. Rather, the Scottish Executive's only wider economic role, beyond the distribution of public money, regards the promotion of economic regeneration in the context of an economic system that it does not control (leaving aside the issue regarding the ability of *any* government to control its economy in an era of economic globalisation). In this context, the early reports suggest that the role of the finance department of the Scottish Executive is nothing like a Scottish equivalent of the Treasury (see, for example, November 2000: 34; Mitchell, February 2001: 5).

This limited role is largely explained by the role of the UK Treasury. The Treasury is still the most important figure in Scotland's financial process, controlling not only the money that Scotland receives but also the wider macroeconomic and monetary policies of the UK as a whole (although note the independent role of the Bank of England in setting interest rates): 'in comparison with other unitary states, there is highly centralised and unified control over public expenditure and taxation, exercised directly by, or on behalf of, the Treasury' (Heald and McLeod, 2002: 147). Indeed, the Scottish Executive as a whole is often treated by the Treasury merely as 'any other [UK Government] department' (Cairney, May 2006: 17). Consequently, the reports state regularly that the Scottish Government is tied to the Treasury when it comes to raising (and sometime spending) money (May 2000: 12; Trench, May 2006: 50; Trench, May 2008: 55; Trench, January 2009: 73-4; Christie, May 2006: 61; Christie, September 2006: 57; Trench, May 2008: 69).

The Scottish Executive's role is restricted primarily to economic development using the more limited levers that it has available (for discussions of economic policy in this context see Winetrobe, May 2002: 64; November 2002: 36; February 2003: 44; June 2003: 65; August 2003: 38; February 2004: 41; May 2004: 58; November 2004: 42; April 2005: 41; Cairney, January 2006: 122; May 2006: 73; September 2006: 73; May 2008: 96; January 2009: 44-7; May 2009: 51-6; see also Cairney, September 2009: 55 which discusses the increasing Scottish Government focus on modern apprenticeships, as part of its cooperation with Labour). This is reflected in the Scottish Executive's first economic framework which effectively focuses on 'supply side' policies regarding Scotland's 'physical infrastructure and human capital', with some suggestion (perhaps in contrast to old Labour thinking) that the private sector has a key role to play (November 2000: 35; it also produced a fairly symbolic cut in business rates—Christie, January 2007: 62). While devolution has provided greater political impetus for economic development (or a new direction for Scottish Enterprise), there are 'few 'immediate political gains' and the Executive still relies on the stability created by UK economic policy (Bell, May 2001: 45). Indeed, Bell (February 2004: 31) argues that the single biggest factor determining Scotland's growth rate from 1963 to 2002 has been 'the performance of the UK economy as a whole' (see also the SNP criticisms of the lack of effect of supply side policies without the ability to cut corporation tax—Christie, January 2007: 60).

The Scottish Executive also did not have a finance department with the capacity and centralising role of the Treasury (November 2000: 34). In particular, it did not have a department that could hold spending departments to strict performance and expenditure targets and therefore shape the direction of public policy. Indeed, departing Finance minister Tom McCabe criticised the ability of departments to block the movement of spending towards other portfolios and called for 'a new Scottish Treasury with the clout to get tough on spending departments that continue to squander cash without proper scrutiny' (Cairney, January 2008: 11). To some extent this call was backed by the Scottish Executive commissioned Howat report that recommended a more strategic approach to public spending (Cairney, January 2008: 12). In its absence, the coalition Partnership Agreements served as a proxy mechanism for coordination.

Nor did the Scottish Executive have a powerful unit built around the First Minister. While FM Jack McConnell mooted the idea of heading a new 'Performance Improvement and Innovation Unit' to help 'drive up the quality of public services', his position quickly shifted towards more ad hoc arrangements, with civil servants and external advisers working together on specific projects. Work done at the centre remained 'supervisory' before McConnell appointed a figure form the private sector to take that agenda forward (Winetrobe, November 2002: 5; Winetrobe, February 2003: 5-6; Winetrobe, February 2004: 4).

McConnell did experiment further with measures to coordinate policy, but much of it was symbolic: the revised title of Minister for Finance and *Public Services* was described in the media as accentuating Andy Kerr's '"cabinet enforcer" function' (Winetrobe, February 2002: 7); and, his successor, Tom McCabe, was given the title of Minister for Finance and Public Sector Reform. Yet, 8 years of generous public expenditure deals negated much of the need for tough spending decisions. Instead, the First and Finance Ministers have generally pursued the 'Scottish policy style', 'seeking consensus and working with departments and public bodies' (Cairney, January 2006: 16). Further, although the Finance Committee recommended that the Scottish Executive emulate the UK Government approach, and in particular the Prime Minister's Delivery Unit's concentrated focus on fewer targets, this agenda was hampered by the relatively fixed nature of the coalition Partnership Agreements (Cairney, January 2006: 16–17).

Public Sector Reform and Finance

The monitors report highly critical voices in local government and the unions regarding public sector reform (to the extent that some unions threatened to defect from Labour to SNP — Mitchell, May 2002: 57; see also Mitchell, November 2003: 49 on union leaders speaking at the SNP conference; and Mitchell, February 2004: 37 on the Rail, Maritime and Transport workers' union (RMT) split from Labour (given their differences on rail privatisation) to support the SSP). They suggest that the Scottish Executive, under McLeish, undermined the ability of local authorities to control public services by accepting the 'Blairite public sector modernisation programme' and emphasising the 'positive contribution of the private sector to public services' (McGarvey, November 2001: 44–5; see also Winetrobe, May 2001: 11; November, 2001: 64; February 2002: 8). This general approach included an increased use of public-private partnerships to deliver services and the large scale voluntary transfer (LSVT) of council housing to housing associations (McGarvey, November 2001: 45). The latter was opposed in particular by Unison (the main public services union) which described housing associations as 'privately-financed, unelected quangos' (McGarvey, May 2002: 47–8).

Yet, both cases highlight the extent to which the Scottish Executive made a virtue out of necessity by promoting policies effectively under Treasury control (McGarvey and Cairney, 2008: 139; 192). In other words, PPP may be 'the only show in town' (Heald and McLeod, 2002: 155 — although this charge was disputed by the Scottish Executive's Finance Minister when highlighting its small command of the overall capital budget — Winetrobe, May 2002: 62). Further, Treasury power in housing stock transfer became fairly explicit when it agreed to write off Glasgow's council housing debt if there was a 'yes' vote to transfer (which there was) (McGarvey, May 2002: 48; Winetrobe, May 2002: 65; see Curtice, May 2002: 29 which shows that 87% in Glasgow would prefer to rent from their local authority, suggesting that the 'financial inducement' to vote yes was successful).

The ascension of McConnell did not lead to the reversal of policies on PPP or LSVT (Mitchell, May 2002: 57; McGarvey, August 2002: 36; Winetrobe, November 2002: 35; August 2004: 47; perhaps with the exception of the scrapping of the Skye Bridge tolls — Bell, May 2004: 52; Winetrobe, April 2005: 43). Although the rhetoric sometimes changed under McConnell (Bell, February 2003: 36; compare with Winetrobe, June 2003: 64; August 2003: 37; Cairney, September 2006: 75), the rate of PPP for schools became higher in Scotland than any other part of the UK (McGarvey, August 2004: 36; Cairney, January 2006: 120; January 2007: 84; although note that PPP accounted for less than 19% of all Scottish capital spending in 2004-5 — Bell, February 2004: 33). Perhaps the only notable Scottish agenda relates to moves by the Scottish Executive to 'end the so-called "two-tier workforce" than can arise from PPP and similar arrangements for private sector delivery of public services' (Winetrobe, February 2003: 43).

In housing, McConnell was also unlucky enough to reign during the problems associated with Glasgow Housing Association (McGarvey, November 2002: 28) which were in part caused by its move from direct provider of housing to regulator of registered social landlords (McGarvey, November 2003: 39; McGarvey, May 2004: 49; Scott, January 2007: 56). The Scottish Executive was buoyed by an Accounts Commission report suggesting that most of the aims of LSVT — more investment in repairs and refurbishment, reduced rent increases — were met (Scott, May 2006: 56-7). However the experience of several 'no' votes suggested that LSVT was not inevitable, at least in the short term (Cairney, January 2006: 116; January 2007: 76; Scott, January 2007: 55-6; Scott, September 2007: 59). McConnell also oversaw Scottish Executive policy on private prisons, an issue which combined with general concern over prison facilities and possible closures, to produce partly successful 'cross-party parliamentary opposition' to its policy (i.e. fewer private prisons were announced — Winetrobe, August 2002: 45-6; November 2002: 34; but see Cairney, January 2007: 87 on the proportion of people jailed in private prisons).

Finance and the SNP Government

In the months before the SNP's election, it engaged in a bitter debate with Labour about the extent to which Scotland pays its way within the UK. As Christie (January 2007: 60) suggests, although there is 'a general acceptance by most economists that Scotland runs a deficit of some form', the means of demonstrating this via the Scottish Executive produced *Government Expenditure and Revenue in Scotland* (GERS) is problematic, because it makes significant assumptions about the amount of tax raised in Scotland. Therefore, while unionists pointed to the 2004–5 deficit of £6bn or £11.2bn (including North Sea revenues or not) as proof of the benefits of the Union to Scotland, the SNP criticised the calculation of the figures and, in particular, the underestimation of Scotland's entitlement to North Sea oil revenue. In addition, it argued that spending would be lower (with less defence and overseas expenditure) and revenue higher (when reducing corporation tax to boost economic growth) in an independent Scotland (Christie, January 2007: 61). Interestingly, given that ministers have no involvement in the production of the figures, the first GERS under an SNP Government suggested that Scotland's 'fiscal deficit' is much smaller than previous editions had indicated, and indeed may be non-existent (depending on whether and how North Sea oil revenues are taken into account) (Trench, September 2008: 79).

The election of an SNP Government also coincided almost exactly with an end to the big public expenditure increases that characterised the first 8 years of devolution (the shift from 'financial good times' to 'belt-tightening was predicted by Christie, January 2007: 59). Further, issues that would have been dealt with behind closed doors before 2007 were now played out in the press between competing parties (see McGarvey and Cairney, 2008: 192). Following its Comprehensive Spending Review, the Treasury announced that Scotland's DEL would rise from £26.059 billion in 2007–08 to £27.244 billion in 2008–09, £29.584 billion in 2009–10 and £33.309 billion in 2009–10. This represents an average real annual rise of 1.8 per cent and, for then Scottish Secretary Des Browne, 'a very good PBR/CSR for Scotland' (Trench, January 2008: 80). The SNP countered this claim by pointing to a shift in the 'baseline' to calculate the figures. The 2007–08 baseline figure for Scotland's budget was reduced by £340 million to take into account lower levels of spending in England by the Department of Health in previous years. Therefore, the annual real rise is 1.4 per cent. Further, the SNP Government pointed out that since the baseline was reduced, the increase in 2008–09 is £845 million. This represents a real rise of 0.5 per cent. The SNP argued that this was the lowest real annual rise since the early 1980s, further hampered by the Treasury's unwillingness to release the Scottish Government's EYF reserves, unless it was spent on capital projects, and its unwillingness to treat London Olympic spending as English spending producing Barnett consequentials (Trench, January 2008: 81–2; see also Trench, May 2008: 69; Trench, September 2008: 78 on the Treasury refusal of consequentials on prison spending in England and Wales and police pensions). Indeed, Trench (January 2008: 82; May 2008: 70; January

2009: 73) highlights the irony of narrowing devolved control over finance (and a harder line by the Treasury, particularly on efficiency savings) following the election of a nationalist government. The SNP has also come to terms very quickly with the idea that, in the eyes of the Treasury, the Scottish Government is merely another UK Government department (Cairney, 2012a).

The SNP Government provided a novel and partial solution to the 'Scottish Treasury' problem: by moving a huge range of policy responsibilities to the finance department under the direct control of the Finance Secretary and two supporting ministers (McGarvey and Cairney, 2008: 111; 120). It was also able to preside over some quick wins, albeit not always followed up by longer term success. For example, it devoted considerable resources to healthcare waiting times—representing not only key policy battleground within Scotland but also a proxy measure of devolved success when compared to England (Trench, January 2008: 84; chapter 8). Further, and most notably, it was able to persuade local authorities to freeze council taxes for its entire first term of office (in part through extra funding, at the marginal expense of rail and rural development spending). However, its eventual aim, a local income tax, was dropped (Scott, May 2009: 74). This perhaps marks a defeat on more than one level—by the Scottish Parliament that opposed the LIT policy (Scott, January 2009: 63) and the Treasury which neither played ball with the effects of a local income tax on reserved benefits (worth £400m per year) nor presented the Scottish Government with a side-deal as compensation (as in free personal care—Cairney, 2006a). The Treasury also questioned the Scottish Government's ability to pass a bill on taxation, a reserved area, and signalled that the effect of its efficiency savings agenda would be a reduction of the £500m in the Scottish budget for two years—making it a bad time to introduce a new tax that may not raise as much as council tax (Trench, May 2008: 73; Trench, September 2008: 83; Bort, September 2008: 35; Scott, May 2009: 75; Trench, May 2009: 88).

The SNP Government also made a commitment to reform the financing of capital projects, but a key feature of the devolution monitors is that they struggled to identify the distinctiveness of SNP policy. The Scottish Government set up the Scottish Futures Trust as a way to address the excessive costs of PPP projects associated with the profit-seeking motives of private companies (by, for example, pooling the borrowing power of local authorities to fund capital projects directly) (Cairney, September 2008: 97). It was described by Trench (January 2008: 86) as 'a vehicle to boost capital investment in infrastructure by the public sector by providing an alternative to

Private Finance Initiative schemes' (Trench, January 2008: 86) but by one of the Scottish Government's economic advisers as PPP 'with window dressing' (Cairney, January 2009: 44). It soon became clear that, although the scheme would operate on a 'non-profit distributing model', the Scottish Futures Trust was not an alternative to PPP (Scott, September, 2008: 73; Scott, May 2009: 80). Rather, it was an attempt to use PPP but to reduce *excessive* profits. It is a 'close relative of PFI' which involves private contractors and private finance, and the cap on the ability of firms to make profits from PFI projects has had an uncertain effect (Hellowell and Pollock, 2009: 406; 416; compare with Scottish Futures Trust, 2011).

The initial confusion about this point contributed to criticisms of the policy and scepticism about its likely effectiveness (Trench, May 2008: 73; see also Bort, September 2008: 36–7 on unions branding the SFT as an unnecessary quango). Perhaps in response, the SNP changed the remit of the SFT, towards a body that would act more as a 'focus for expertise and co-ordination' of PPP arrangements and the use of private capital (Trench, September 2008: 83; Cairney, May 2009: 55). However, the uncertainty seemed also to delay council decisions to commission new schools and to fulfil its pledge to 'match the school-building programme of the previous administration "brick by brick"' (an assertion denied by the SNP — Scott, January 2009: 61; Bort, January 2008: 29; Cairney, May 2008: 90; Scott, May 2009: 80). It also proved to be the wrong vehicle to finance the Forth Road Bridge, an issue which again demonstrated the centrality of the Treasury in Scottish Government decisions (Trench, January 2009: 74; Cairney, May 2009: 55).

Perhaps more promising is the SNP's attention to regulation. As Cairney (January 2008: 13) suggests, Scotland's reputation for hands-off government, when compared to the 'target-based, top-down regime caricature in England' does not extend to the regulatory landscape that surrounds public bodies. Some statutory bodies may be subject to inspection from as many as six agencies all with different methods and questions, while small voluntary agencies may have to devote a member of staff to maintain audit records (undermining governmental rhetoric on shifting personnel from 'backroom' to 'frontline' services). Such problems prompted the Scottish Executive to commission the Crerar review which reiterated the need to balance the benefits (service quality and public assurance) of scrutiny with their costs. It recommended (in the long term) a move towards a single, national scrutiny body (Cairney, January 2008: 13; Scott, January 2008: 73–4). While the Scottish Government was sympathetic, and the tone of the report was consistent with the SNP's professed desire towards decentralisation, it effectively rejected the idea of a single regulatory body in favour of a 25% reduction in bodies and a reform of the scrutiny process (Scott, May 2008: 65–6; Scott, September 2008: 75)

Conclusion

The early years of devolution may go down in history as unusual, since attention to public expenditure was generally low and spending was generally high. Indeed, these factors are closely linked, since high levels of spending across the UK helped reduce attention to issues of Scottish advantage and reduced the need for tough bargaining between the Treasury and the devolved territories (Heald and McLeod, 2005: 514). They perhaps also contributed to low attention to the issue of fiscal autonomy as part of further constitutional reform, since high funding allowed the Scottish Executive to pursue policy innovation without worrying too much about how to finance it. Indeed, devolution and high public expenditure produced a raft of expensive policies — including free personal care, the reduction and then abolition of student tuition fees, and a rise in salaries for teachers — that may not have been introduced under current economic circumstances. As Mitchell et al (2003: 139) note, 'Good times make governing easier ... If the economic context was to change that could create very different conditions against which the public would judge both the Executive and devolution'.

The monitors suggest that attention to the Barnett formula, as a symbol of devolved finance, could 'explode' at any time. Yet, it has been remarkably low key. One reason for such low attention, beyond the agenda setting design of the Barnett formula itself, is that the formula seems to have had enough of an effect to satisfy its critics. There is some evidence of a Barnett squeeze. While the term 'squeeze' is misleading, and the idea of a squeeze in some areas is problematic, it often *looks* like spending in key areas such as health and education is converging. This may often be enough to reduce attention, or for it to lurch to other areas in a congested agenda, even if Scottish Executive income is supplemented by other funds (such as the removal of council housing debt). Scotland is occasionally described as a 'land of milk and honey', introducing expensive policies that are effectively subsidised by taxpayers in England (see chapter 8), but there are many other social cleavages more likely to attract sustained attention in the UK (such as between public and private workers or those who claim or subsidise benefits).

There have also been few high profile instances in which the Scottish Executive has created intergovernmental tensions by using funding to go its own way. Further, the experience of devolution has shown us that the Scottish Executive has very limited economic powers and is tied strongly to the UK. There is no Scottish equivalent to the Treasury, partly because the UK Treasury still controls most of the main economic policies, and partly because the Scottish finance department does not have the same ability to control departments by linking funding to targets. There is also no distinctive Scottish way on capital finance, with Scottish developments on PPP and housing stock transfer reflecting the need to make a 'virtue of necessity' regarding Treasury rules.

This is the context in which we can view the SNP Governments from 2007 and 2011. The 2007–11 term showed us that the Scottish Government often had very little room to manoeuvre. It produced some quick wins in relation to the centralisation of government responsibilities, and the pursuit of symbolically important targets, but was generally frustrated by its inability to innovate in areas such as capital finance and local taxation. The 2011–16 period may not diverge significantly from that position, at least in the absence of further constitutional reform. As things stand, economic policy in Scotland is heavily dependent on the UK Treasury and the Scottish Government's role is relatively difficult to detect (which perhaps explains why relatively limited measures, such as the funding of 'modern apprenticeships', command such high stakes in the annual budget rounds). We have also entered a new era of economic retrenchment, in which Scottish governments can no longer use generous budgets (or their EYF) to make up for their overall lack of powers. The Scottish Government's room for manoeuvre has never seemed so limited. The next few years will be dominated by attention to the effects of budget cuts across the public sector landscape, to be interrupted sporadically by the prospect of 'fiscal autonomy', or some other form of arrangement associated with constitutional change, coupled with the occasional elite attention in England to Scotland's advantageous position.

Chapter 10

Changes in the Constitution

There have been very few major changes to the devolved settlement since 1999. Further, as chapter 5 suggests, surprisingly few issues of constitutional tension have arisen. Yet, as chapter 7 suggests, the issue of *potential* constitutional change sometimes seems ever-present in Scottish political debate and there has long been tangible public support for some sort of extension to devolution without going as far as independence. This chapter explores levels of government, political party and parliamentary attention to that potential for change and highlights the potential for change in the next few years. It would be an exaggeration to say that, before 2007, we heard nothing about independence and, after 2007, it's all people talk about, but this gives us an idea of the effect on an SNP win on the shift of attention.

To some extent, we can divide attention to constitutional change into a game of two halves (of approximately six years, from 1999–2005 and 2005–11). In the first half, discussions of independence or further devolution were relatively infrequent, with attention focused on minor issues or sporadic attention to major issues (for example, during the 2003 election). Only a few issues, such as the UK Supreme Court and the 'West Lothian Question', received sustained attention in the monitors. In the second half, attention to constitutional change rose as an SNP election win seemed increasingly likely and the 2007 election involved more intense Labour-led discussions about the value of the Union and perils of independence. The SNP's election win in 2007 then prompted two separate reviews of devolution: the Scottish Government's 'National Conversation' and the Scottish Parliament-commissioned and UK Government-supported Calman Commission exploring the options to extend devolution. Further, the SNP's electoral avalanche in 2011 has made it inevitable that Scotland will vote on an independence referendum before the next Scottish Parliament election.

To explore these issues, the chapter is structured as follows. First, it considers why the constitution received less attention in the first half of devolution, exploring initial attention to new politics and the role of the Labour party as a key defender of the constitutional status quo. Second, it highlights the particular importance of the UK Supreme Court problem and the West Lothian question and explores why both issues have yet to be resolved. Third, it charts the rise of attention to independence before and after the 2007 election. Fourth, it outlines the National Conversation and Calman Commission processes, with particular emphasis on their proposals to change Scotland's financial relationship with the UK. Finally, it considers the likely outcome of these deliberations.

The First Half

Discussion of independence in Scotland was relatively infrequent until the lead up to, and outcome of, the 2007 Scottish Parliament election. Public and elite attention in the first four years in particular was much more likely to be directed to the success or failure of new politics and the new devolved institutions (chapter 1). There have long been signs that a small majority of the population favours more tax powers and responsibilities for the Scottish Parliament (chapter 7), but this did not translate into anything concrete. Serious discussions of an extension of devolved powers arose rarely. Constitutional discussions often proved to be little more than attention to the implementation of devolution or the Scotland Act 1998. For example, Presiding Officer David Steel became increasingly frustrated with the need for a revision of the Act to make changes (such as electing a third deputy presiding officer) to the operation of the Scottish Parliament, and the Procedures Committee subsequently considered if 'Holyrood should be entitled to "reform itself"' (Wright, February 2002: 27; February 2003: 27; note that the deputy issue is addressed by the new Scotland Bill).

Or, larger constitutional issues arose sporadically, often with no resolution, before attention shifted to other issues. For example, while the SNP used the 2003 Scottish Parliament election campaign (and a question in the Scottish Parliament—Wright, November 2003: 31) to further its idea of a referendum on independence, the Labour and Conservative manifestos merely referred to the benefits of devolution and the need for good Scottish-UK partnerships (Wright, June 2003: 42–3). A more interesting discussion can be found in the Liberal Democrat manifesto, which proposed a second Constitutional Convention in 2009 (the first Scottish Constitutional Convention was the main vehicle for devolution debate in the 1990s—see McGarvey and Cairney, 2008: 12;

34-6). By 2009, 'we will be in a good position to see how the Scottish Parliament has worked to improve the quality of life and governance in Scotland. The Convention will be able to identify any helpful improvements to the Parliament's powers and methods of working' (Liberal Democrat manifesto in Wright, June 2003: 42-3).

One explanation for this general lack of attention to further devolution is that Scottish Labour figures, including First Minister Jack McConnell, were aware of the potential for the issue to create further significant (and electorally damaging) tensions within the Labour party. The 'interfering' role of MPs in devolved policymaking in Scotland, and the opposition to devolution or further devolution, has never been of the scale and longevity we see in Wales (see for example, Seaton and Osmond, 2005: 10-12; Bodden, 2011). However, the MP/MSP relationship was quite uncertain in the early years of devolution and there were some examples of turf wars. For example, the Boundary Commission for Scotland began in 2001 a two-stage review of Westminster and then Scottish Parliament constituencies. The consequence of reducing the number of Scottish MPs from 73 to 59 was the potential to reduce the number of MSPs from 129 to 106 (Wright, May 2003: 35-6; Wright, August 2002: 24; Wright, February 2003: 25; Curtice May 2002: 24-5; January 2006; 70).

The prospect of a reduced Scottish Parliament *now* seems very unlikely.[27] However, the continuous attention in the monitoring reports suggests that it was a live issue for some time, particularly among Scottish Labour MPs, and that the Scottish Executive needed to secure Scottish Secretary and/or Prime Ministerial support for the maintenance of 129 (and, therefore, different constituency boundaries for Scottish Parliament and UK elections) (Wright, May 2002: 35; November 2002: 18; Wright, November 2001: 37; Wright, June 2003: 43-4; Wright, August 2003: 26; Wright, February 2004: 20-2; Wright, May 2004: 29; McGarvey, May 2004: 47). Indeed, the issue gave Labour MPs an excuse to make their views about devolution known; to warn 'overworked' MSPs that their numbers would be more likely to be cut if they were spending too much time debating reserved issues and '"straying" onto Westminster's turf' (Wright, August 2001: 24-5; for

---

[27] Indeed, by mid-2004 the agenda had moved on to the issue of confusing boundaries and voting systems in Scotland, prompting Alistair Darling to establish the Arbuthnott commission (but not to devolve control of Scottish Parliament elections to the Scottish Parliament) (Wright, August 2004: 24; Wright, April 2005: 24-5; Trench, September 2008; 64; for a discussion of the four different electoral systems in Scotland and Arbuthnott's recommendations, many of which were not accepted, see McGarvey and Cairney, 2008: 69-72).

examples, see Wright, February, 2003: 31–2; April 2005: 30 on the Scottish Parliament's debates on Iraq, and Wright, April 2005: 24 on the motion to retain six Scottish regiments). There were also reports that 'senior figures in Blair's Government had told MSPs to stop 'badmouthing' their MP colleagues if they want to keep their present number of 129' (Wright, November 2001: 37). The same threat was made later, by MPs, to pressure (in vain) Jack McConnell to reject the Liberal Democrat call for STV in local government elections (Wright, August 2003: 26).

It is in this context that we should view First Minister Jack McConnell's conciliatory noises to his UK Labour colleagues, who were less keen on the further-devolution agenda so soon after devolution (treated by many Labour MPs as an event rather than a process): 'I believe firmly in the devolution settlement agreed in the referendum. I don't believe we should be arguing about the powers of the Scottish Parliament for the next five or six years. We should get on with the business of delivering improved public services. For that to happen requires a partnership with our colleagues at Westminster' (McConnell in Wright, February 2002: 29). McConnell made similar comments ('now is not the time to go into consideration of changing the powers of the Scottish Parliament') when Wendy Alexander called for a Royal Commission to explore 'fiscal federalism' (Wright, November 2004: 20; see also Wright, February 2004: 16–17 on an early fiscal autonomy debate in the Scottish Parliament and Wright, August 2004: 29 on potential UK Conservative support for fiscal autonomy).

Notably, the two most prominent constitutional issues came from UK-led initiatives (note that both issues are yet to be resolved). The first issue regards the UK Government decision to introduce a UK Supreme Court to perform the judicial functions previously carried out by the House of Lords. It raised issues about the proper institution to hear civil appeals in Scotland. The potential legal problem was that the Union of 1707 perhaps precluded cases in Scotland being heard by any courts in 'Westminster Hall' (the Lords was effectively exempt) (Wright, August 2003: 23). The political problem was that the reform exposed what seemed to be an anomaly in Scottish politics—Scotland maintained its own legal system under the Union of 1707 but the final appeal for civil (*but not criminal*) cases was held outside Scotland (Winetrobe, February 2004: 35). The UK Government did not help matters by failing to consult (well, or at all) on the implications of a move in the UK which had the potential to produce unintended consequences in Scotland (Winetrobe, August 2003: 33; see also chapter

5 on the UK Government's periodic failure to consult with the Scottish Executive).

While the issue attracted particular attention from the SNP, it was 'by no means a lone political voice' (Wright, August 2003: 24). For example, Gordon Jackson (Labour MSP and QC) called for the new body to be able to resolve constitutional disputes between Holyrood and Westminster—an initiative rejected by the UK Government (Lord Falconer) on the basis that, in the UK system, Parliament is sovereign and should not be overruled by what would be an equivalent to the US Supreme Court (a stance that is increasingly untenable while the UK is a member of the EU) (Wright, August 2003: 24; Winetrobe, August 2003: 34). Both sides also made an appeal to the idea of progress, with reformers keen to portray the Supreme Court as a move away from archaic practices (and towards addressing its new position in regard to EU and European Convention of Human Rights law), and critics suggesting that a system in which civil appeals in Scotland go to a non-Scottish institution was outdated. There were also some concerns that legal decisions made in reference to English cases would affect Scots law (before the issue was addressed in amendments to the bill) and about the numbers of Scottish judges on the Supreme Court (the convention was two, with scope for more representation on Scottish-only issues) (Wright, February 2004: 14–16; Winetrobe, May 2004: 53–4).

The UK legislation required a Sewel motion, passed in 2005 (Wright, April 2005: 25). Yet, legislation did not mark the end of the debate. Rather, Alex Salmond made some strong criticisms of the Supreme Court following its involvement in a criminal case in 2011 (one month after the Scottish Parliament election). The stakes were raised when the Supreme Court made a ruling on Nat Fraser (regarding the prosecution's use of evidence heard by a Scottish High Court) not long after it ruled on the 'Cadder case' (regarding the right to legal representation during police questioning). In both cases, the Supreme Court became involved because both appeals were based on the defendants' human rights in relation to the ECHR (Robertson, 2011). The Supreme Court was effectively the next stage before a possible final appeal to the European Court of Human Rights (although note that the Supreme Court's ruling sent the issue back to Scotland, with the Court of Criminal Appeal asked to rule on a retrial (agreed) or Fraser's release). The Fraser case prompted Salmond to highlight 'the principle that Scotland has, for hundreds of years, been a distinct criminal jurisdiction, and the High Court of Justiciary should be the final arbiter of criminal cases in Scotland, as was always the case' (Whitaker and Robertson, 2011). Salmond also appeared to criticise

Supreme Court justice Lord Hope personally to highlight a perception that Scottish rulings are made by one or two Scottish judges (BBC News 5.6.11). Salmond's solution seems to be to allow a Scottish court to hear such cases before they go to the ECtHR in Strasbourg, but the issue as yet remains unresolved (Salmond appointed a committee, chaired by Lord McCluskey, to investigate the issue—Scottish Government 2011b; BBC News 5.6.11). It has also been sidelined to some extent by opposition, media and Lord Steel's criticisms about Salmond's attempts to personalise a constitutional issue (BBC News 16.6.11; Cochrane, 2011; Scott, 2011; Dinwoodie, 2011).

The second issue regards the unintended constitutional consequences of devolution, including the 'West Lothian' question ('the inability of English MPs to vote on devolved Scottish issues while Scottish MPs can still vote on the equivalent English issues [e.g. health, education, local government]' but not devolved Scottish issues— McGarvey and Cairney, 2008: 31; 165). The West Lothian question has always rumbled on in the background, but became a salient issue from 2003 for two main reasons. First, Scotland-based MPs (John Reid and Alistair Darling) were given UK ministerial posts in areas (health and transport) in which they had predominantly English responsibilities but minimal influence on those policy areas in Scotland (Wright, August 2003: 25). Second, Scotland MP votes were required to pass legislation applying primarily to England when England-based MPs rebelled in large numbers. The issue arose in November 2003 when Scotland and Wales MPs were needed to clinch the Labour Government vote on NHS foundation hospitals (John Reid was Health Secretary—Wright, August, 2003: 25–6). Interestingly, the SNP argued that in some cases there is effectively no West Lothian question because, for example, the decision to pursue private funding for the NHS in England has huge consequences for public provision in Scotland (they voted against foundation hospitals and tuition fees). In contrast, UK Shadow Health Secretary Tim Yeo called the matter a 'constitutional outrage' (Wright, February 2004: 17–19).

In January 2004 Scottish Labour votes were required to pass the bill introducing student top-up fees in England, prompting Conservative calls to prohibit Scottish MPs voting on 'purely English' matters. This solution was rejected by Alistair Darling (Scottish Secretary), who argued that MPs in devolved territories still had the right to help decide how Parliament allocated tax-raised UK resources, and worried that such measures would produce two classes of MP and perhaps 'federalism or even independence' (Wright, February 2004: 18–20; Wright, August 2004: 29; note that survey respondents in Scotland seem to favour Scots abstaining from such votes—Curtice, February 2001: 24; May 2004: 19; January 2006: 52; Wright, February 2004: 20; Ormston and Curtice, 2011). Jack Straw (Leader of the Commons) expressed similar concerns about the breakup of the UK in 2006 (but note that critics feared the West Lothian question would also lead to separatist claims) (Trench, September 2006: 44–6). Various other schemes were mooted, including: giving Parliament's Speaker the discretion to choose which votes were English-only (Wright, May 2004: 33); legislating to stop Scotland MPs voting on English matters; producing a new 'covenant' between Scotland, England and Wales; and even replacing MSPs with Scottish MPs (Trench, September 2006: 44–6; see also Bort, January 2008: 31–2 on the West Lothian Question and the wider issue of English attitudes to Scotland). They were rejected by the UK Labour Government as impractical and potentially harmful to the stability of the UK (Trench, September 2006: 44–6; January 2007: 46). Further, no solution has been accepted even under a Conservative-led UK Government, largely because the West Lothian question is small beer at a time of economic and political crisis (it did not support a member's bill in September 2011 but intends to establish a commission in October—Settle, 2011; note that an e-petition on West Lothian currently has 126 of its 100000 signatories required by the UK Government to ensure parliamentary debate).[28]

The Second Half

The 2007 election result was the single biggest cause of a rise of attention to constitutional change (followed by the 2011 result which gave the SNP a majority in the Scottish Parliament and made an independence referendum inevitable). However, the independence issue had begun to receive more attention from the end of 2005. The SNP published the wording of its proposed referendum on independence in November 2005 in the lead up to its part in the 'Independence Convention' with the Greens and SSP. As Lynch (January 2006: 113; May 2006: 65) suggests, the title was supposed to associate the independence project with the Scottish Constitutional Convention's role in the push for devolution, and it marked 'an acceptance by the SNP that its efforts alone are unlikely to win independence', but it was also primarily a 'campaigning tool'. In this regard, we should be careful to distinguish between campaigning for election and for independence. The SNP was certainly successful in its attempts to secure media and public attention and an election win in

---

[28] http://epetitions.direct.gov.uk/petitions/1047 'English votes for English MPs'

2007. Lynch (January 2007: 66–9; April 2007: 76–9) notes that the SNP began to secure heightened attention from the end of 2006 as: polls suggested that it was ahead of Labour and that support for independence was there under some circumstances (chapter 7); its policies were received quite favourably in the press; the SNP secured high profile donations from business owners keen to see a 'level playing field' on the independence debate (including Brian Souter and Sir Tom Farmer), and declared a 'fighting fund' of over £1m; the Catholic Church began to appear more open to the idea of independence; and, tensions arose within Scottish Labour on SNP-led issues such as Trident and nuclear power. However, its success in promoting independence is another matter (see below), particularly since its elections in 2007 and 2011 did not coincide with a rise in support for independence (chapter 7).

The independence agenda rumbled on at the same time as the Liberal Democrats completed the 'Steel Commission' report into the future of devolution and reiterated their desire to see a second Constitutional Convention (Lynch, May 2006: 66–7). It was then followed by 'a reprise of Labour's negative campaigning over independence', with Tony Blair arguing that independence would undermine Scotland's economy and Jack McConnell predicting 'decades of constitutional upheaval' (Lynch, January 2007: 68). UK ministers and McConnell also made more positive speeches about the importance of Britishness, the social and economic (and security service) integration between Scotland and the rest of Britain and the general value of the Union. Indeed, Labour's position proved to be highly unusual ('the only party supporting the status quo') when McConnell rejected the idea of further devolution in favour of using existing powers more effectively (Lynch, January 2007: 68; this stance was criticised quite heavily in the print media, before and after the 2007 election – Bort, January 2007: 39–40; September 2007: 28–9). The Liberal Democrats also committed themselves to a rejection of coalition government with the SNP unless they dropped their plans for an independence referendum – a move that Lynch (January 2007: 70–1) relates to the number of seats in which the SNP and Liberal Democrats would go 'head-to-head'.

The pre-election discussions of constitutional change were notable for their separation: independence and devolution were often discussed and promoted almost entirely separately in self-contained conventions or commissions. While Labour often criticised the SNP's stance on independence, and the SNP seemed open to the idea of a multi-option referendum to attract support from the Liberal Democrats

(Lynch, April 2007: 80), there was little party engagement outside of the electoral arena. This position set the tone for much of the constitutional debates and developments from 2007–11. The SNP Government initiated its 'National Conversation' to consult on, and encourage support for, independence, while the main opposition parties got behind the 'Calman Commission' inquiry into the future, and possible extension, of devolution. While both sides could not completely ignore each other's arguments and agendas, it often seemed like they tried their best. The two constitutional reviews continued on parallel tracks, displaying different styles of consultation and with minimal discussion between them (Trench, May 2008: 58). The National Conversation considered devolution in some detail but largely to reject it in favour of independence. The Calman Commission's remit did not include consideration of independence. Such was the distance between them that, 'The unionist parties have declined invitations to contribute to the National Conversation, and the SNP government has instructed its officials to provide assistance to the Calman Commission "on factual matters" only' (Jeffery, January 2009: 9; see also pp 15–16 on the lack of coordination between Scottish, Welsh and UK reviews of the constitution).

There were some notable exceptions. For example, Alex Salmond reiterated his possible support for a multi-option referendum including both independence and further devolution (Lynch, May 2008: 76; September 2008: 92–3). The SNP also agreed to consider both fiscal autonomy under devolution and independence as part of a deal with the Liberal Democrats during the annual budget round in 2009 (Cairney, May 2009: 34). Further, some Conservative and Labour voices called for a referendum to settle the matter quickly—including, most notably, Wendy Alexander's ill-fated call to 'bring it on' (Bort, May 2008: 29–33; September 2008: 24–5). Still, as Bort (January 2008: 35–6) notes, the appearance of two separate reviews exacerbated their partisan image and diminished the legitimacy of both—particularly since UK Labour support for a review of devolution was lukewarm at best (Lynch, May 2008: 78).

As Keating (May 2009: 11; see also Keating, 2009) notes, the parallel process 'has allowed both sides to avoid difficult questions that might be raised by the other'. In particular, there has not been a substantive debate on the 'political economy of independence'—what economic model it would adopt (such as the Irish model of low tax and 'minimal welfare standards' or the Nordic model of 'high taxes, high welfare standards') and what the transitional arrangements would look like. Nor has there been a substantive debate on Scotland's part in the EU

(Keating, May 2009: 7). Instead, the debate quickly descended to superficial comparisons with countries first described as part of an 'arc of prosperity' before being disparaged as part of the 'arc of insolvency' following the global financial crisis (Keating, May 2009: 7). This seems particularly unfortunate, given that the SNP's modern form of independence within the EU and in cooperation with the UK (and with a recognition of the limited powers any small nation has, independent or not) may not be too far from the 'devolution-max' option considered by the Calman Commission (Jeffery, January 2009: 15).

The SNP and the National Conversation

The SNP began official preparations for the independence agenda in 2007. It published a White Paper *Choosing Scotland's Future* (Scottish Government, 2007) on constitutional change, discussing devolution but expressing a preference for independence and linking an independence referendum to the idea that, under the Union of 1707, the 'people of Scotland' still have the 'fundamental political right to determine their own constitutional future' (2007: 19). It then goes on to discuss the practical implications, including: the need for an Act of the UK Parliament to settle the new arrangements; negotiations with the UK Government over transition economic arrangements and more fundamental issues regarding the armed forces and diplomatic role of each country; stating that it would remain a member of the EU and other international organisations such as the UN; and stating that the Queen would remain as Head of State in Scotland (2007: 20-4; it leaves open the question of joining the Euro, but Salmond previously stated his intention to keep the pound before considering the Euro – a plan that would be problematic if Scotland was obliged to seek membership of the EU). It also published a draft bill on the independence referendum in 2007, promised to hold its 'National Conversation' and introduced an economic plan designed to both 'make itself credible and effective' (as part of its strategy on governing competence) and create the 'economic conditions for Scottish independence' (by making 'Scots families £10,000 wealthier come 2017' – Lynch, September 2007: 68; January 2008: 93; see also Cairney, September 2007: 76).

There is surprisingly little to report about the National Conversation. Jeffery (January 2008: 9) reports that in early 2008 it 'ticked over more or less invisibly', while Cairney (September 2009: 11) remarks that it was 'low key' in 2009. Trench (January 2008: 63) suggests that the National Conversation has been fairly limited, with its main presence on the internet (which lists ministerial speeches and some public comments), due to a lack of finance and a lack of clarity about its intentions. Jeffery (January 2009: 10–11) suggests that this format was perhaps the intention, with a series of 'Minister's Blogs' and other materials designed to prompt online debate on particular themes (but see Keating's May 2009: 6 comparison with the major research done in Quebec before its referendum in 1995). In 2008, the National Conversation entered a 'second phase', with consultation extended to 'pressure groups and civic Scotland' and the public in a series of roadshow meetings introduced by Alex Salmond, and debates chaired by Scottish ministers (Lynch, May 2008: 76; McEwen, May 2008: 7). There was also an online questionnaire 'fielded at 5000 young people' (Jeffery, January 2009: 10–11).

The National Conversation ended in 2009, followed by the Scottish Government's (2009b) second White Paper *Your Scotland, Your Voice: A National Conversation* which: reported on the results of the conversation (5300 attendees at events; 500000 visitors to the website — 2009b: 5; see also Harvey and Lynch, 2010); discussed briefly the Calman Commission (it supports some proposals and calls for them to be 'implemented as soon as possible', but also criticises its stance on fiscal reform and other matters — 2009b: 12–13; 28); provided a more detailed account of the benefits of independence in comparison with devolution (it is 176 pages long); and, set out its plans for a referendum bill (2009b: 136–9). Yet, its efforts came to nothing in the 2007–11 period because it could not secure enough votes in the Scottish Parliament to pass its referendum bill (despite periodic claims that at least one party might change its mind — Cairney, September 2009: 11). Instead, it decided not to introduce the bill at all, preferring to use the platform of the 2011 election campaign and the prospect of re-election to further its plans (Hutcheon, 2010). Its manifesto (SNP, 2011: 28) does not set a date and its avalanche win produced some calls for an early vote, but its plan seems to be to hold the vote in the second half of its five-year term. This provides enough time to resolve outstanding issues regarding the changes to the Scotland Act associated with the Calman Commission.

The Calman Commission

The National Conversation was quickly criticised by the UK Government which argued that Unionist parties commanded two-thirds of the Scottish Parliament's voters (Trench, September 2007: 49; it is now closer to 50/50 — see chapter 11). The case for further devolution, not independence, began with talks between the main opposition parties (Labour, Conservative, Liberal Democrat) on the back of the Liberal Democrats' Steel Commission and call for a second Constitutional Convention (Lynch, September 2007: 73) and a series of key Labour and Conservative speeches on the value of the Union, including Scottish Labour leader Wendy Alexander's St Andrew's Day speech which focused most on the need for a review of devolved finance and the Barnett formula (Trench, January 2008: 64–5). This agenda was furthered by an unusual arrangement in which the opposition parties would seek to establish the 'Scottish Constitutional Commission' (chaired by Sir Kenneth Calman — Lynch, May 2008: 81–2) via a motion in the Scottish Parliament, but it would be funded by the UK Government and supported administratively by UK Government-employed civil servants (Lynch, January 2008: 98). Lynch (January 2008: 99) also suggests that the initial process was odd because Labour had recently committed itself to no-further-devolution (Alexander's speech 'put the seal on this constitutional U-turn for Scottish Labour' — Bort, January 2008: 34), and the Conservatives did not have a clear position (David Cameron expressed a vague commitment to 'an imperfect Union' — Bort, January 2008: 33). Rather, all the three parties could agree on was that the Commission should not consider independence (Bort, January 2008: 34; it was also asked to consider what devolved responsibilities could usefully be reserved — Lynch, May 2008: 78).

Subsequent reports suggest that the aims of, and control over, the Calman Commission were initially contested by the Unionist parties, with some confusion about who (or which Whitehall department) was funding and servicing its activities, followed by calls by the Conservatives and Liberal Democrats to make the Commission independent rather than Labour-led (Trench, May 2008: 58–9). These issues were addressed and the Commission bore 'all the hallmarks of a UK independent commission: it is chaired by a senior figure in public life; its members have been picked to provide party-political balance, but also a range of expertise within and beyond formal politics; and it is serviced by the civil service' (Jeffery, January 2009: 9). It also established the 'Independent Expert Group on Finance' chaired by Anton Muscatelli, to advise on what proved to be a key aspect of the Commission's work: 'how the financial accountability of the Scottish Parliament might be improved' (see Jeffery, January 2009: 10). The Calman Commission operated in a more 'traditional' way to the National Conversation (Jeffery, January 2009: 10). Although it maintained a website and invited comments, it generally operated by seeking written and oral evidence from the UK and Scottish Governments, politicians, pressure participants and some academics (the Independent Expert Group consisted almost entirely of academics).

The monitors provide three detailed commentaries on the Calman Commission. Jeffery (January 2009: 11–15) comments on the first report of the Independent Expert Group on Finance and the Commission's interim report. The former has three related themes: first, 'there is a trade-off between territorial financial arrangements focused on inter-regional equity ... and arrangements focused on fiscal autonomy'; and, second, any choice on which model to select and how to balance equity and autonomy is political rather than technical. In other words, the Expert Group is only in the position to make recommendations based on the requirements of policymakers, or to give them enough information with which to make a choice. The third theme—how will new fiscal arrangements affect the Union?—arose in comparisons between the Expert Group's work and reports by other academics (including Andrew Hughes Hallett and Drew Scott) and the think tank Reform Scotland, which proposed quite ambitious tax raising and borrowing powers for the Scottish Parliament. In contrast, the Expert Group was more cautious, largely because it could not 'visualise how full fiscal autonomy for the Scottish Parliament might be consistent with the maintenance of the union' (see Jeffery, January 2009: 13). The latter theme was central to the interim report of the Calman Commission, which produced considerable material (to demonstrate that it is 'rigorously based on evidence', perhaps in contrast to the National Conversation) on the history of devolution and current practices and '"principles" of union'—largely to foster further debate and help it gather more evidence before making its final recommendations (Jeffery, January 2009: 13–14).

Keating's (May 2009: 7–10) assessment is more critical of the philosophy underpinning Calman's interim report, commenting in particular on its discussion of British social citizenship. The interim report tries to articulate a coherent view about a widespread desire to have the best of both worlds: devolution, to recognise different identities and attitudes; and, the Union, to foster a sense of social solidarity and citizenship and, in particular, to ensure that people across the UK have some sort of common access to public services and a welfare state (see Greer, 2009). As chapter 7 discusses, a small majority of Scottish respondents want both the devolution of responsibility for health, education, welfare and social security *and* an assurance that greater autonomy does not lead to differences in public service standards and levels of benefits (Curtice, May 2004: 19). First, Keating argues that that the report does not recognise the idea of Scottish social citizenship, in which equal access to public services and the welfare state is pursued within Scotland rather than the UK (and the broader issue of political and human rights is pursued by Scottish institutions within a European framework). Second, he suggests that devolution may provide 'more fertile territory' for the sort of social democratic state envisaged in discussions of social citizenship. Third, he points to a series of problems related to intergovernmental relations and the control of devolved institutions when we try to maintain a UK-wide standard of service (in a non-federal system).

While the Calman Commission's (2009) final report does not resolve these points, it does provide a much more ambitious set of recommendations than its interim report (and its rather constrained remit) would suggest (see Cairney, May 2009: 5–9). It recommends:

- Various fiscal reforms, including reducing UK income tax by 10 pence in the pound to oblige the Scottish Parliament to make a decision on how much tax should be raised, and devolving a series of smaller taxes which could be used to further devolved policy aims (below).

- Devolving responsibility for Scottish Parliament elections, airgun regulation, drink-driving limits, national speed limits, animal health funding, marine nature conservation, the Deprived Areas fund, discretionary elements of the reformed Social Fund, the appointment of the Scottish member of the BBC Trust and the prescribing of controlled drugs (e.g. heroin) to treat addiction.

- Maintaining reserved control in areas that require policy and/or administrative uniformity (such as charity law and regulation, food labelling and regulation, and the regulation of all health professions) and areas such as research funding (to ensure that resources are pooled), as well as better coordination in problematic areas such as health and safety, the children of asylum seekers and welfare to work programmes.

- Formalising and improving the process of IGR.

The Barnett Formula Revisited?

Chapter 9 suggests that there was very little to report on the Barnett formula because Scotland's fiscal relationship with the UK changed very little and the Barnett formula remains to this day. It also suggests that the UK Government had relatively little incentive to revisit the formula in the first half of devolution, because public expenditure was rising rapidly and it was able to argue that the formula was successfully producing convergence in per capita expenditure (see for example Howarth in Hazell, 2001: 259–60). Consequently, the most vocal discussion of Barnett was likely to be a *principled* objection to the system since that objection would not be as susceptible to shifts in public expenditure. One such example comes from the Liberal Democrat manifesto in 2003 (Scottish Parliament elections) which argues that, while Barnett provided short term financial stability, it should be replaced by a needs-based formula. However, it received almost no attention during the campaign (Wright, June 2003: 43).

The election of an SNP Government lifted (elite) attention to Barnett to its highest level since devolution. Further, it signalled its support for the replacement of Barnett in its White Paper *Choosing Scotland's Future* which considers the options for fiscal autonomy (within a devolved settlement) alongside the option of independence. While the SNP obviously favoured the latter option, there was some scope for a (very) loose coalition with its counterparts in the opposition parties around the former option—a possibility signalled by Wendy Alexander's speech trailing the Calman Commission (Trench, January 2008: 87–8). In other words, there now seems to be public cross-party support in Scotland to revisit the Barnett formula.

Yet, fiscal autonomy may not come any time soon. The Calman report (2009) argues that it would be difficult to maintain the Union if the UK Government granted full fiscal autonomy to Scotland. Therefore, macro-economic policy must remain reserved and Barnett (which provided stability during devolution's first decade) should be maintained until the UK Government commissions a needs assessment to determine a more equitable system of funding. A Lords report made a similar recommendation for a needs assessment and the replacement of Barnett (Cairney, September 2009: 12) (but note that neither outline in detail *how* a needs assessment should be conducted, largely because this is a fiercely political exercise). In the meantime, to produce more accountability for money spent in Scotland, there should be a devolution of some economic powers when the differences would not undermine overall macroeconomic policy—the Stamp Duty on property transactions, the Aggregates Levy, Landfill Tax and Air Passenger Duty.

More importantly, it argues that the Scottish Parliament should be obliged to make a positive and more visible decision about its level of taxation in relation to the UK rather than benefiting from the relatively hidden status quo position in which it accepts the same levels by not using the tartan tax. It recommends reducing UK income tax in Scotland by 10p in the pound (for the lower and higher income tax thresholds, with no ability to tax on one but not the other) and reducing Scotland's grant accordingly, meaning that Scottish Parliament would have to set the Scottish rate at 10p to stay the same as the UK. It suggests keeping benefits such as housing/council tax reserved but to give much more scope for Scottish Ministers to amend their use when developing their own policies. It also recommends allowing the Scottish Government, like local authorities, to borrow on a Prudential basis (i.e. based on its capacity to repay debt—allowing the Scottish Government to fund the Forth Road Bridge in a more straightforward way), and to consider further tax devolution—on VAT and a share of fuel duty—when these recommendations have 'bedded in'. This suggests that, again, the recommendations do not mark the end of the Scottish 'settlement'.

The Next Steps

The opposition parties expressed enthusiasm about the Calman report, but did not fall over themselves to further its recommendations. Indeed, the SNP gained some political capital by recommending the early implementation of some measures—largely the further devolution of responsibilities—while expressing criticism of the recommendations on fiscal reform (largely because they seem designed to give the *appearance* of Scottish Parliament financial responsibility without producing much change in its ability to influence the economy). Notably, while Labour and the Conservatives welcomed the report's recommendations in principle, there was no serious commitment to take them forward quickly, much to the frustration of the Liberal Democrats (Cairney, September 2009: 11). Indeed, the latter joined forces with the SNP and Greens to pass a Scottish Parliament motion calling for '... the UK Government to work with the Scottish Parliament to ensure that, where there is consensus, all such recommendations are implemented before the dissolution of the current UK Parliament' (Scottish Parliament Official Report 9.12.09 Col 22020).

The UK (Labour) Government did not respond positively to that timescale, largely because *Scotland's Future in the UK* (Cm7738, 2009) made a commitment to implementing Calman in the next Parliament (from May 2010). It accepted most of Calman's recommendations (the main exceptions are the devolution of air passenger duty, given EU state aid rules, and the application of the income tax plan to income on savings), but also defended the Barnett formula and stated that it had no plans to review it (2009: 11). It agreed to replace the Scottish Variable Rate ('tartan tax') with a new ability to, effectively, vary income tax by 10 pence in the pound (up or down) – by estimating the tax yield and deducting 'a sum equivalent to a ten pence reduction in the rate of income tax' from the Scottish block grant (2009: 10). This would happen 'as soon as economic and fiscal circumstances permit' (2009: 11). It also agreed to give the Scottish Government more capital borrowing powers (2009: 11).

Following the 2010 general election, the UK (Conservative and Liberal Democrat) Government put constitutional reform quite high on its agenda, promising legislation that year. It produced *Strengthening Scotland's Future* (Cm 7979, 2010) in November. The paper introduces few differences, although it does propose giving Scottish ministers greater borrowing powers (for capital projects *and* current spending if tax yields are lower than expected), recommend delaying the devolution of the aggregates levy (while it is subject to court action) and address miscellaneous issues, such as introducing the power to devolve some powers temporarily (to address problems associated with the Somerville case on 'slopping out') and requiring that all Scottish Parliament bills are deemed to cover devolved issues and consistent with EU law and the ECHR (see Trench 2010a).

Unusually, the Scotland Bill was subject to scrutiny from both Parliaments. The Scottish Parliament's Scotland Bill committee (which, at the time had an SNP minority) approved the bill conditionally, subject to a recommendation to reconsider some issues (regarding, for example, how to address a shortfall in income related to income tax volatility and the limits to Scottish ministerial borrowing) and return an amended Scotland Bill to the Scottish Parliament for further approval via a second Sewel motion (Scotland Bill Committee Report, 2011). While the SNP criticised the bill and sought to amend it in Westminster, and its members of the Scottish Parliament's Scotland Bill committee presented 'minority views', it voted to support the Sewel motion giving Westminster the power to legislate. As Trench (2011a) argues, this move is not as inconsistent (or a U-turn) as many media accounts suggest. Rather, the Sewel motion gives conditional support to the Scotland Bill and proposes the need for a second motion. Following the 2011 election, this puts the SNP in a much stronger position, with a Scottish Parliament committee now much less likely to accept the Bill as it stands. As Trench (2011b) notes, Scottish Secretary Michael Moore had previously suggested that the UK Government could pass the Scotland Bill without Scottish Parliament consent, but this seems unlikely given the size of the SNP win and the general tendency of the Conservative-led UK Government to seek consensus on territorial issues. Instead, the Scottish Parliament's new Scotland Committee Bill, with an SNP majority, will reconsider its provisions and use its new inquiry to explore issues such as the devolution of corporation tax before reporting at the end of 2011 (Trench, 2011c).

Conclusion

At one stage from 2010–11 it looked like there might be at least a temporary resolution to the constitutional question. The SNP Government did not have the votes to secure an independence referendum. Instead, it was obliged to engage with the UK Government and opposition parties in the Scottish Parliament on amendments to the Scotland Bill, to introduce a small number of new devolved responsibilities and a new financial setup in which it was more responsible for income tax variation and a small number of other taxes. Now, that process is subject to uncertainty. The SNP's avalanche win has produced in UK policymakers a greater desire *not* to challenge the SNP on constitutional matters and perhaps reconsider the Scotland Act process. It has also given the SNP the confidence to insist on a fundamental review of the Scotland Bill in the run up to its introduction of a bill to conduct a referendum on independence. At the same time, there is little evidence to suggest that the 'people of Scotland' will vote for independence. Instead, the likely outcome will be further devolution, perhaps furthered by the stronger hand given to the SNP in 2011.

As such, further devolution will be a very messy compromise, with a miscellany of further devolved powers accompanied by the devolution of some economic powers but the reservation of the major economic levers on interest rates and taxation. If the Calman process is a useful guide, the result will be the appearance of greater Scottish accountability for its own spending without a parallel ability to make a profound difference to the way that the Scottish Government budget is determined (its budget is £30bn; each one pence change to income tax represents approximately £4–500m). The Scottish Government will be able to vary income tax by up to ten pence in the pound, but in the context of twelve years in which no Scottish government has exploited its ability to vary income tax. The economic conditions have changed since the initial period of devolution in which there was almost no incentive to vary income tax (a rise was unnecessary given the high budget; a reduction would expose Scotland's generous financial settlement). However, a rise in taxes would still be unpopular and a reduction would still expose Scotland's generous settlement (or lead to an unpopular reduction of public services) and the income tax status quo is not *that* much harder to maintain.

Perhaps the biggest saving grace of devolution so far is that the UK and Scottish Governments and Parliaments appear well equipped to manage that messy compromise. Few serious issues with constitutional aspects have arisen since devolution and those issues have been addressed without any fundamental disagreements likely to undermine Scotland's position within the Union.

Chapter 11

Conclusion: Has Devolution Been a Success?

It is commonplace in the Scottish devolution literature to express scepticism about the idea of 'new politics' and to question the success of Scottish devolution on that basis. In this sense, Scottish devolution was a victim of the context in which it was created. First, the design of devolution arose largely from discussions held in the Scottish Constitutional Convention—a body with all the characteristics of working groups used later by devolved governments in the early years of devolution. The environment is one of cooperation between a small number of policymakers and a large number of optimistic pressure participants. As such, the result was a series of very ambitious (and often contradictory) recommendations, not only about the structure of the political system and its institutions, but also the behaviour of its participants. Second, the plans were created in an atmosphere of perceived political disenchantment, with the Scottish Parliament and its associated bodies occasionally likened to an additional layer of expensive and unnecessary bureaucracy. Consequently, proponents of devolution felt obliged to prove that Scottish devolution would be something more; that it could lead to a better style of politics and policymaking and really make a difference to people's lives. In both cases, the result was an incredibly high bar that we would not expect anyone to clear. Instead, we can see many aspects of new politics as ideals to aspire to but not to reach. In other words, it is inappropriate to consider the success of devolution in these terms. It may also be impossible because the term 'new politics' means too many things to too many people. It is a vague term referring to a series of often contradictory visions (Winetrobe, 2001: 2).

If so, we need a more realistic discussion of the success of devolution. This chapter adopts the framework of policy success outlined by McConnell (2010). McConnell (2010: 46) and Marsh and

McConnell (2010: 571) initially distinguish between political, process and programmatic success (for an application to Scottish devolution, see McGarvey and McConnell, 2011). Political refers simply to the effect of the policy on the government's credibility, popularity and chances of re-election. Process measures include a focus on a policy's legitimacy, or the extent to which the government learned from more established and successful initiatives elsewhere, passed the policy through accepted democratic channels, secured a body of support and/or passed legislation with no significant opposition or amendment. Programmatic refers to implementation success, in terms of the link between its objectives and outcomes, the extent to which it represented an efficient use of resources, and the question of benefit to a particular social group.

In these terms we are more likely to be able to identify *types* of policy success. For example, devolution itself was popular, and remains popular, and may have contributed to a short-term boost to the popularity of Labour (although it was rather popular in 1997 anyway). This is instant success, although it is also fleeting and may have been shared with other political parties. We can also identify process success, particularly because the UK Labour Government learned the lessons of the past (the 1979 experience) and held a referendum before passing the legislation to introduce devolution in Scotland (McGarvey and Cairney: 30–1; 36–7). As such, the legislation passed with relatively low opposition and there is a strong link between ideas proposed by the SCC, the UK Government's White Paper, The Scotland Act 1998 and the eventual outcome. There is also *some* evidence of learning from the more established 'consensus democracies', and the Nordic countries in particular, even if Scottish devolution was more likely to be built using a caricature of Westminster as a 'negative template' (Mitchell, 2000; Arter, 2003).

Perhaps most importantly, the process to introduce devolution itself was an excellent example of new politics in action. It involved unusually strong cross-party cooperation, both during the SCC negotiations (between the Labour, Liberal Democratic and Green parties, with fleeting SNP involvement) and during the 'Yes, Yes' to a Scottish Parliament (with tax raising powers) campaign which brought together the leaders of Labour, the Liberal Democrats and the SNP (the Conservatives opposed devolution at the time). It also took in a large number of local authority, voluntary, small business, religious, trade union, women's and ethnic minority groups and was still able to produce pro-devolution reports based on considerable consensus (2008: 34–5). We may *now* be sceptical about new politics, but it is more difficult to dismiss the success of pre-devolution consultation and cooperation.

Programmatic success is more difficult to assess although, again, we can identify several positive aspects of the devolution process if we extend the 'policy success' framework further, to consider: *whose* success we are measuring primarily (policymakers, their stakeholders, their target group?); how they might measure their own success when they have multiple, and sometimes contradictory, objectives; how they measure success when there is imperfect information and some choice regarding the 'benchmarks' they can adopt; and how long we should wait before assessing success and failure (McConnell, 2010: 82–7; Marsh and McConnell, 2010: 575). We can also make a useful distinction between the type of success we associate with an adherence to important *principles*, and the success we associate with the longer term outcomes of *behaviour* (and whether or not we can relate it to those principles).

The introduction of devolution itself may be seen by many as a sign of success in its own right, as might the endurance of devolution (it seems to be here to stay). We may then explore the related objectives or priorities that different people use to assess success in more detail. For example, Hazell (2000: 3; 5) argues that devolution was an 'extraordinary achievement' because it represented the transformation of 'a highly centralised unitary state into a devolved and quasi-federal system of government' in a short period of time without leading to the 'break-up of Britain.' For others, devolution was an instant success because it partly solved the democratic deficit (chapter 2). Following the introduction of a Scottish Parliament, Scottish voters have received the Scottish government they voted for (albeit generally in a minority or coalition form). This is only partial success because devolution covers a limited number of policy areas and Scotland still generally votes Labour in UK elections, with the potential (realised in 2010) for a non-Labour UK Government. However, it may be the highest level of success that most supporters of devolution would have expected, particularly if they support the Union. We may also relate devolution objectives to further constitutional change. For example, George Robertson may welcome devolution but be disappointed that it did not 'kill nationalism stone dead', while Alex Salmond may welcome devolution as a platform for the SNP but be disappointed that it has not prompted the majority of the 'people of Scotland' to support independence. Each example shows that a lack of complete success does not mean failure. Rather, it means that we assess devolution success according to our expectations and in relation to other objectives.

We can point to similar examples of success in terms of the adoption of new Scottish political institutions favoured by the SCC and other supporters of devolution, such as: a Scottish Parliament built on the 'consensus democracy model', with members elected using a mixed-member-proportional system; a set of parliamentary principles and practices built on a modernisation of 'old Westminster' and rejection of the House of Lords; and, a set of measures to increase the potential for members of the public to participate directly in politics, including a Scottish Civic Forum and a petitions system administered by the Scottish Parliament (chapter 1). In other words, our assessment of these measures becomes at least a two stage process. Our first question is 'did supporters of devolution secure the institutions they demanded?', and our second question is 'did those institutions behave in the way they wanted or expected?'.

Similar issues arise with the social background of elected representatives in the Scottish Parliament. For example, partial success may be found in the commitment of some parties (and Scottish Labour in particular) to take gender seriously and take greater steps to address the representation gap than in Westminster. Then, further success may be measured in terms of the level of representation of women in the Scottish Parliament. This issue also shows the importance of the benchmark we select, since we will find more success in comparisons with the proportion of women in Westminster than when using a 50/50 benchmark.

Despite some concerns in 2011 about the departure of key Labour women, and a reduction in the parliamentary Labour party (traditionally the source of more than half of the Scottish Parliament's female members), the gender balance improved slightly at 65% men and 35% women because very similar numbers of women and men left and returned. The Parliament is also now not exclusively white (note that Bashir Ahmad served from 2007 until his death in 2009), with two new Scottish–Asian MSPs representing 1.6% of MSPs (black and ethnic minorities represent 2% of the Scottish population). More work is required to tell if the occupational background of MSPs has changed. Political parties in many countries have an increasing reputation for recruiting candidates from 'politics facilitating' occupations (such as party, interest group and think tank staff) and the Scottish Parliament is no exception (Keating and Cairney, 2006; McGarvey and Cairney, 2008: 229–30). Overall, we can identify relative success if our expectations are pegged to the Westminster experience, and relative failure if pegged to pre-devolution hopes and dreams.

The Success of New Politics, the Scottish Parliament and Political Parties

It is in this context that we can view the success of measures related to the idea of new politics. For example, there is almost no evidence to suggest that the civic forum or petitions processes have had a tangible effect on public policy, but the petitions process still represents the *potential* for members of the public to become directly involved in politics that did not exist before 1999 (and its processes are often studied by members of other legislatures). That potential could have been enhanced with other measures, such as the devotion of resources to encourage people to participate in these processes, or the introduction of other measures, such as regular referendums (as in Switzerland and US states). The fact that it was *not* suggests that we make choices and that direct participation may be low on our list of priorities. For example, although the barriers to petition entry are low (requiring one signature to get attention), the rewards for a well-subscribed petition are also low (including three minutes to describe the petition in a Scottish Parliament committee). Similarly, neither the Scottish Parliament nor the Scottish Executive felt that the Scottish Civic Forum was worth funding for longer than seven years (partly because it struggled to attract a not-previously-involved-in-politics audience). Therefore, we may conclude that the success of these measures was roughly proportionate to the resources devoted to them.

The Scottish Parliament is a more complicated case and we can identify a more balanced scorecard. As chapters 1–3 show, it is easy to be negative about the role of political parties, particularly given the tendency of the governing party to dominate the policymaking role of the Scottish Parliament, even under minority government. Yet, these evaluations are generally made in relation to the unrealistic expectations associated with new politics that few of us hold. Our evaluation of success changes when we change the benchmark. For example, Scottish Parliament was not designed to be a legislature in the US mould (in which there is a clear separation of powers between executive, legislature and judiciary) and its proponents may generally hold a sense of realism about what we can expect from a parliamentary system. In this context, if we compare the Scottish Parliament, as an institution, to *Westminster* then we can identify a series of improvements associated with UK parliamentary reform movements since the 1960s (many of which are now being adopted in Westminster — Winetrobe, in correspondence). This includes the fusion of Westminster's standing and select committee functions, to enable members scrutinising legislation to develop subject based expertise (although the success of this measure is now questioned by some Scottish Parliament clerks), and the reform of legislative procedures to allow committees to consider both the principles of legislation and specific amendments to bills before they are discussed in plenary. Members of the Scottish Parliament also find it less difficult to introduce (but not pass) legislation, and committees also have this ability even if they use it sparingly.

These powers have not translated into a major shift in the relationship between the executive and legislature. The Parliament has generally been a peripheral part of the Scottish policy process for the majority of its 12 year existence. In the first eight years, the Labour and Liberal Democrat coalition performed the role of a majority government, controlling the vote in plenary and committees and passing so much legislation that most committees devoted most of their activities to scrutiny (instead of, say, agenda setting inquiries). There was little evidence of 'power sharing' or 'new politics' and much more evidence of a concentration of power in the government combined with an adversarial atmosphere that we associated so much with 'old Westminster'.

We might have expected a big difference in the latter four years, with the Scottish Government finally having to negotiate with opposition parties in the Parliament to secure its policy aims. Yet, four years of minority government showed that, while the Scottish Government passed fewer bills in four years (42, compared to 50 from 2003–7 and 53 from 1999–03) and required the support of other parties to pass annual budgets, the balance of power did not change dramatically. With the exception of some high profile government retreats (on the independence referendum, local taxation reform and minimum alcohol pricing), there was a muted parliamentary effect. The Scottish Government produced and amended the vast majority of the legislation and found that they could pursue many of their aims without recourse to Parliament—through public spending, the use of legislation already on the statute books and its new relationship with local government. The experience of the Conservatives perhaps sums up the executive-legislature relationship best. They may look back on their position from 2007–11 and treat it as their longest period of success given the circumstances they face (low popularity and no likelihood of forming a government) and the peripheral role in the Scottish Parliament that they enjoyed from 1999–2007. From 2007–11 they often propped up the SNP, providing support on key votes (most notably on the budget) for quite small policy concessions. Committees were no more effective. Indeed, at times, they seemed *less* effective after 2007 either because: the main opposition parties seemed disinterested in committee business; party politics got in the way of business-like committee decision making; or, simply because they did not have the resources to find out how local and health authorities were spending public money.

The Scottish Parliament's role is limited largely to departmental and legislative scrutiny under any type of government formation — coalition, minority or majority. It does not have the resources to present an alternative legislative agenda or budget. For example, committee bills are generally limited to parliamentary reform and standards. Members' bills either take a long time to produce (the fox hunting ban took two years) or relate to issues in which non-complex legislation can be used (in areas such as dog fouling and the ability of shops to open at Christmas). The committees' ability to undertake agenda-setting inquires is also limited and few lead to a memorable government response.

However, it is difficult to equate this outcome with policy failure because Scotland did not introduce a US-style system with a clear separation, and sharing, of powers. The outcome is not surprising given the (UK Government sponsored) Consultative Steering Group's emphasis on the 'need for the Executive to govern' (see McGarvey and Cairney, 2008: 90). In other words, the lack of parliamentary influence on legislation and public policy is not an indicator of devolution policy failure when viewed through the eyes of organisations such as the Labour government (and supportive parties) responsible for the Scotland Act 1998, the CSG or the Scottish Government of the day. Further, even the Scottish Parliament is reluctant to call for more resources to improve scrutiny or take a more active policymaking role. Again, we can gauge success in terms of multiple objectives: the Scottish Parliament has been a qualified success given the strong commitment of the UK Government and others to an executive-centred parliamentary system in which parliamentary committees and their staffs do not enjoy the resources to do much more than scrutinise governmental legislation. How much success can we demand realistically of a Scottish parliamentary committee when it has, say, seven MSPs (with multiple responsibilities and demands) and is supported by three members of staff, monitoring a department with hundreds or thousands of staff and processing the legislation produced by that department?

We can identify a similar set of multiple, and often contradictory, objectives associated with new politics and the role of parties. On the one hand, we want parties to work together constructively in Parliament to produce robust legislation and to ensure that the Scottish Government is held to account. On the other hand, we want parties to compete to win elections and recruit members, and for parties to engage in robust debates on policy to help educate the public and help us think through hard decisions in which there may not be a consensus. We should assess the success of new politics in this light, exploring what we can realistically expect from political parties who try to balance their need to cooperate in Parliament with their right to express political differences and seek electoral success at the expense of their competitors. In other words, it is difficult to know what new politics would really look like and if we would recognise it if we saw it. Certainly, we would not find it in the regular set-piece exchanges between government and opposition party leaders in First Minister's Questions. Rather, much of that sort of cooperation takes place behind the scenes and before matters come to a head in plenary.

As chapter 2 highlights, there are additional elements of party practice that make it difficult for us to provide a straightforward analysis of success. For example, most parties are part of a wider UK party system. While the SNP has no counterpart in the UK, and the Liberal Democrats have a 'federal' system, the Conservatives and (in particular) Labour maintain systems in which ultimate control still resides in London. Labour also engaged in the most extensive vetting process of its candidates. Therefore, we can say that the UK parties have multiple objectives—to see their devolved parties enjoying electoral success and perhaps engaging constructively in the Scottish Parliament, but not if it comes at the expense of the electoral standing of the party in Westminster. This is a consistent theme in the history of Scottish Labour, with the devolved party seeking further devolution to engage in Scottish terrain, but the UK party conscious of the effect of that devolution on policy uniformity—and attitudes to further Scottish devolution. In these terms, a change in the behaviour of Scottish parties may take much more than twelve years if it requires the further evolution of UK political parties operating in Scotland.

The Success of the Scottish Government: Strength and Stability

If we treat their relationship as a 'zero-sum game', a lack of Scottish Parliament success may equate to Scottish Government success: minimal parliamentary influence may be a good indicator of the strength and stability of the executive. This is certainly a key finding in chapter 4 which discusses the ability of the Scottish Executive coalition to dominate parliamentary proceedings from 1999–2007. Strength in this sense means an ability to 'dominate Parliament and its legislative process', while stability refers to the fact that coalition governments generally have longer lives than their minority counterparts because they are less vulnerable to votes of no confidence in Parliament (Cairney, 2011a: 261). These factors were key indicators of success for Scottish Labour. It sought a sense of control that it feared would be lost if Labour ministers were forced to cooperate on a regular basis with the SNP: 'We have to have a settled programme rather than a programme where we could be ambushed every time' (Maureen Macmillan, Labour MSP, in Arter, 2004: 83). Therefore, Labour's ability to form a coalition government with the Liberal Democrats, without conceding too much policy ground, is an example of short term success. However, as chapter 4 suggests, the pursuit of success in one arena may involve a trade-off in another. Labour conceded policy ground in key areas such as tuition fees, free personal care and the introduction of STV in local elections (some of the policy decisions that we remember most).

In contrast, while the SNP minority government was less able to dominate the Scottish Parliament vote, and more vulnerable to a vote of no confidence (although none were passed), it was stronger and more stable within government because it did not have to negotiate its policy programme, or share ministerial posts, with another party. Perhaps most importantly, the single party and streamlined SNP Government became associated with an extended period of governing competence — something that had an immense effect on its popularity and subsequent election as a majority government.

The complication to this discussion regards the locus of power within government. Scottish governments operate within a system of 'multi-level governance' (Bache and Flinders, 2004; Cairney, 2012b) in which power is dispersed across levels of government (EU, UK, Scottish, local) and shared with other actors such as civil servants, quangos and pressure participants such as interest groups, private sector and third sector bodies. Early reports identify problems of Scottish Executive effectiveness based on the potential for UK ministers to intervene in policy decisions, a lack of clarity about which Scottish ministers were responsible for certain quangos and a lack of clarity about the Scottish Executive's role within the Scottish justice system. There was also some doubt about the ability of ministers to control the civil service (or at least give them the direction required to implement policy), with examples such as relocation exposing the limits to their new powers, and issues such as freedom of information demonstrating the time it takes for the civil service to adapt to its new role. Most importantly, our discussion of territorial policy communities reminds us that most policy is processed by civil servants in consultation with pressure participants. Ministers may control this process when they become involved, but they only have the ability to pay attention to a small proportion of government business. These examples of power diffusion were compounded by occasional power struggles between parties within the coalition and between Labour ministers.

In this light, policy success relates more to the ability of a Scottish government to present an *image* of power or governing competence, rather than to actually take control of policymaking as if power was held centrally in one place by a small number of actors (it is not!). The SNP's period of minority government demonstrated that a small streamlined single party government, with no need to cooperate with another party in government, was more able to support this image by: accepting the need for a greater degree of cooperation with the Scottish Parliament; fostering a very public devolution of powers (and political responsibility) to organisations such as local authorities; and, pursuing a set of policy ambitions consistent with its limited abilities to guarantee that they came to fruition.

The Success of Intergovernmental Relationships

The issue of IGR exposes the potential for conflicting objectives — between, for example, the principled pursuit of open cooperation between UK and Scottish parliaments, and the pragmatic pursuit of relatively secret practical arrangements that generally suit both executives. Scottish governments were generally successful in pursuing the latter. From 1999–2007 the Scottish-UK government relationship was low key; discussions were conducted informally and almost entirely through political parties, ministers and civil servants. Formal mechanisms for negotiation and dispute were used rarely and the Scottish Executive played a minimal role in EU policy making.

This issue reinforces McConnell's (2010: 82) focus on *whose* success we are describing. For example, we can relate informal IGR to several Scottish Executive (1999–2007) and UK Government objectives, including a desire within the Labour Party to maintain an image of policy uniformity by managing policy quietly and between ministers, or a desire by most actors in both governments to minimise attention to the Scotland-UK financial relationship, by preferring the Barnett formula to more frequent and formal budget negotiations. We may also identify a general desire within government to coordinate IGR through the civil service, to ensure the smooth delivery of policy in both territories. If we evaluate outcomes on those terms, we can identify high levels of success punctuated by embarrassing instances of policy divergence, periodic attention to Barnett, levels of Scottish Executive dissatisfaction when civil servants in UK Government Departments fail to consult them on measures relevant to Scotland, and early tensions between the First Minister and Scottish Secretary. The Scottish Executive was also often-frustrated by its inability to influence the EU agenda. In general, the informal arrangements seemed to suit both executives, but in a context in which the Scottish Executive was clearly the junior partner (and could only expect so much from any IGR arrangements). In contrast, members of both Parliaments would struggle to find many instances in which they became involved successfully in IGR (since the Sewel motion process was driven by government) — although they are perhaps not much more excluded from this process than in general.

These measures of success change somewhat from 2007, with Labour no longer driven in the same way to manage policy uniformity, and the SNP less likely to benefit from relatively quiet arrangements. Yet, their relationships did not change remarkably following the election of the SNP in 2007. Nor did they change in 2010 when the Conservatives and Liberal Democrats formed a coalition government in the UK. Although there were more instances of high profile disagreements from 2007, there was a still tendency for this charged atmosphere to give way to a more humdrum, day-to-day relationship as civil servants worked through the details. The 2011 election result prompted a shift in intergovernmental relations to some extent. David Cameron's promise to govern Scots with respect had already translated into a partial acceptance of the need for more frequent JMCs, and the 2011 election may boost a general tendency to tread carefully in Scottish territory (although we should not go too far — issues such as the budget are still driven by the UK Government with the devolved governments, at best, consulted on its measures). Success for the UK Government in this context may relate to its ability to manage territorial affairs without exacerbating Scottish attitudes to constitutional change, while the SNP Government may seek electoral advantage by standing up for Scotland's interests in a small number of low profile cases. Evaluating the success of IGR beyond those types of motivation is difficult unless we appeal to a more principled yardstick stressing the role of parliaments and the transparency of the process (in which case we would generally identify failure).

A greater SNP effect can be found in the Scottish Government's relationship with local government. This example demonstrates well the significance of multiple objectives and the need to assess success in terms of the perceptions of different actors according to their aims. We can detect in the Scottish Executive a greater willingness to use short-term targetry and ring-fenced funding to direct local authorities to implement government policies (compared to the Scottish Government, not the UK Government). In that context, the targets themselves became proxy measures of success. In contrast, the Scottish Government had a clear agenda to reduce ring fenced funding (from 22% to 11%) and to agree longer term targets (single outcome agreements) with individual local authorities. Further, while both governments sought to develop meaningful partnerships with local authorities, that aim has a different meaning in different eras. From 1999–2007, the Scottish Executive often had conflicting objectives and seemed happy to trade some local authority goodwill for an adherence to its policy aims, producing an often publicly-tense relationship with COSLA (perhaps made worse, in the short term, by its introduction of STV in local elections). From 2007, the Scottish Government aims of devolving responsibility and fostering good relationships were consistent. It also used that relationship to deliver a freeze in council taxes—a successful policy outcome in terms of the SNP's short term aims (to freeze taxes and secure electoral gains) but not, as yet, its long term aim (the freeze was sold as the first step in reforming local taxation).

The Scottish Government experience presents us with an interesting set of different measures of success in terms of the perceptions of the Scottish Government and its opposition. For the latter, the new central-local relationship failed because the Scottish Government could not deliver on its policy promises. Indeed, a failure to reduce class sizes or introduce free school meals uniformly tended to dominate parliamentary debate from 2007–11. This is a top-down measure of success, solely in terms of a small number of government aims, without a thoughtful consideration of the multiplicity of government aims and how it might trade-off one for another. In contrast, the Scottish Government often presented a bottom-up interpretation of its policy aims, arguing that it provided the strategic direction and funding for policy aims (such as a reduction in class sizes), but respected the ability of local authorities to set their own priorities given the multiplicity of Scottish Government aims and their limited resources. In this context, the evaluation of success becomes fiercely political. Indeed, the issue of class sizes was a big factor in Fiona Hyslop's reshuffle, as the opposition parties began to set the agenda and both the Scottish Parliament and Scottish Government became frustrated about the shifting balance between strategic direction and local discretion.

Success and the Image of Devolution

Public opinion evidence on the success of devolution is mixed. On the one hand, there is a wealth of data which suggests that most respondents do not think that devolution has made a positive difference — whether it is a question about the performance of the Scottish Parliament, the difference it has made to Scotland, its achievements, its effect on the way that Britain is governed or the effect it has had on particular policy areas such as health or education. On the other hand, there is more positive support for the idea that it has made Scotland's 'voice' in the Union stronger or that Scottish institutions are more likely than their UK counterparts to act in Scotland's interests. More importantly, respondents tend to think that devolution has made little difference, not that it has made things worse. Further, many blame the UK Government for problems with policy areas such as health. Consequently, a key finding is the perception that people want devolution to be extended far enough to make a difference. This finding chimes with more direct questions which find that the majority of respondents would like devolution extended to areas such as social security, welfare and taxation (without going as far as independence). In other words, the public may question the success of devolution, so far, in *practice* but this experience has helped maintain or reinforce a belief in the *principle* of devolution and demand for further devolution.

The Success of Scottish Public Policy and Policymaking

There is very limited evidence linking Scottish social attitudes to the demand for markedly different public policies. If we look at the flagship (and other notable) policies since devolution — free personal care, the reduction and then abolition of higher education tuition fees, the smoking ban, STV in local elections (plus mental health reform and the acceleration of differences in health services and schools) — it is difficult to find a clear link between social attitudes and policy divergence. In broader terms, is difficult to demonstrate the success of devolution because the Scottish public opinion-policy link is weak at best. In fact, chapter 7 highlights as many examples of Scottish policymakers going *against* public policy (most notably when removing section 28).

Instead, this policy change and divergence represents the devolved institutional effect, caused by a combination of factors, including differences in party success (Labour/LD coalition, SNP victory) and party systems (including a centre-left Parliament with no significant Conservative opposition) which influence the ways in which new

Scottish institutions deal with policy demands. In some cases, the decisions can be linked strongly to deals made within the coalition (the graduate endowment and tuition fees, free personal care, STV). In others, we may link them to the role of territorial policy communities and the stronger links between Scottish governments and public sector professions in areas such as health and education. There are also instances of important differences in policy style, such as when the Scottish Executive passed important mental health legislation in a much more straightforward way than its UK counterpart. In some cases, there may be a role for Parliament—such as when it recommended free personal care and expressed support (initially quite quietly, to Labour ministers) for a smoking ban.

In each case, we see that devolution has made an *impact* on public policy. However, again, success is more difficult to measure. Chapter 8 identifies a number of relevant themes. First, the UK Government has a clear role in setting the agenda for the measurement of success. In particular, senior ministers regularly criticised the lack of Scottish Executive 'modernisation' and pointed to proxy measures of success, such as waiting times, to back up their argument. Second, most policy areas demonstrate short-term success for some actors. Perhaps the best example is STV in local elections—a decision related clearly to the demands of the Liberal Democrats, which was successful as soon as the policy was adopted (although note the amount that it had to trade to secure that commitment), even if the new electoral system did not boost its electoral fortunes (if anything, the reverse is true).

However, most areas also demonstrate an 'implementation gap', or a gap between the expectations of actors involved in the formulation of policy and the eventual outcomes. Success in this context may occur when that gap is small. Again, this is a political rather than a technical issue, since much depends on the objectives that we identify and the measures we use to gauge success (such as when we consider the policy of reducing class sizes). However, in many cases we can say that there is a fairly visible gap: such as when arguments over funding undermined free personal care policy or when the uptake of ASBO legislation was remarkably low. The most successful policy may be the smoking ban, because compliance rates have been close to 100%. However, this example also shows us the importance of timeframes and short versus long term success, since the policy is designed to reduce smoking and passive smoking and therefore improve the health of the population (something that may take decades to gauge). Third, it is difficult to assess the success of one policy in isolation, since government is about making choices based on multiple, often conflicting, objectives. Fourth, policymaking involves allocating limited resources – suggesting that, in this age of austerity, we may have to start talking about success in terms of the reduced money available to the policy (even in the land of milk and honey).

The election of an SNP government did not cause a radical shift in the direction of public policy. It is associated with some distinctive policies, most notably on alcohol, council tax reform and tuition fees, but most legislation passed from 2007–11 generally received cross-party support, while much represents an inherited legacy from its predecessor. In this context, we might measure its success in other terms, such as its image of governing competence and the role this played in its re-election (since, surely, the primary aim of political parties is re-election). We might also return to the idea of two visions for a devolved Scotland: one in which we expect much policy innovation linked to the idea of 'Scottish solutions to Scottish problems'; and, one in which we expect more limited innovation, reflecting the hope that devolution would remove Scotland from the UK Government's policy conveyor belt and halt the introduction of inappropriate policies. In this light, we might argue that a good measure of success is the *lack* of policy innovation, summed up briefly by Jack McConnell's phrase 'doing less, better'.

The Success of the Barnett Formula

The Barnett formula may, at one stage, have looked like it could satisfy all camps: maintaining Scotland's advantage in the short term, with the promise of greater fiscal equity in the long term; and, allowing Scottish and UK government actors to keep attention to the issue low, to avoid regular and fierce debates on an issue that they did not want to debate. In these terms, for some, it provides a classic example of successful politics but bad policy, resulting in a policy that no-one appears to want (or can admit that they want) but few are in the position to change. Success may refer to the issue's low-key progress despite its potential to 'explode' at any moment.

Our evaluation is complicated by three main factors. First, no-one is sure what the primary aim was when the formula was introduced. It is often described as an interim measure put in place before the Treasury negotiated a new settlement with the Scottish Assembly in 1979. Yet, since *any* interim measure could have been introduced, we also need to know what it was designed to do while in place: stabilise or reduce Scotland's advantage; reduce Scotland's advantage to the level identified in the needs assessment or below? Yet, since we don't know, it is difficult to gauge success. Second, there is constant debate about the effect of Barnett on Scotland's share of public expenditure since the outcomes are subject to interpretation—particularly around the (problematic) idea that although Scotland's share has remained stable we can identify a squeeze in some policy areas.

Third, our assessment takes place in the context of a much wider debate about Scotland's limited economic powers before and after devolution. For example, Barnett may be part of a system designed to compensate Scotland for UK economic policies geared towards economic growth in the south east of England. Scotland's lack of fiscal autonomy also makes it very difficult to consider policy success, in areas such as public-private partnerships and the large scale voluntary transfer of housing, when the Scottish Government would not have chosen the policy. The SNP Government's Scottish Futures Trust is a particularly difficult policy to judge, since it involves using very limited powers to subvert a UK Government tendency towards PPP, as much as an effort to deliver capital projects with private funding, in a new era of economic retrenchment in which private and public funding is much harder to secure. Consequently, it may not be appropriate simply to measure success by asking if it matched the previous Executive's building programme 'brick by brick'.

The Constitutional Agenda: Success for the Union or the SNP?

If we were asked to describe the National Conversation or Calman Commission, the word 'success' would not spring to mind instantly. Yet, we may view them as successful given the aims of their supporters. For the SNP Government, the aim may have been to keep the issue of independence alive without rushing into an independence referendum agenda (an agenda that was undermined by opposition parties), or merely to demonstrate a commitment to independence when everyone knew it could not pursue the matter properly under minority government. We can assess Calman in a similar way. If treated as an exercise designed to solve the apparent contradictions of devolution (e.g. we want more powers but not to use them to undermine British citizenship) and to produce a coherent blueprint for further policy and fiscal devolution, then it may go down as a partial success at best. If treated as a political exercise designed to compete for attention with the National Conversation, and to provide a series of recommendations consistent with its rather limited brief, it seems to have been successful (particularly since the UK Government has, so far, used it to underpin its constitutional reforms).

Of course, the success of both endeavours has been overshadowed by the 2011 election. The result produced quite an odd effect on the agenda for constitutional change. The main effect has been an almost unquestioned argument by the SNP that it has a mandate to introduce a referendum on independence, since this was a clear plank in its 2011 manifesto. In 2007 this argument was less effective because the unionist parties pointed out that most people voted for parties who did *not* support independence and, more importantly, signalled that they would vote against a bill in the Scottish Parliament to introduce a referendum. In 2011 the voting split was closer to 50/50 (the three main opposition parties secured just over 50% of the constituency votes, but 44% of the regional vote) but, more importantly, the SNP has the majority in Parliament to ensure that a bill will pass without significant opposition.

The 2011 election result had a further impact—it seemed to produce almost a reversal of positions from the main opposition parties and the UK Government. From 2007–11 they questioned the SNP mandate for an independence referendum and latterly criticised the SNP for being obsessed with the constitution at a time of economic crisis. From 2011 they accepted the SNP mandate, with opposition parties fairly invisible on the issue and the UK Government appearing very reluctant to say anything that looks like it is questioning the SNP Government's moral authority. This is the slightly odd part, for two reasons. First, the SNP mandate is not clear because its electoral success is generally attributed to its image of governing competence. The Scottish Election Studies of 2007 and 2011 have both pointed to valence issues (the image of the leader, the party's vision for government, perceptions about the party's ability to govern) rather than substantive policy differences as the explanation for increased SNP success. Further, as chapter 7 shows, a vote for the SNP is not a vote for independence. In fact, support for independence has generally been slightly above and below one-third of the population for the duration of devolution.

Second, its mandate is not clear because its manifesto was not clear on the details of an independence referendum. There is little detail on the questions to be asked and what we should do with the results. For example, the plan in 2007 seemed to be to ask the electorate to give the Scottish Government permission to negotiate a new constitutional settlement with the UK Government. Such a process would require a second referendum on the negotiated outcomes. Yet, the SNP is now criticising the UK Government's (or Scottish Secretary Michael Moore's) suggestion that two referendums are required and the UK Government seems reluctant to argue. This reluctance is largely based on the popularity of the SNP as demonstrated by its majority in the Scottish Parliament. This situation shows us the greatest legacy of 'old

Westminster'. The SNP commanded less than half of the popular vote, but the election result is portrayed by most as a thumping victory that leaves an SNP mandate in no question. This is a majoritarian democratic view of politics, not a consensus democratic view.

Conclusion

For most people, the policy of devolution was based on one simple aim: to have an enduring set of policymaking institutions in Scotland. In turn, that aim was based on the general desire for Scottish governmental arrangements to reflect high levels of national identity and to get the government it voted for, without going as far as independence. In those terms, devolution was a success as soon as it happened and everything else is just detail. A narrative of new politics may have been useful to further the devolution movement and ensure a successful referendum vote, but we should avoid assessing the success of devolution with regard to a set of aims that will never be met (particularly since it is such a vague term referring to a series of often contradictory visions). We should be similarly cautious about the idea of devolution as the solution to Scotland's distinctive set of policy problems, since we then begin to confuse what is good policy with what is good policymaking and, more importantly, we confuse good policymaking with the place we want policy decisions to be made. In other words, we should not place too much faith on solving problems by making decisions locally, particularly when we consider the interdependence between Scotland and its institutions with the EU and wider world and their institutions. The same can be said for issues such as economic growth. It is difficult to say that devolution failed because it did not aid Scotland's economy (leaving aside the lack of economic levers in Scotland) simply because, for most people, this was a peripheral aim at best. It makes little sense to begin to attach all sorts of aims for devolution retrospectively and use them to gauge the success of the devolution project.

In broader terms, no measure of policy success can be objective. Rather, evaluations of success are just as political as any other aspect of politics. As such, it makes more sense to assess success in the eyes of those involved than it does to seek common agreement or a technical answer. We may have our views on what are the most relevant measures of success, but should not confuse those views with objective criteria, however principled they may be.

References

Andrews, R. And Martin, S. (2006) 'Has Devolution Improved Public Services?' *Public Money and Management*, 27, 2, 149-56

Arter, D. (2003) *The Scottish Parliament: A Scandinavian Style Assembly?* (London: Frank Cass)

Agranoff, R. (2004) 'Autonomy, Devolution and Intergovernmental Relations', *Regional and Federal Studies*, 14, 1, 26–65

Arter, D. (2004) 'The Scottish Committees and the Goal of a "New Politics": A Verdict on the First Four Years of the Devolved Scottish Parliament', *Journal of Contemporary European Studies*, 12, 1, 71–91

Asare, B., Cairney, P. and Studlar, D. (2009) 'Federalism and Multilevel Governance in Tobacco Policy: The European Union, the United Kingdom and the Devolved UK Institutions', *Journal of Public Policy*, 29, 1, 79-102

Bache, I. and Flinders, M. (2004) 'Multi-level Governance and the Study of the British State', *Public Policy and Administration*, 19, 1, 31–52

Baumgartner, F. and Jones, B. (1993) *Agendas and Instability in American Politics* (Chicago: Chicago University Press)

Baumgartner, F. and B. Jones (2009) *Agendas and Instability in American Politics* 2nd edition (Chicago: University of Chicago Press).

Barnes, E. (29.7.11) 'Scottish Labour struggled to match SNP's £2.1m war chest, figures show' *The Scotsman* http://news.scotsman.com/scotland/Scottish-Labour-struggled-to-match.6809382.jp

BBC News (4.12.03) 'MSPs' expenses revealed' http://news.bbc.co.uk/1/hi/scotland/3292269.stm

BBC News (23.9.09) 'Primary 1 class size to be capped' http://news.bbc.co.uk/1/hi/scotland/8269996.stm

BBC News 25.11.10 'Alex Salmond sorry over tartan tax decision' http://www.bbc.co.uk/news/uk-scotland-11839173

BBC News (9.2.11) 'Scottish government budget passed by MSPs' http://www.bbc.co.uk/news/uk-scotland-12400444

BBC News (5.6.11) 'Salmond appoints experts to look at Supreme Court' http://www.bbc.co.uk/news/uk-scotland-13656147

BBC News (16.6.11) 'No Alex Salmond apology in Supreme Court row' http://www.bbc.co.uk/news/uk-scotland-13793330

BBC News (8.8.11) 'Row within SNP over John Mason's gay marriage motion' http://www.bbc.co.uk/news/uk-scotland-14435856

Bell, D. (2001) 'The Barnett Formula' http://www.economics.stir.ac.uk/staff/dnfb1/Barnett%20Formula.pdf

Bell, D. and Christie, A. (2001) 'Finance—The Barnett Formula: Nobody's Child?' in A. Trench (ed.), *The State of the Nations: The Second Year of Devolution in the UK* (London: The Constitution Unit)

Bennett, M., Fairley, J. and McAteer, M. (2002) *Devolution in Scotland: The Impact on Local Government* (York: Joseph Rowntree Foundation)

Bodden, T. (2011) 'End MPs role in devolved Welsh law-making says Lord Elis-Thomas', *Daily Post* http://www.dailypost.co.uk/news/north-wales-news/2011/01/28/end-mps-role-in-devolved-welsh-law-making-says-lord-elis-thomas-55578-28069720/

Bradbury, J. (2006) 'Territory and Power Revisited: Theorising Territorial Politics in the United Kingdom after Devolution', *Political Studies*, 54: 559–82

Bradbury, J. and Mitchell, J. (2007) 'The Constituency Work of Members of the Scottish Parliament and National Assembly for Wales', *Regional and Federal Studies*, 17(1): 117–45

Brown, A., McCrone, D. and Paterson, L. (1997) *Politics & Society in Scotland*. (Basingstoke; MacMillan)

Buckland, L. (11.8.11) 'Concern at mental patient treatment' *The Scotsman* http://news.scotsman.com/scotland/Concern-at-mental-patient-treatment.6816531.jp

Bulpitt, J. (1983) *Territory and Power in the United Kingdom* (Manchester: Manchester University Press).

Cairney, P. (2006a) 'Venue Shift Following Devolution: When Reserved Meets Devolved in Scotland', *Regional and Federal Studies*, 16, 4, 429-45

Cairney, P. (2006b) 'The Analysis of Scottish Parliament Committees: Beyond Capacity and Structure in Comparing West European Legislatures', *European Journal of Political Research*, 45, 2, 181-208

Cairney, P. (2007a) 'Using Devolution to Set the Agenda? Venue shift and the smoking ban in Scotland', *British Journal of Politics and International Relations*, 9,1, 73-89

Cairney, P. (2007b) 'A Multiple Lens Approach to Policy Change: the Case of Tobacco Policy in the UK', *British Politics*, 2, 1, 45-68

Cairney, P. (2008) 'Has Devolution Changed the British Policy Style?, *British Politics*, 3, 3, 350-72

Cairney, P. (2009a) 'The "British Policy Style" and Mental Health: Beyond the Headlines', *Journal of Social Policy*, 38, 4, 1-18

Cairney, P. (2009b) 'The SNP and Minority Government in Scotland', Paper to the Study of Parliament Group, Westminster, April http://paulcairney.blogspot.com/2009/05/scottish-national-party-and-minority.html

Cairney, P. (2009c) 'Intergovernmental Relations and the Scottish National Party', APSA 2009 Toronto Meeting Paper. Available at SSRN: http://ssrn.com/abstract=1451744

Cairney, P. (2009d) 'Implementation and the Governance Problem: A Pressure Participant Perspective', Public Policy and Administration, 24, 4,

Cairney, P. (2009e) 'The role of ideas in policy transfer: the case of UK smoking bans since devolution', *Journal of European Public Policy*, 16, 3,471-488

Cairney, P. (2011a) 'Coalition and Minority Government in Scotland: Lessons for the United Kingdom?' *Political Quarterly*, 82, 2, 261-9

Cairney, P. (2011b) 'The New British Policy Style: From a British to a Scottish Political Tradition?', *Political Studies Review*, 9, 2, 208-20

Cairney, P. (2011c) 'Comparing Policy Styles in the UK and Scotland: Beyond the Headlines', Paper to Seminar on Policy Styles, Graduate School of Law, Hokkaido University, September

Cairney, P. (2012a) 'Intergovernmental Relations in Scotland: what was the SNP effect?', *British Journal of Politics and International Relations*, forthcoming

Cairney, P. (2012b) *Understanding Public Policy: Theories and Issues* (Basingstoke: Palgrave)

Cairney, P. and M. Keating (2004), 'Sewel Motions in the Scottish Parliament', *Scottish Affairs*, 47: 115-34

Cairney, P., Halpin, D. and Jordan, G. (2009) 'New Scottish Parliament, Same Old Interest Group Politics?' in C. Jeffery and J. Mitchell (eds.) *The Scottish Parliament, 1999-2009: The First Decade* (Edinburgh: Luath Press)

Cairney, P., Studlar, D. And Mamudu, H. (2012) *Global Tobacco Control: Power, Policy, Governance and Transfer* (Basingstoke: Palgrave)

Cm 5240 (2001) Memorandum of Understanding and Supplementary Agreements Between the United Kingdom Government, Scottish Ministers, the Cabinet of the National Assembly for Wales and the Northern Ireland Executive Committee http://www.dca.gov.uk/constitution/devolution/pubs/odpm_dev_600629.pdf

Cm7738 (2009) Scotland's Future in the United Kingdom (London: The Stationery Office) http://www.scotlandoffice.gov.uk/scotlandoffice/files/Scotland%27s%20Future%20in%20the%20United%20Kingdom.pdf

Cm 7979 (2010) Strengthening Scotland's Future (London: The Stationery Office) http://www.scotlandoffice.gov.uk/scotlandoffice/files/Scotland_Bill_Command_Paper.pdf

Cochrane, A. (2.6.2011) 'Childish conduct is hurting Alex Salmond's Supreme Court attack' The Telegraph http://www.telegraph.co.uk/news/uknews/scotland/8552140/Childish-conduct-is-hurting-Alex-Salmonds-Supreme-Court-attack.html

Commission on Scottish Devolution (2008b) 'Oral evidence session with Jack McConnell MSP' http://www.commissiononscottishdevolution.org.uk/uploads/transcript-1-October.pdf

Commission on Scottish Devolution (2008c) 'Oral Evidence Session With Lord Sewel And Alan Trench' http://www.commissiononscottishdevolution.org.uk/uploads/2009-02-03-lord-sewel-&-alan-trench---for-website.pdf

Condor, S. (2010) 'Devolution and national identity: the rules of English (dis)engagement', *Nations and Nationalism*, 16, 3, 525-43

Currie, B. (19.4.11) 'SNP councils warn Cosla: You do not speak for us' *The Herald* http://www.heraldscotland.com/news/election/snp-councils-warn-cosla-you-do-not-speak-for-us-1.1096992

Curtice, J. (2004) 'Restoring Confidence and Legitimacy?' in A. Trench (ed.), *Has Devolution Made a Difference? The State of the Nations 2004* (Exeter: Imprint Academic).

Curtice, J. (2009) 'Devolution, the SNP and the Electorate' in (ed.) G. Hassan *The Modern SNP: From Protest to Power* (Edinburgh: Edinburgh University Press)

Davidson, L. (2008) 'SNP 'abuse' of executive power is making Holyrood irrelevant, say angry opposition', *The Times* November 21 http://www.timesonline.co.uk/tol/news/uk/scotland/article5209490.ece

Denver, D., Mitchell, J., Pattie, C. and Bochel, H. (2000) *Scotland Decides: The Devolution Issue and the Scottish Referendum* (London; Frank Cass)

Denver, D. and Johns, R. (2010) 'Scottish Parliament Elections: 'British Not Scottish' or 'More Scottish Than British'?', Scottish Affairs, 70 (Winter),

Dinwoodie, R. (16.8.11) 'Lord Steel quit over SNP attacks on Supreme Court' *The Herald* http://www.heraldscotland.com/news/politics/lord-steel-quit-over-snp-attacks-on-supreme-court-1.1117772

Dinwoodie, R. (5.9.11) 'Yes voters take lead in new independence poll' *The Herald* http://www.heraldscotland.com/news/politics/yes-voters-take-lead-in-new-independence-poll-1.1121712

Earle, M. (2007) 'Parliamentary Pay and Allowances', SPICe Briefing 07/09 http://www.scottish.parliament.uk/business/research/briefings-07/SB07-09.pdf

Earle, M. (2009) 'Parliamentary Pay and Expenses 207-8 and Pay and Expense rates 2008-9', SPICe briefing 09/06 http://www.scottish.parliament.uk/business/research/briefings-09/SB09-06.pdf

Elvidge, J. (2011) *Northern Exposure: Lessons from the first twelve years of devolved government in Scotland* (London: Institute of Governance) http://www.instituteforgovernment.org.uk/publications/44/

Ford, M. and Casebow, P. (2002) 'The Civil Service' in G. Hassan and C. Warhurst (eds), *Anatomy of the New Scotland: Power, Influence and Change* (Mainstream: Edinburgh)

Gay, O. (2006) 'The Lyons and Gershon reviews and variations in civil service conditions', House of Commons Library SN/PC/2588 www.parliament.uk/briefing-papers/SN02588.pdf

Gordon, C. (2002) 'From War of Attrition to Roller-coaster Ride: Local and Central Government in Scotland', *Public Money and Management*, April-June, 6-8

GPC Scotland (April 2000) *Devolution and Health Monitoring Project: First Quarterly Report* (London: Constitution Unit)

GPC Scotland (June 2000) *Devolution and Health Monitoring Project: Second Quarterly Report* (London: Constitution Unit)

GPC Scotland (September 2000) *Devolution and Health Monitoring Project: Third Quarterly Report* (London: Constitution Unit)

Green-Pedersen, C. (2001) 'Minority Governments and Party Politics: The Political and Institutional Background to the "Danish Miracle"', *Journal of Public Policy*, 21, 1, 53-70

Greer, S. (2001) *Divergence and Devolution* (London: The Constitution Unit and Nuffield Trust)

Greer, S. (2004) *Territorial Politics and Health Policy* (Manchester: Manchester University Press)

Greer, S. (2009) (ed.) *Devolution and Social Citizenship in the UK* (Bristol: Policy Press)

Greer, S. and Jarman, H. (2008) 'Devolution and Policy Styles', in A. Trench (ed.) *The State of the Nations 2008* (Exeter: Imprint Academic)

Harvey, M. And Lynch, P. (2010) 'From National Conversation to Independence Referendum?: The SNP Government and the Politics of Independence', paper to Political Studies Association Conference, April, Edinburgh

Hazell, R. (2000) 'Introduction: The First Year of Devolution' in R. Hazell (ed.) *The State and the Nations: The First Year of Devolution in the United Kingdom* (Exeter: Imprint Academic)

Hazell, R. (2001) 'Conclusion: The State of the Nations after Two Years of Devolution' in A. Trench (ed.) *The State of the Nations 2001* (Exeter: Imprint Academic)

Hazell, R. (2003) 'Conclusion' in R. Hazell (ed.) *The State of the Nations 2003* (Exeter: Imprint Academic)

Heald, D. And McLeod, A. (2002) 'Beyond Barnett? Financing Devolution' in J. Adams and P. Robinson (eds.) *Devolution in Practice: Public Policy Differences Within the UK* (London: IPPR)

Heald, D. And McLeod, A. (2005) 'Embeddedness of UK Devolution Finance within the Public Expenditure System', *Regional Studies*, 39, 4, 495–518

Healthcare Improvement Scotland (2011) 'Healthcare Improvement Scotland process for assessing the applicability of Technology Appraisal Guidance published by the National Institute for Health and Clinical Excellence for NHS Scotland' http://www.healthcareimprovementscotland.org/idoc. ashx?docid=dd6a00a5-978a-4258-9d21-bc15d7192d49&version=-1

Hellowell, M. and Pollock, A. (2009) 'Non-Profit Distribution: The Scottish Approach to Private Finance in Public Services', *Social Policy and Society*, 8, 3, 405-18

Holyrood.com (28.6.08) 'Labour launches plans for private members bills' http://www.holyrood.com/component/content/article/68-scottish-parliament/1719-%20

House of Lords Select Committee on the Constitution (2002) *Devolution: Inter-institutional Relations in the United Kingdom*, HL Paper 28 http://www.parliament.the-stationery-office.co.uk/pa/ld200203/ldselect/ldconst/28/28.pdf

HM Treasury (2009) *Public Expenditure Statistical Analyses 2009* http://www.hm-treasury.gov.uk/pespub_pesa09.htm

Horgan, G. (2004) 'Inter-institutional Relations in the Devolved Great Britain: Quiet Diplomacy', *Regional and Federal Studies*, 14, 1, 113–35

Hutcheon, P. (5.9.10) 'Salmond shelves plans for referendum on UK break-up' *The Herald* http://www.heraldscotland.com/news/politics/salmond-shelves-plans-for-referendum-on-uk-break-up-1.1052924

Jeffery, C. (2002) 'Devolution: Challenging Local Government?' *Joseph Rowntree Foundations paper* http://www.jrf.org.uk/node/3643

Jeffery, C. And Hough, D. (2003) 'Regional Elections in Multilevel Systems', *European Urban and Regional Studies*, 10, 3, 199-212

Jeffery, C. (2006) 'Devolution and divergence: public attitudes and institutional logics', in J. Adams and K. Schmueker (eds), *Devolution in Practice 2006* (Newcastle: IPPR North)

Jeffery, C. and Herbert, S. (2011) 'The Outcome of the 2011 election and the likely impact on the fourth session of the Parliament', paper to the Scottish Study of Parliament Group, Scottish Parliament, Edinburgh, June

Jervis, P. and Plowden, W. (2000) 'Introduction' in Jervis, P. and Plowden, W. (eds.) *Devolution and Health* (London: The Constitution Unit and Nuffield Trust)

Jervis, P. and Plowden, W. (2001) 'Health in the UK — the differences of approach begin to emerge' in Jervis, P. and Plowden, W. (eds.) *Devolution and Health: Second Annual Report* (London: The Constitution Unit and Nuffield Trust)

John, P. (1998) *Analysing Public Policy* (London: Continuum)

Johns, R., Denver, D., Mitchell, J. and Pattie, C. (2010) *Voting for a Scottish Government: The Scottish Parliament Elections of 2007* (Manchester: Manchester University Press)

Jordan, G. and Maloney, W.A. (1997) 'Accounting for Subgovernments: Explaining the Persistence of Policy Communities', *Administration and Society*, vol.29, 5, 557-583

Jordan, G., Halpin, D. And Maloney, W. (2004) 'Defining Interests: Disambiguation and the Need for New Distinctions?' *British Journal of Politics and International Relations*, 6, 195-212

Jordan, G. and Halpin, D. (2006) 'The Political Costs of Policy Coherence? Constructing a "Rural" Policy for Scotland', *Journal of Public Policy*, 26: 21–41

Kellas, J. (1989) *The Scottish Political System*, 4th edition (Cambridge: Cambridge University Press)

Keating, M. (2005) *The Government of Scotland: Public Policy Making after Devolution* (Edinburgh: Edinburgh University Press)

Keating, M. (2009) *The Independence of Scotland: Self-government and the Shifting Politics of Union* (Oxford: Oxford University Press)

Keating, M. and Cairney, P. (2006) 'A New Elite? Politicians and Civil Servants in Scotland after Devolution', *Parliamentary Affairs*, 59, 1, 43-59

Keating, M., Stevenson, L., Cairney, P. and MacLean, K. (2003) 'Does Devolution Make a Difference? Legislative Output and Policy Divergence in Scotland', *Journal of Legislative Studies*, 9(3): 110–39

Keating, M., Cairney, P. And Hepburn, E. (2009) 'Territorial Policy Communities and Devolution in the United Kingdom', *Cambridge Journal of Regions, Economy and Society*, 2, 1, 51-66

Keating, M., Cairney, P. And Hepburn, E. (2012) 'Policy Convergence, Transfer and Learning in the UK under Devolution', *Regional and Federal Studies*

Keating, M. (2012) 'Intergovernmental relations for what?', *British Journal of Politics and International Relations*, forthcoming

Leicester, G. (2000a) 'Scotland' in (ed.) R. Hazell *The State and the Nations* (Exeter: Imprint Academic)

Leicester, G. (2000b) 'Scotland' in Jervis, P. and Plowden, W. (eds.) *Devolution and Health* (London: The Constitution Unit and Nuffield Trust)

Lijphart, A. (1999) *Patterns of Democracy* (New Haven, Conn: Yale University Press)

Lundberg, T. (2006) 'Second-Class Representatives? Mixed-Member Proportional Representation in Britain', *Parliamentary Affairs*, 59, 1, 60-77

MacGregor, S. (2010) 'Voting Behaviour in the Scottish Parliament', paper presented to the Elections, Public Opinion and Parties Annual Conference, Essex, September

MacLeod, A. (2.11.09) 'Fantasy of education portfolio sealed Hyslop's fate', *The Times*, http://www.timesonline.co.uk/tol/news/uk/scotland/article 6940021.ece

Maddox, D. (5.10.09) 'Bureaucrats tell MSPs: We can't cope with draft bills workload' *The Scotsman* http://news.scotsman.com/politics/Bureaucrats-tell-MSPs-We-can39t.5702505.jp

Maddox, D. (11.5.11) 'Ed Miliband: Scottish Labour won't cut off London again' *The Scotsman* http://www.scotsman.com/holyroodelections/Ed-Miliband-Scottish-Labour-won39t.6766140.jp

Maddox, D. (24.5.11) 'Alex Salmond warns of Holyrood powers "stalemate"' *The Scotsman* http://news.scotsman.com/scottishnationalparty/Alex-Salmond-warns-of-Holyrood.6773300.jp

Marsh, D. and McConnell, A. (2010) 'Towards a Framework for Establishing Policy Success', *Public Administration*, 88, 2, 564–83

McConnell, A. (2010) *Understanding Policy Success: Rethinking Public Policy* (Basingstoke: Palgrave Macmillan)

McCrone, D. and B. Lewis (1999) 'The 1997 Scottish Referendum Vote', in B. Taylor and K. Thompson, *Scotland and Wales: Nations Again?* (University of Wales Press)

McGarvey, N. and Cairney, P. (2008) *Scottish Politics* (Basingstoke: Palgrave)

McGarvey, N. and McConnell, A. (2011) 'Has Scottish Devolution Been a Success?' Paper presented to the Public Administration Conference, University of Birmingham, September

McGarvey, N. (2012) 'Scottish Devolution and Local Government', *British Journal of Politics and International Relations*, forthcoming

McGlauchlin, M. (22.8.11) 'Government fights bid to outlaw fees for English students' http://news.scotsman.com/scotland/Government-fights-bid-to-outlaw.6822760.jp

Midwinter, A.F. (2004a) 'Financing Devolution in Practice: The Barnett Formula and the Scottish Budget, 1999-2003', *Public Money and Management*, June, 137-44.

Midwinter, A.F. (2004b) 'The Changing Distribution of territorial Public Expenditure in the UK', *Regional and Federal Studies*, 14, 4, 499-512

Miller, B. (2008) 'Muslims and Multicultural Nationalism in Scotland', paper to Nanovic Institute for European Studies, University of Notre Dame, October http://nanovic.nd.edu/assets/8824/miller_paper_muslims_in_scotland.pdf

Mitchell, J. (2000) 'New Parliament: New Politics in Scotland' *Parliamentary Affairs* 53, 3, 605-621

Mitchell, J. (2003) 'Third Year, Third First Minister', in R. Hazell (ed.), *The State of the Nations 2003* (Exeter: Imprint Academic).

Mitchell, J. (2004) 'Scotland: Expectations, Policy Types and Devolution', in A. Trench (ed.), *Has Devolution Made a Difference? The State of the Nations 2004* (Exeter: Imprint Academic).

Mitchell, J. (2005) 'Scotland: Devolution is Not Just for Christmas', in A. Trench (ed.), *The Dynamics of Devolution: The State of the Nations 2005* (Exeter: Imprint Academic)

Mitchell, J. (2008) 'Minority governments, constitutional change and institutional cultures in Scotland' in A. Brazier and S. Kalitowski (eds.) *No Overall Control? The impact of a 'hung parliament' on British politics* (London: Hansard Society)

Mitchell, J. and the Scottish Monitoring Team (2001) 'Scotland: Maturing Devolution', in A. Trench (ed.), *The State of the Nations 2001* (Exeter: Imprint Academic).

Ormston, R. and Curtice, J. (2011) 'Resentment or contentment? Attitudes towards the Union 10 years on' in A. Park, J. Curtice, E. Clery and C. Bryson (eds.) *British Social Attitudes: Exploring Labour's Legacy* (The 27th Report) (London: Sage)

Parry, R. (1993) 'Towards A Democratised Scottish Office?', *Scottish Affairs*, 5, Autumn, 41-57

Parry, R and Jones, A. (2000) 'The Transition from the Scottish Office to the Scottish Government', *Public Policy and Administration*, 15(2): 53–66

Pyper, R. (1999) 'The Civil Service: A Neglected Dimension of Devolution', *Public Money and Management*, 19(2): 45–9

Review of SPCB Supported Bodies Committee (2009) *1st Report 2009: Review of SPCB Supported Bodies Committee*, SP Paper 266, http://www.scottish. parliament.uk/s3/committees/rssb/reports-09/rssb09-01.htm

Robertson, J. (26.5.2011) 'Why the Supreme Court of UK has power to overturn Scots convictions' *The Scotsman* http://thescotsman.scotsman.com/legalissues/Why-the-Supreme-Court-of.6774511.jp

Rokkan, S. and Urwin, D. (1983) *Economy, Territory, Identity, Politics of West European Peripheries* (London: Sage)

Rosie, M. and Bond, R. (2003) 'Identity Matters: The Personal and Political Significance of Feeling Scottish' in Bromley, C., Curtice, J., Hinds, K. and Park, A. (2003) *Devolution – Scottish Answers to Scottish Questions?* (Edinburgh: Edinburgh University Press)

Seaton, N. and Osmond, J. (2005) 'Assembly Government' in J. Osmond (ed.) *Nations and Regions: The Dynamics of Devolution* (Quarterly Report, April 2005) (London: The Constitution Unit)

Scott, J. (2.6.11) 'Alex Salmond's attack on the UK supreme court smells political' *The Guardian* http://www.guardian.co.uk/law/2011/jun/02/alex-salmond-attack-supreme-court

Scottish Futures Trust (2011) 'About Us' http://www.scottishfuturestrust.org.uk/a.asp?a=5

Seyd, B. (2002) *Coalition Government in Britain: Lessons from Overseas* (London: The Constitution Unit) http://www.ucl.ac.uk/constitution-unit/publications/unit-publications/84.html

Simeon, R. (2003) 'Free Personal Care' in in R. Hazell (ed.) *The State of the Nations 2003* (Exeter: Imprint Academic)

Sandford, M. (2011) 'Political developments in Wales to April 2011' House of Commons Library SN/PC/05965 www.parliament.uk/briefing-papers/SN05965.pdf

Schattschneider, E.E. (1960) *The Semi-Sovereign People* (New York: Holt, Winehart & Winston).

Schmueker, K. and Adams, J. (2005) 'Divergence in Priorities, Perceived Policy Failure and Pressure for Convergence' in (ed) Schmueker, K. and Adams, J. *Devolution in Practice 2006* (Newcastle: IPPR North)

Scotland Bill Committee Report (2011) 'Report on the Scotland Bill and relevant legislative consent memoranda'
http://scottish.parliament.uk/s3/committees/scotBill/reports-11/sbr11-01.htm#1

Scottish Constitutional Convention (1990) *Toward's Scotland's Parliament* (Edinburgh: SCC).

Scottish Constitutional Convention (1995) *Scotland's Parliament: Scotland's Right* (Edinburgh: Convention of Scottish Local Authorities)
http://www.almac.co.uk/business_park/scc/

Scottish Government (2007) *Choosing Scotland's Future* (Edinburgh; Scottish Government)
http://www.scotland.gov.uk/Resource/Doc/194791/0052321.pdf

Scottish Government (2009a) *Scottish Ministerial Code*
http://www.scotland.gov.uk/Publications/2009/06/18095600/16

Scottish Government (2009b) *Your Scotland, Your Voice: A National Conversation*
http://www.scotland.gov.uk/Resource/Doc/293639/0090721.pdf

Scottish Government (27.10.10) 'New cap for P1 class sizes'
http://www.scotland.gov.uk/News/Releases/2010/10/27115654

Scottish Government (2011a) *An Evaluation of Football Banning Orders in Scotland*
http://www.scotland.gov.uk/Publications/2011/07/22120711/0

Scottish Government (2011b) 'Independent Review Group examining the relationship of the High Court of Justiciary and the United Kingdom Supreme Court' http://www.scotland.gov.uk/About/supreme-court-review

Scottish Government (2011c) *Advancing Professionalism in Scottish Teaching: Report of the Review of Teacher Employment in Scotland* (McCormac Review)
http://www.scotland.gov.uk/About/reviewofteacheremployment

Scottish Government and COSLA (2007) 'Concordat between the Scottish Government and COSLA' (Edinburgh: Scottish Government)

Scottish Information Commissioner (2010) *Freedom of Information Annual Report*
http://www.itspublicknowledge.info/uploadedfiles/AnnualReport2010PrintVersion.pdf

Scottish National Party (SNP) (2011) *Re-elect a Scottish Government working for Scotland* (2011 Scottish Parliament Election Manifesto)
http://manifesto.votesnp.com/

Scottish Office (1998a) *Shaping Scotland's Parliament: Report of the Consultative Steering Group on the Scottish Parliament* (Edinburgh: Scottish Office).

Scottish Parliament (2006) 'SPCB Commissions Full Issues Paper On Allowances' http://www.scottish.parliament.uk/nmCentre/news/news-06/pa06-086.htm

Scottish Parliament (2007) 'SPCB announces a full scale review of parliamentary allowances'
http://www.scottish.parliament.uk/nmCentre/news/news-07/pa07-057.htm

Settle, M. (9.9.11) 'Coalition stalls on West Lothian Question' The Herald http://www.heraldscotland.com/news/politics/coalition-stalls-on-west-lothian-question-1.1122657?localLinksEnabled=false

Siebert, S. (2009) 'Gender Balance in Scottish Local Authority Councils', *Public Policy and Administration*, 24, 2, 175-93

SPICe (Scottish Parliament Information Centre) (1999) *Commission on Local Government and the Scottish Parliament (McIntosh Committee)*, Research Note 99/14 http://www.scottish.parliament.uk/business/research/pdf_res_notes/rn99-14.pdf

SPICe (2000a) *Ethical Standards in Public Life etc. (Scotland) Bill*, Research Paper 00/05 http://www.scottish.parliament.uk/business/research/pdf_res_papers/rp00-05.pdf

SPICe (2000b) *The Cubie Report* Research Note 00/06 http://www.scottish.parliament.uk/business/research/pdf_res_notes/rn00-06.pdf

SPICe (2010) *Patient Rights (Scotland) Bill* Research Note 10/52 http://www.scottish.parliament.uk/business/research/briefings-10/SB10-52.pdf

Stirling, T. and Smith, R. (2003) 'A Matter of Choice? Policy Divergence in Access to Social Housing Post-devolution', *Housing Studies*, 18, 2, 145-58

Strøm, K. (1990) *Minority Government and Majority Rule* (Cambridge, Cambridge University Press)

Trench, A. (2004) 'Devolution: The Withering-away of the Joint Ministerial Committee', *Public Law*, 513-17

Trench, A. (2010) 'The constitutional provisions of the Scotland bill' http://devolutionmatters.wordpress.com/2010/12/17/the-constitutional-provisions-of-the-scotland-bill/#more-1878

Trench, A. (2011a) 'The Scotland bill: debated at Westminster and provisionally approved at Holyrood' http://devolutionmatters.wordpress.com/2011/03/12/the-scotland-bill-debated-at-westminster-and-provisionally-approved-at-holyrood/

Trench, A. (2011b) 'Whither the Scotland bill?' http://devolutionmatters.wordpress.com/2011/05/09/wither-the-scotland-bill/#more-2388

Trench, A. (2011c) 'The Scotland bill in the Lords and at Holyrood' http://devolutionmatters.wordpress.com/2011/07/13/the-scotland-bill-in-the-lords-and-at-holyrood/

The Herald (17.8.11) 'Sheriffs shun Football Banning Orders' http://www.heraldscotland.com/news/home-news/sheriffs-shun-football-banning-orders-1.1118058

Watts, R. (2007), 'The United Kingdom as a Federalized or Regionalized Union', in A. Trench (ed.) *Devolution and Power in the United Kingdom* (Manchester: Manchester University Press)

Whitaker, A. and Robertson, J. (26.5.11) 'Supreme Court threat to Scots law – Alex Salmond', *The Scotsman* http://thescotsman.scotsman.com/news/Supreme-Court-threat-to-Scots.6774512.jp

Winetrobe, B. (2001) *Realising the Vision: a Parliament with a Purpose* (London: The Constitution Unit) http://www.ucl.ac.uk/spp/publications/unit-publications/82.pdf

Winetrobe, B. (2005) 'A Principled Approach to the Sewel Parliamentary Processes', Submission to Procedures Committee Sewel Convention

Inquiry.
http://www.scottish.parliament.uk/business/committees/procedures/inq
uiries/sewel/07-winetrobe.htm

Woods, K. (2001a) 'Scotland' in Jervis, P. and Plowden, W. (eds.) *Devolution and Health: Second Annual Report* (London: The Constitution Unit and Nuffield Trust)

Woods, K. (2001b) *Devolution and Health: Quarterly Monitoring Programme* — March (London: The Constitution Unit)

Woods, K. (2001c) *Devolution and Health: Quarterly Monitoring Programme* — June (London: The Constitution Unit)

Woods, K. (2002) *Devolution and Health: Quarterly Monitoring Programme* — March (London: The Constitution Unit)

Index